Praise for *Investing Between the Lines*

Investing Between the Lines captures the essence of successful executives: Communicate strong values that ALL employees understand and emulate, put safety and customers at the top of the corporate agenda, and maintain the agility to change. L.J. Rittenhouse reminds leaders that yes, their words matter.

—JAMES P. TORGERSON, President and CEO,
UIL Holdings Company

Rittenhouse has done it again! Wise investors, executives, directors, and employees will empower themselves with the knowledge and techniques recommended by L.J. Rittenhouse. If you are searching for leaders who build sustainable businesses, *IBTL* offers the important clues needed to find these long-term value creators. I highly recommend *Investing Between the Lines*.

—JAMES A. SEYERS, Portfolio Manager, Personal Investment
Management Group, ScotiaMcLeod

The ability to inspire confidence lies at the heart of creating value. It is also difficult to measure. L.J. Rittenhouse's insightful book presents a creative approach to developing metrics that identify confidence-building executives. Investors looking to find and back such leaders are advised to read this book!

—DR. VINAY NAIR, Founding and
Managing Principal, Ada Investments

That a man is as good as his word is a truism that underlines L.J. Rittenhouse's *Investing Between the Lines*, a guide to ferreting out a company's "business morality." She makes a compelling argument that executive letters are the best barometers of leadership qualities. This book is required reading for the long-suffering investing pub-

lic, as well as for officers and board members looking to see how well their CEO fares in informing others about the company's progress.
—IRENE NATIVIDAD, Chair,
Corporate Women Directors International

Confirming the deep insight of every faith tradition, Rittenhouse offers convincing proof that integrity matters. Words are sacred and CEOs who honor this truth are more likely to be trustworthy stewards of capital.
—DR. RON PATTERSON, Sr. Minister,
Naples United Church of Christ, Naples, Florida

L.J. Rittenhouse explains in this well-written manual why it is necessary to pay close attention to CEOs' words. By espousing the principles and practices used by Warren Buffett and other straight-talking leaders, Rittenhouse shows how to make sound judgments in separating companies that build long-term relationships from those preferring one-night stands. Executives and communication teams will gain important lessons in how to make wealth-creating communications.
—MARK O'HARE, Senior Partner, Grant Thornton, Australia

Rittenhouse's ideas are critical for individual investors like me. Unlike portfolio managers running mutual funds who limit their viewpoint to the next quarter, we can be more patient. That demands having someone in charge who knows what he's doing, and can effectively communicate. If a business can't be made understandable to the shareholders, how can we assume the CEO understands it? And if he can't communicate it to us, how does he communicate it to the people who work for him?"
—TOM ROBBINS-MILNE, Individual Investor, New York City

INVESTING BETWEEN THE LINES

HOW TO MAKE SMARTER DECISIONS BY DECODING CEO COMMUNICATIONS

L.J. RITTENHOUSE

New York   Chicago   San Francisco   Lisbon   London
Madrid   Mexico City   Milan   New Delhi
San Juan   Seoul   Singapore   Sydney   Toronto

1 2 3 4 5 6 7 8 9 0   DOC/DOC   1 8 7 6 5 4 3 2

ISBN   978-1-26-592269-6
MHID   1-26-592269-6

e-ISBN   978-0-07-174324-2
e-MHID   0-07-174324-3

This publication is designed to provide accurate and authoritative information in regard to the subject matter covered. It is sold with the understanding that neither the author nor the publisher is engaged in rendering legal, accounting, securities trading, or other professional services. If legal or financial advice or other expert assistance is required, the services of a competent professional person should be sought.

—From a Declaration of Principles Jointly Adopted by a Committee of the American Bar Association and a Committee of Publishers and Associations

McGraw-Hill books are available at special quantity discounts to use as premiums and sales promotions or for use in corporate training programs. To contact a representative, please e-mail us at bulksales@mcgraw-hill.com.

Library of Congress Cataloging-in-Publication Data
Rittenhouse, L. J.
  Investing between the lines : how to make smart investment decisions by decoding CEO letters / by L.J. Rittenhouse.
      pages cm
  ISBN-13: 978-1-26-592269-6
  ISBN-10: 1-26-592269-6
  1. Investments. 2. Financial statements. 3. Commercial correspondence.
  4. Business ethics. I. Title.
  HG4521.R584   2012
  332.6—dc23
                                                        2012039734

My word is my bond
Since 1801 the motto of the London Stock Exchange
(in Latin, "dictum meum pactum"), where bargains
are made with no exchange of documents
and no written pledges being given.
—*Urban Dictionary*

I should be very surprised if the story I have to tell is anywhere
near the whole truth. We are all, as Huxley says someplace,
Great Abbreviators, meaning that none of us has the wit
to know the whole truth, the time to tell it if we believed we did,
or an audience so gullible as to accept it.
—*Neil Postman,* Amusing Ourselves to Death

Acknowledgments

Investing Between the Lines represents the contributions of many people. Special thanks go to Stephen Dandrow and Rahel Abebe, who reviewed chapters, checked facts, and analyzed data, while continuing to conduct "business as usual." John Taylor's insights on corporate finance and forensic intelligence sharpened ideas, led to new discoveries, and spurred us onward. Bob Emmott offered his wisdom and experience on leadership, while Gary Zahokos, Roger Marvinney, Erich Korngold, Tom Robbins-Milne, John Freund, Caren Byrd, and Rick Kool helped to clarify important concepts. Greg Icenhower challenged and guided our Candor and strategy reporting throughout as he has done over the decade.

Thanks go to Lisa Norton, Laura Berman, John Finck, and Justine Hoechst for reviewing chapters and to Michelle Sauvage for her graphic representation and data development expertise. Without Warren Buffett's permission to quote generously from his shareholder letters, there would have been no first book, *Do Business with People You Can Tru$t* and no present book. My gratitude to him and to Debbie Bosanek, his assistant, is immeasurable.

Thanks go to McGraw-Hill editors Zachary Gajweski, Mary Glenn, and also to Patricia Wallenburg, who composed *IBTL*. Jill Totenberg and the team at Monaco Associates, Carolyn Monaco and Alicia Simons, guided the transition from book production to book release and set us on a firm course.

No ambitious project like this is possible without the support of friends and family. This group of stalwarts includes, but is not limited to, David Dowd, Sahil Ghandi, as well as Neel, Sarita, and Ashima, Betty Robbins and Moses Silverman, Gordon and Carole Hyatt, Eve Burton, Barbara Cooperman, Enid and Nan Elliot, Jesse Guardina, Sam Murkatovic, and my daughter, Lianne.

Finally, and not least of all, is the debt I owe my clients who have worked with us over the years and used Rittenhouse Rankings Candor metrics to build and rebuild trustworthy cultures that produce excellent results. Your dedication has launched this essential approach to twenty-first-century business. This book is dedicated to you and all that you have done and are doing to usher in a new era of corporate Candor.

Contents

Introduction

There is a stretch on Pacific Street in Omaha, Nebraska, that is lined with trees, homes, churches, and a small shopping center called the Countryside Village. It is home to the Bookworm Book Store. Founded in 1986 by Phil and Beth Black, the Bookworm is now an Omaha institution that specializes in books about Berkshire Hathaway and its CEO, Warren Buffett. When you open the door and enter, a bell rings.

Each year in early May, traffic in the store grows. The bell rings constantly as Berkshire Hathaway investors arrive from around the world. They have come to attend the company's annual meeting, an event Buffett calls the Woodstock of Capitalism. Beth and Phil know many by name.

On the day of the meeting, the Bookworm sales team rises before dawn. Bleary-eyed, they arrive at the CenturyLink Center to prepare for tens of thousands of investors, many of whom are clutching coffee cups and standing in long lines outside the auditorium until the doors open at 7 a.m.

The team enters the 194,000-square-foot exhibition hall and navigates the maze of exhibits to find the Bookworm Bookstore. When they find it, some check inventory and others take positions behind the long row of cash registers. Stacks of books are piled high on tables. All have been recommended by Buffett and Vice Chair Charlie Munger. Among them is one that I wrote, *Buffett's*

Bites, about the principles found in Berkshire Hathaway shareholder letters.

Buffett's decision in 2003 to create a faux bookstore at this annual meeting underscores his CEO-as-teacher mission. He wants Berkshire's owners to understand the economic and managerial principles that account for the company's success. From 7 a.m. until 4 p.m., the Bookworm sells thousands of books. Investors stagger to the cash registers holding stacks of books they will send to their homes and offices. Company representatives in nearby exhibits are selling See's Candies, Fruit of the Loom T-shirts, Pampered Chef cookware, and other Berkshire products.

I've known the Bookworm staff ever since 2002, when they sold my first book, *Do Business with People You Can Tru$t*. From time to time, I call Bookworm manager Diana Abbott to catch up on book sales and local news. She has her pulse on the comings and goings in Omaha. Knowing how close I live to Wall Street, Diana asks, "How is the market doing?" I answer, "It's up and down. Why do you care?" She explains, "Our customers are worried about their investments."

"They should listen to native son Warren Buffett," I advise. "He says it is folly to follow the market." She counters, "They don't know what companies to buy. They don't know whom to trust." I tell her, "That is why I am writing *Investing Between the Lines*."

This book offers significant findings from over a decade of research based on coding CEO communications. Over this time, my company has identified linguistic clues to help investors decide if a company and its leadership can be trusted. Our research is based on two principles:

1. Trust is the necessary foundation for long-term business success.
2. Candor is the language of leaders who choose to be trusted.

Investing Between the Lines is intended for three audiences.

First, CEOs and boards of directors will discover best practices of corporate candor. They will learn how the Rittenhouse Model of a Sustainable Business serves as a checklist to diagnose the health of a business. It allows executives to compare their patterns of corporate communication and content with those of their competitors. Companies that communicate candidly will build trusting relationships and protect corporate reputations. They can be expected to outperform their peers.

A second audience includes individual investors like my mother, who was blessed with smarts and common sense, but had no business training. Mom lacked the confidence to analyze the information in a shareholder letter. As a shareholder in a number of companies, she ignored the annual reports that arrived in the mail. But after learning the clues to detect candor in corporate communications, Mom could pick out key words with her red pen. She began to see which CEOs deserved her trust and capital and which did not.

The third audience includes business students and professional long-term investors who study company fundamentals. Pension fund managers, for instance, tell me they keep five years of annual reports on hand so that they can track the continuity of management's promises—a key indicator of trust. This group seeks to find leaders who steward capital and are accountable for their words and actions.

If you didn't know this before, you will soon learn: some CEOs' words and deeds can put profits in your pockets, while the words and deeds of others can destroy value—sometimes overnight.

It pays to know the difference.

CHAPTER 1

Executive Communications and Performance

Disclosure, noun

1. Something that is disclosed.

2. The act of disclosing; revelation.[1]

When journalists learn it is possible to search for meaning in CEOs' shareholder letters—the ones found in company annual reports—they laugh, or worse, they complain the letters are full of lies. They don't expect to find meaningful disclosures. Once, while interviewing me on CNN, anchor Daryn Kagan confessed that she threw out stacks of unread annual reports each spring. She asked, "Why bother reading them?"

Anyone looking for information in shareholder letters knows how difficult this can be. Many are littered with jargon and platitudes. But when investors tell me they can't understand what a CEO is trying to say, they have already gained vital information. If the communication doesn't make sense or is full of spin, ask yourself: Does the CEO not understand the business, or is he hiding something? Did the board of directors and the executive team read the letter? If so, why didn't anyone tell the CEO it needed a critical review?

If investors cannot make sense of this communication, why would they trust the corporate leadership, let alone the company's accounting numbers?

Executive communication reveals the character of the CEO. Is a letter written in a personal or an impersonal style? Is the CEO comfortable with disclosing his unique persona, or is he protected by handlers? Does he offer a frank report about mistakes that were made and challenges that were met, or does he report only successes? Authentic leaders write balanced reports that build trust. Inauthentic leaders will twist facts and weaken trust.

Shareholder letters can reveal a CEO's underlying motivations. If the primary goal is to promote the company without informing or educating investors about the business, expect fluff, not facts. The ratio of facts to fluff is an important indicator of financial integrity and shareholder value. This is the goal of *Investing Between the Lines*.

INVESTING BETWEEN THE LINES AT ENRON

In early 2001, it seemed impossible that Enron could be in trouble. It had been named the "Most Innovative Company" by *Fortune* magazine for six years in a row and was one of the most highly valued stocks on the market. When the company's 2000 annual report was published in early 2001, the stock was trading at $70 a share, or more than 60 times earnings. The company's board of directors included the chairman of Alliance Capital International, a retired dean and professor emeritus of accounting at the Stanford Business School, the former head of the U.S. Commodities and Trading Commission, and a former U.K. energy secretary.

Yet the 2000 shareholder letter, signed by Chairman Kenneth Lay and CEO Jeff Skilling, signaled trouble. The first paragraph reported: "The Company's net income reached a record $1.3 billion in 2000." This was an impressive figure. But when I checked the middle of the annual report to find this number on Enron's audited income statement, it was missing. Instead of $1.3 billion, Enron's net income was listed as $979 million.

Searching through Management's Discussion and Analysis of Results, I discovered an explanation for this discrepancy in a financial footnote under the heading: "IBIT [Income before Interest and Taxes] before items impacting comparability." Reading between the lines, it appeared that Enron had written down its investment in the troubled Azurix water company and triggered an operating earnings loss of $326 million.[2] This $326 million plus the reported net income of $979 million totaled $1.3 billion—the number reported in the shareholder letter.

Now I could explain how the numbers added up, but this raised an important question: Why did Enron include a loss as income in the shareholder letter? In time, legions of lawyers and accountants would learn that the accounting for Azurix was one of a number of "financial innovations" that Enron used to report fictitious income.

When the company declared bankruptcy on December 2, 2001, Enron's employees saw their pensions evaporate overnight, stockholders lost their capital, suppliers were stuck with unpaid bills, and customers wondered who would honor their power delivery contracts. On December 28, 2001, Enron's stock, which had traded as high as $70 a share eight months earlier, closed out the year at $0.60 per share.

After a four-month trial in 2006, Lay and Skilling were convicted of fraud and conspiracy. Lay died two months later, before he was sentenced, and Skilling was fined $45 million and sentenced to 24 years in prison. It was a tragic end to a company that defined an era of limitless ambition.

SHAREHOLDER LETTERS AND SILENT CENSORSHIP

In 2002, not long after the Enron bankruptcy, I attended a panel discussion about the state of financial journalism that included, among others, the distinguished reporters from national newspapers and magazines. During the Q&A session, the panel was asked how the financial media had failed to recognize and expose problems at Enron.

The answer was surprising. Reporters said they had suspected that there were problems at Enron but were discouraged from pursuing investigations. They were quick to add that no one had ever said, "Don't report on Enron." Instead, the speakers implicitly understood that editors would not welcome stories about the company's problems.

Over the past decade, the financial media, corporate directors, and also many of the institutions charged with protecting the public interest have been caught asleep on the job. Financial industry "watchdogs," including credit rating agencies, the Securities and Exchange Commission (SEC), the U.S. Justice Department, and investment analysts, all failed to expose massive problems in companies favored by investors. The names are familiar: Bear Stearns, AIG, Lehman Brothers, Merrill Lynch, Wachovia, HealthSouth, Qwest, and others.

Anyone who has lost faith in our public and corporate institutions is advised to critically read executive communications. As I will demonstrate in this book, careful readers can discover problems that are hiding in plain sight. After a decade of analyzing executive candor in thousands of CEO letters and other reports, I have learned that most companies are highly transparent, often unintentionally so. In fact, Rittenhouse Rankings has shown repeatedly that serious problems at well-known companies could have been spotted before they turned into headline-grabbing disasters.

PREVENTING FUTURE ENRONS

In April 2002, Warren Buffett was invited to speak at the Securities and Exchange Commission Roundtable at the Hotel International in New York City. He joined a distinguished panel that included James Copeland, the CEO of Deloitte & Touche; Dick Grasso, the chairman and CEO of the New York Stock Exchange; Martin Lipton, of the law firm Wachtell, Lipton, Rosen, and Katz; and Dwight Churchill, head of Fixed Income at Fidelity Investments. The topic was "How to Prevent Future Enrons."

Buffett spoke first. He stated that the amount of information companies provided to the Securities and Exchange Commission and accountants was more than satisfactory. The problems at Enron and other companies, he explained, were due not to the quantity of company disclosure, but to its quality. In his view, the CEO was responsible for quality disclosure. He said:

> Under any rules, if the CEO, wants to obfuscate, they can do that; and if they want to make it clear, they can do that. If they want to provide you with fluff, they can do that. If they want to provide you with substance, they can do that. The CEO will look at any rules through his own particular glasses, and either look at them as a way to give his shareholders more information, or to do some kind of tap dance number.[3]

His recommendation to the panel was simple: "[A]s the chief disclosure officer of a company, [the CEO] should write his own letter."

Buffett described the approach he used in writing his letters: "[T]he CEO should write that letter as if he had one partner, and that partner has been away for a year. The partner is intelligent. He's somewhat versed in accounting terminology and finance terminology, but he's no expert. He's interested because he has a large section of his net worth in the company and is ready to be a shareholder for an indefinite period, if he's treated well."

In other words, Buffett followed the Golden Rule of successful partnerships. He imagined what he would want to hear if he were an investor in Berkshire rather than its CEO.

The moderator, Marty Lipton, asked Buffett to comment on the effectiveness of new proposed legal standards that would impose penalties for inadequate and misleading disclosures. Buffett had strong views about this: "I think it's much better to have the CEO disciplined by his owners than attempt to discipline him by courts. . . . [W]hatever rules you came up with on that, I think that the CEO would go to his lawyers and say, 'How do I stay out of jail and tell them the least?'"

Lipton was surprised by Buffett's answer and asked: "Am I correctly interpreting what you said? You say that imposing more legal rules, whether increased liability or specific line item disclosure, would not, in your opinion, further the objective of making the appropriate information available? It would have just the opposite effect?"

Buffett replied: "I really think it would, Marty."

Sitting in the audience that day at the meeting, I took careful notes. Buffett was repeating ideas we had discussed since 1997, when I wrote him about analyzing CEO shareholder letters. This mission began in 1991 when I left Lehman Brothers, where I had worked as an investment banker in the corporate finance department. Back then I never imagined my new career would take me to Berkshire Hathaway's world headquarters on Farnum Street in Omaha, Nebraska.

THE JOURNEY FROM WALL STREET TO FARNUM STREET

When I joined Lehman Brothers in 1981, the firm was one of the most respected investment banking houses on Wall Street. Its culture was steeped in private partnership traditions dating back to the Civil War.

Walking down the halls to attend meetings, I passed paintings by Old Masters and new artists. The plush carpeting muffled voices from behind partly closed doors. Eating in the partners' dining room, I watched reflections bounce off the dark wainscoting that shone from frequent polishing. A chandelier studded with Austrian crystals sparkled and hung precariously over the massive oval dining table.

These outward signs of wealth, privilege, and security were deceptive. They masked internal tensions that threatened Lehman's values and traditions.

Lehman had two businesses: investment banking and trading. Each had a unique culture. The bankers occupied offices on the upper floors of Lehman's leased space at 55 Water Street, while the traders worked on the floors below them.

Dressed in striped shirts, suspenders, and polished wing tips, the bankers levered their Ivy League connections to cultivate long-term, trusting relationships with influential business leaders. Clients rewarded the bankers for advice on financings, restructurings, and mergers and acquisitions and brought profitable business to the firm.

Street-smart traders were deal jockeys. They executed underwritings and initial public offerings (IPOs) of stock for the firm's clients and traded securities. Arriving at the trading floor early in the morning, the traders removed their jackets, loosened their ties, rolled up their sleeves, and swapped outrageous jokes. They shouted out buy and sell orders from desks littered with phones, computer monitors, and half-eaten sandwiches. While Lehman's bankers earned multi-million-dollar fees, the traders measured profits in cents per trade.

But the line drawn between these two cultures was cracking. The introduction of new computerized technologies had accelerated the volume and speed of Lehman's trading business. It was becoming a profit center, not just a cost center. In 1983, Lewis Glucksman, the head of Lehman's trading business, leveraged this new financial clout and was named co-CEO with Peter Peterson, Lehman's top invest-ment banker and former U.S. secretary of commerce under President Richard Nixon. It was an uneasy alliance.

In fact, several months later, Glucksman ousted Peterson in a bloodless coup. His victory was short-lived. On May 11, 1984, the firm was bought by American Express, and Lehman was merged into the Shearson/American Express investment banking subsidiary. The new company would be called Shearson Lehman/American Express. In 1987, American Express acquired the old-line Wall Street firm E.F. Hutton. Now the bank was called Shearson Lehman Brothers Hutton American Express.

Merging multiple cultures and integrating complex systems and procedures was difficult and at times seemed impossible. Each new leadership and policy change was disruptive and unsettling. I escaped the infighting and scheduled meetings around the country to bring in new clients and business. But each visit back to the World Financial Center office offered more evidence that Lehman's "partnership" val-ues were endangered. Its "clients first" philosophy was being replaced by a "me-first" culture. Bankers were expected to sell clients the finan-cial product du jour, regardless of their need.

Instead of a meritocracy, the firm had become a bureaucracy. In the spring of 1991, I submitted my resignation and closed the door on an office with spectacular views of the New York harbor, the prospect of six-figure bonuses, and colleagues I had grown to respect and trust.

THE FIRST INVESTOR RELATIONS CLIENT

I decided not to join another Wall Street bank and started an investor relations business. It was an interesting value proposition. At Lehman, I had learned that clients were knowledgeable about raising and spending money. But I also knew that they were ignorant about what investors truly thought of their businesses and leadership styles.

The emergence of the dot-com era was changing the financial paradigm. Instead of tangible assets like plant, property, and equipment, intangibles such as CEO and corporate reputations, intellectual property, customer and employee satisfaction, and even advertising were all becoming significant indicators of future value. Business executives needed to know how investors valued these intangible assets.

Projections of earnings and earnings growth were becoming key factors in investing decisions. Instead of focusing on the management of cash and creation of economic value, investors were increasingly basing their decisions on whether or not companies met quarterly earnings targets. CEOs needed to know how to present each quarter's earnings results in a credible longer-term context.

As part of a comprehensive program of investor relations services, Rittenhouse Rankings offered to survey financial analysts and investors to gauge how they valued management and the company's financial prospects. These findings guided executives in developing reports that anticipated investor skepticism and bridged information gaps. Aligning investor and management expectations helped to ensure that the stock traded at a fair and reasonable price. It was a cost-effective way to add shareholder value.

Rittenhouse Rankings, perceptual surveys affirmed certain management assumptions and challenged others. When investors failed to understand a client's value proposition, we determined whether this was due to overly optimistic projections, unreliable execution, a flawed business model, or other factors. Then clients were guided to take corrective actions. Acting on this strategic intelligence helped them build investor trust.

In a survey for one CEO client, we learned that investors questioned the company's competitive advantages and future outlook. To correct these misperceptions, the CEO composed a shareholder letter with detailed and meaningful information. However, we soon realized there was no objective standard by which to judge what was *meaningful*. To fill this gap, I read his letters and compared them to those of his competitors.

After reading dozens of letters multiple times, distinct patterns began to emerge. We saw that certain topics were repeated in almost every CEO letter, such as strategy, business opportunities, and customer programs. When our client read the many different ways that his competitors framed their strategies, he was amazed. Like other Rittenhouse Rankings clients, he exclaimed, "I had no idea anyone was doing this."

THE GOLD STANDARD OF SHAREHOLDER LETTERS

The Rittenhouse Rankings mission to create a gold standard in executive reporting made a quantum leap after we discovered Warren Buffett's shareholder letters. At more than 10,000 words, his letters were almost five times longer than the average shareholder letter. Buffett's letters stood alone. Not only did he offer humorous stories, he also explained how the concept of "float" was essential to estimating the cash flows of insurance companies, the source of most of Berkshire's earnings. Even more surprising, Buffett discussed the year's mistakes and took personal responsibility for them.

In his 1996 letter, for example, Buffett described the errors he made in choosing to buy USAir's preferred stock:

> When Richard Branson, the wealthy owner of Virgin Atlantic Airways, was asked how to become a millionaire, he had a quick answer: "There's really nothing to it. Start as a billionaire and then buy an airline." Unwilling to accept Branson's proposition on faith, your Chairman decided in 1989 to test it by investing $358 million in a 9.25% preferred stock of USAir.
>
> I liked and admired Ed Colodny, the company's then-CEO, and I still do. But my analysis of USAir's business was both superficial and wrong. I was so beguiled by the company's long history

of profitable operations, and by the protection that ownership of a senior security seemingly offered me, that I overlooked the crucial point: USAir's revenues would increasingly feel the effects of an unregulated, fiercely-competitive market whereas its cost structure was a holdover from the days when regulation protected profits. These costs, if left unchecked, portended disaster, however reassuring the airline's past record might be. (If history supplied all of the answers, the Forbes 400 would consist of librarians.)

Buffett had expected the company to reduce its costs, including labor costs, a notoriously difficult thing to do in an industry with strong unions. He reported that between 1990 and 1994, USAir lost a total of $2.4 billion, wiping out the book equity of its common stock. During this period, the company still paid the dividends on its preferred stock. But in mid-1994, it was forced to suspend payments. Unable to predict when the situation would improve, Buffett wrote down his preferred stock investment to $89.5 million. He tried throughout 1995 to sell the shares for half of their face value, but was unsuccessful in finding buyers.

Then Buffett got lucky. In 1996, a new CEO, Stephen Wolf, stemmed USAir's losses. The company began to report profits. Not only was Buffett paid the dividends that had been suspended, but he also received money for penalties owed when they were not paid.

Buffett could have ended this story in his 1996 letter on a happy note. Instead, he confessed that before receiving the $47.0 million dividend payment from USAir, he had tried to unload the shares at a price below their par value. Buffett wrote: "[Once again], I failed in my attempt to snatch defeat from the jaws of victory. . . . In another context, a friend once asked me: 'If you're so rich, why aren't you smart?' After reviewing my sorry performance with USAir, you may conclude he had a point."

SHAREHOLDER LETTERS AND FINANCIAL VALUE

Buffett devours annual reports and shareholder letters. When I wrote him in 1997 about Rittenhouse Rankings's work to measure candor in shareholder letters, he responded, "You are doing the work of the angels." He invited me to attend the 1998 Berkshire Hathaway annual meeting.

In a 2001 interview I learned that Buffett grades a company higher if he finds the CEO actually wrote the shareholder letter. When I asked why this was important, he replied,

"I look for someone who talks to me frankly and honestly about the business, the way a partner would. That's a significant plus. . . . If the CEO doesn't write [the letter], it's a black mark against them for one reason—they may not know their business very well. Plenty of CEOs don't understand their business as well as a lot of people outside their business, or even the people who work for them. They do not want to be seen as they really are."[4]

Then Buffett described his creative process:

I just sit down in late November and I dictate the whole thing very quickly. It reads like a bunch of garbage when I get it back, but at least it gets my train of thought in a logical formation. Then I clean it up, and I clean it up, and I clean it up. After that I send it to Carol Loomis [of *Fortune* magazine] for editing. When she sends it back, I almost have to start all over again.

The last five percent of it takes about 95 percent of the time. That's the way it works. Once I sat next to Agnes Nixon, who created *All My Children* and other soap operas. I met her at the Calgary Olympics. She studied under some famous writing professor at Northwestern who told her, there is always the "right" word. I believe that. Until you get the right word, forget about the rest. You've got to have the right word. If you can't explain an idea, you haven't got your own thinking correct yet. So you're searching to get it just right.

Buffett expects his managers to adopt similar candid communication standards. He wants them to find the "right" word. His shareholder letters not only serve as the company's investor relations program but also strengthen the principles that define the Berkshire culture: investor partnership, choosing economic results over accounting results, candid disclosure, treating all investors fairly, and doing business with people you trust.

These principles have guided Buffett throughout the years and turned him and many of his early investors into billionaires. They form the core of the Berkshire Hathaway culture, which Buffett intends to preserve by picking successors who share these same principles. Do companies that publish letters like Buffett's perform better than companies that do not? Can investors gain an investing advantage by reading shareholder letters and getting insights into the corporate culture?

Financial reporter and historian Jason Zweig seemed to think so. That was the subject of his 2004 article, "A Tale of Two Washingtons," for *Money* magazine.[5]

WORDS AND NUMBERS

In addition to writing the weekly "Intelligent Investor" column for the *Wall Street Journal*, Zweig edited the 2003 revised and annotated edition of Benjamin Graham's investing "Bible," *The Intelligent Investor*. Graham, who died in 1976, is renowned as the father of security analysis and was also Warren Buffett's teacher and Wall Street mentor.

In his 2004 *Money* magazine article, Zweig highlighted two questions that Graham believed every investor needed to consider:

1. Is management reasonably efficient?
2. Are the interests of the average outside shareholder receiving proper recognition?

Zweig advised readers to study the company's financial statements to determine the answer to the first question. To answer the second question, Zweig recommended that investors examine how a CEO communicates with the company's investors. To illustrate his points, he compared two Seattle-based companies, Washington Mutual (WaMu) savings bank and global logistics company Expeditors International.

Zweig noted that WaMu's website described the company as "a powerhouse . . . a high performing company that is driving superior shareholder returns." In contrast, Expeditors' website failed to tout its stock, despite the fact that it had outperformed WaMu over the previous five years. Its philosophy was described in this website posting from Expeditors management: "We have our hands full with earning the profits. The stock price will have to take care of itself."[6]

When Zweig listened in on the quarterly earnings calls of both companies, he discovered that WaMu's calls were as changeable as the weather. Depending on the quarter's results, management guided analysts to higher or lower estimates of future earnings.

In contrast, Expeditors downplayed earnings and offered what Zweig called, "the most radically frank shareholder communications I've ever seen." The 2004 website posting below addressed a question about whether the company had changed its policy of filing written investor questions with the SEC in an 8-K report. Investors had come to expect this filing within 48 hours after the release of Expeditors' quarterly earnings. Management replied:

> No, there hasn't been a change in policy, but there is a difference between policy and practices. We must admit that it has been our practice of late to be taking more time to get an 8-K out than we had promised in our policy.
>
> So what is happening? We could say that this policy was established in the golden days before Sarbanes-Oxley, internal control audits and other well intended distractions that confront a company of our size or we could fall back on the fact that we have always said, "freight comes first." Then again we could assert with some truth that the breadth and depth of the questions we receive requires a great deal of time and effort to craft meaningful and accurate responses.
>
> But, this is all just a bunch of excuses—which whether they are lame or not, are something that we try not to offer. You're right, we're not getting the 8-K's done as timely as we promised and the real reason is that we have just gotten into the bad habit of taking a little extra time. . . .

In September 2008, WaMu declared bankruptcy. At that time, it was the largest bank failure in U.S. history. Not knowing how to value the company's massive portfolio of toxic mortgage securities, JPMorgan Chase bought it for pennies on the dollar. In contrast, the stock of Expeditors International has increased more than 100 percent since 2004.

When Zweig interviewed me for his article, he asked why Rittenhouse Rankings looks for companies that publish candid shareholder letters. I explained that our research shows that companies that value and practice candor outperform companies that do not. In other words, analyzing words is as important as analyzing numbers.

I told him, "We have bought into an illusion that the bottom line is the only thing that matters [in investment analysis]. But where does the bottom line come from? Accounting! Where does that come from? Judgment, because accounting rules can be applied in so many different ways. What determines judgment? The company values and how they reflect the ethical attitudes of the CEO . . . and how can you judge that if *not* from the way the company communicates?"

It seemed obvious: numbers are the product of countless judgments made in a company about when to count cash, when to book revenue and expenses, how much to count, and where to report it. And these decisions are shaped by the values of the corporate culture.

If a company is guided by conservative, prudent values, such as those at Berkshire Hathaway, then investors can expect more conservative and reliable judgments than those made at companies with aggressive and self-serving cultures. Judgments at these latter companies are likely to lead to creative accounting and financial manipulations. Investors who seek sustainable companies with long-term, durable advantages get clear choices: Berkshire Hathaway or Enron, Expeditors or WaMu?

In other words, investors who search for culture clues in executive communications can determine whether a company's financial numbers are trustworthy.

CHAPTER 2

Corporate Culture, Integrity, and Values

Culture, noun

1a. The integrated pattern of human behavior that includes thought, speech, action, and artifacts and depends upon the human capacity for learning and transmitting knowledge to succeeding generations.

b. The customary beliefs, social forms, and material traits of a racial, religious, or social group.[1]

[Derivation: from Latin *cultura* meaning to cultivate, to care, tend agriculture. Used in 1500s to describe "cultivation through education"; in 1805 to describe the intellectual pursuits of a civilization; and in 1867 to describe the collective customs and achievements of a people.][2]

Corporate culture is difficult to define, but its symbols are easy to spot. Walk into a Costco warehouse and notice the high ceilings, the exposed pipes, the bare walls, and the no-frills product displays. These are outward signs of a culture focused on cutting costs to share savings with customers.

Fly JetBlue. You might bond with the pilot who completes his checklist and then greets passengers in the aisle. He introduces himself and describes the flight plan and weather. Notice how the cabin crew pays attention to details. They embody the company's mission to "[bring] humanity back to air travel by combining product innovation with excellent service and communication."

When did you last call your commercial bank with a service question? Was the representative respectful and helpful, or unpleasant and unhelpful? The former experience reveals a bank with a culture that cares about satisfied customers; the latter does not.

Corporate culture has been called the "glue" that holds an organization together. Like a compass, it provides direction. But culture is so ubiquitous that we take it for granted. We don't even see it. Words are needed to name the tools, assumptions, and shared values that make up a culture. Culture cannot exist without language.

Neil Postman, author of the classic *Amusing Ourselves to Death*, described culture as a "corporation of conversations conducted in a variety of symbolic modes [and technologies]."[3] For instance, the digital and print technologies that transmit American culture today include tweets, social media pages, videos, blogs, websites, digital journals, videos, television, movies, and also newspapers, magazines, and books.

The complexity and variety of a corporate culture are revealed in the richness of its technologies and vocabulary. Language gives meaning to cultural artifacts such as company logos, unique practices, and tall tales, so these can be shared and passed along to future generations. Consider this passage from Wells Fargo CEO Richard Kovacevich's 2001 shareholder letter. It describes the iconic Wells Fargo stagecoach that carried mail and money across the continent in the mid-1800s and that symbolizes the bank's culture:

> The stagecoach carried valuables for customers to help them pursue prosperity, achieve their dreams of financial success, connect and correspond with their friends and families. It visually represents our values—trust, security, dependability, outstand-

ing service and convenience. It also represents one of the founding values of America: "the pursuit of happiness."

The images found in his passage—"carried valuables" and "dreams of financial success"—evoke emotions such as optimism, confidence, and pride in an pioneering heritage. Kovacevich adds that the bank's vision of financial services is firmly grounded in a longstanding "commitment to safeguard our customers' assets and financial information."

ORIGINS OF CORPORATE CULTURE

The word *culture* was first popularized by social anthropologists in the late 1880s who traveled to the South Seas and other remote places to study the customs, knowledge, belief systems, arts, morals, laws, and other habits of societies very different from those in the Western world. One hundred years later, the word began to be used to describe organizational and corporate culture.

Books like the bestseller *In Search of Excellence* popularized this concept of *corporate culture* and introduced a belief that a CEO was responsible for shaping and managing the culture.[4] Organizational expert Andrew Pettigrew observed: "The [leader of a company] not only creates the rational and tangible aspects of organizations, such as structure and technology, but also is the creator of symbols, ideologies, language, beliefs, rituals and myths." *In Search of Excellence* authors Thomas Peters and Robert Waterman cited organizational research that showed that successful companies had "rich networks of legends and parables" and poorly performing companies did not.[5]

The impact of these new studies on the value of corporate culture was widespread. In 1989, a judge blocked a hostile bid made by Paramount for Time Inc. on the grounds that this takeover would destroy Time's corporate culture and harm its customers, its shareholders, and society. The judge ruled that "the law might recognize as valid a perceived threat to a 'corporate culture' that is shown to be palpable [meaning so intense as to be almost touched or felt]."[6]

FINDING VALUES IN SHAREHOLDER LETTERS

Values direct the behavior of people in an organization. They guide employees in making moral and practical decisions. Yet despite the importance of corporate values, few companies meaningfully describe them in shareholder letters and other executive communications.

In the 2001 shareholder letters written after the 9/11 terrorist attacks, only 28 percent of the companies in the Rittenhouse Rankings Culture and Candor Survey (representing about 20 percent of the Fortune 500 companies) used the word *values* in their letters. Of these, only 12 percent, including Charles Schwab, CSX, DuPont, Entergy, Ford, GE, Hewlett-Packard, Johnson & Johnson, Walgreens, and Wells Fargo, directly linked their corporate values to success.

CEO Charles Schwab, for example, described in his letter how the company's values of fairness, empathy, and responsiveness shaped corporate decisions. However, in the post-9/11 economic decline, the company had to lay off hundreds of employees. He admitted that living these values was difficult, and added that Schwab was "very generous with severance packages." Not only did it grant options to departing employees, it also "created a hire-back bonus program."

In his 2001 letter, Walgreens CEO L. Daniel Jorndt reported how the company's values of "hard work, discipline and a strong focus on day-to-day operations and consistent adherence to [its] strategy" had landed it into Jim Collins's bestseller, *Good to Great*. He described the company as being "blessed with thousands of long-serving employees who not only understand the value of such a culture, but enthusiastically pass it on to the next generation."

Among the companies in the 2011 Rittenhouse Rankings survey, only 26 percent mentioned cultural values, down from 28 percent in 2001. Of these, only 9 percent of the companies connected their values with corporate success. The others described values in ways that suggested they were not deeply embedded in the culture.

For example, while Franklin Resources posted its corporate values on the walls throughout its global offices—"Put clients first, build relationships, achieve quality results, and work with integrity"—no mention was made of how these values impacted company performance.

In its 2010 letter, Chevron diluted the power of its value statements by describing them as platitudes: "Above all else, the men and women of Chevron will continue to be guided by our company's values—getting results the right way—and our vision to be the company most admired for its people, partnership and performance."

In contrast, Exxon Mobil's 2010 letter did, in fact, link corporate values to success, but framed them as strategic operating principles rather than as standards to guide moral choices and behavior:

> We succeed by upholding the values that set us apart: *a commitment to safety, operational excellence,* and *risk management; a disciplined, long-term approach to investing;* and *the development and application of advanced technology and innovation.* This *consistent approach* continues to serve us well, weathering the downturns and prospering as opportunities present themselves. [author's emphasis]

Unlike the examples above, Wells Fargo CEO John Stumpf returned to the company's heritage in his 2010 letter and described the bank's values as its corporate "compass, road map, and gyroscope." He reminded readers that "the pioneers who built our communities, the team members who built our company . . . didn't need GPS, smart phones, and electronic tablets to find their way. Their values guided them. . . . At Wells Fargo, [we] don't wake up every morning having to ask ourselves which way we're going." He assured investors they could "expect the company to keep riding the stagecoach in the same direction it's been headed since 1852."

SPOTTING CORPORATE CULTURE IN SHAREHOLDER LETTER STORIES

How can investors find companies with meaningful statements of corporate values? Look in executive communications for engaging stories that describe how the company's business history and strategies have been shaped by its values.

The excerpt below from FedEx's 2010 shareholder letter reveals how founder Fred Smith's entrepreneurial values have defined its culture. Another story about customer service values in Richmond, Virginia–based Dominion Resources reveals a different history and business model.

Global Connection and Collaboration

FedEx founder Fred Smith started his transportation delivery business in 1973 during the height of the Arab Oil Embargo. As oil spiked to $1.30 a gallon, up from just 30 cents, drivers waited in long lines outside of filling stations to get dwindling supplies of gasoline. The experience turned Smith into a passionate advocate for reducing oil consumption in the transportation sector.

His actions as a leader are consistent with the company's mission, restated in his 2010 letter: "to make it possible for people and businesses to connect and collaborate with each other, no matter where they are in the world." His commitment to developing and promoting the use of alternative fuels for truck deliveries and air transportation is evident in this story about electric vehicles:

> We've devoted a great deal of time this past year to advocating a shift in how our nation powers its transportation sector—by using electricity as the power source for short-haul ground vehicles. Electricity is diverse, domestic, stable, and a fundamentally scalable energy source with fuel inputs almost completely free of oil. Vehicle miles fueled by electricity emit less carbon than those fueled by gasoline, even if all of the electricity used to charge the vehicle is generated through conventional sources. High penetration rates of grid-enabled vehicles—propelled in whole or in part by electricity drawn from the grid and stored onboard in a battery—could radically reduce oil consumption in the United States. Electric vehicles would strengthen our economy, reduce national security and economic risks, and dramatically reduce emissions of greenhouse gases.

Smith reported on the company's progress in building a hybrid electric fleet for its daily package deliveries around the country:

> Today, we have our industry's largest fleet of hybrid electric package-delivery trucks. We're still expanding that fleet, but not just by buying new hybrids. We've also learned how to expand the useful lives of some conventional diesel trucks by retrofitting them with hybrid electric drive trains.

Smith described the shortcomings of electricity that required them to invest in developing renewable fuels for aircraft. He even set a goal to get "30 percent of our jet fuel from alternative fuels by 2030" and explained why this was possible:

> Aviation represents a great opportunity for a transition to renewable fuel sources, if only because the infrastructure requirements are much lower. There are about 250,000 gasoline or diesel fueling points in the world, but there are only about 1,700 major aviation fueling points. Transitioning aviation to alternative fuels will be much easier than surface transport if renewable fuels become cost effective. The prospects look brighter every day, with jet fuel already being produced from algae and plants such as jatropha and camelina, albeit at cost levels that are not yet competitive with petroleum.

FedEx's entrepreneurial culture is evident in this work to develop transportation fuels and to meet business and national security goals. Smith's long-term vision allows him to look 20 years into the future and imagine aircraft powered by algae and plant-based fuels. As he educates investors about these possibilities, Smith shows that he values informed owners.

A Reason to Say Thanks

A different story was offered in Dominion Resources CEO Tom Capps's 1998 shareholder letter. For more than 100 years, this company has provided electricity to most of the people in Virginia through its subsidiary Virginia Power, whose rates and returns are regulated by the state utility commission. Even though the word *value* was not used to describe Dominion's customer service–based culture, the corporate values are clearly revealed in the story below:

> In the last week of 1998, beginning the day before Christmas, severe ice storms tested the commitment, strength and ability of our front-line people. Ice broke down an uncountable number of trees, limbs and power lines. More than 440,000 homes and businesses lost power—thousands in need of individual attention. There is no computer known to man that is capable of pulling ice-laden debris off a downed power line, maneuvering a truck or a ladder to restore the wire and hooking it up safely, night or day. Every available Virginia Power crew worked a grueling schedule of restoration, beginning on Christmas Eve and continuing into the New Year.
>
> "We've been inundated with cookies," reported Virginia Power's Joe Murphy, construction team leader, several days into the crisis. "Cookies by the pound, by the box, by the bag, by the sack, satchel, plate, pitcher and handful. We've never been treated like this before. It's been amazing."
>
> Combine great employees and great technology—and give your customers a reason to say "thanks." It's a strategy that works.

Did investors notice this story? Dominion's investor relations vice president reported that institutional investors called him to praise the letter for its candor. One named it the best letter he had read that year. He admitted that the Christmas cookie story had nearly moved him to tears.

Three values were revealed in Capps's story: (1) service and sacrifice, (2) safety first, and (3) execution makes a difference.

When we learn that "every available Virginia Power crew" worked to restore power to hundreds of thousands of customers starting on Christmas Eve, we realize that these crews sacrificed their holiday so customers could heat their homes and cook Christmas meals.

Featuring this story in his letter, CEO Capps recognizes employees who might even be called heroes. The restoration of power lines in freezing temperatures requires expert teamwork. It can mean life or death. From this story, I can imagine the crews maneuvering their trucks on icy roads to lift and restore live wires to poles. When Capps describes these dangers in the letter, we can see that the company values personal courage and a "safety first" culture.

Does Dominion practice these values today? This is what CEO Tom Farrell wrote in his 2010 shareholder letter: "Never forget that the daily tasks of many of our employees are dangerous—from repairing power and gas lines to operating power stations and gas compressors. That is why safety ranks first on our list."

Recognizing employees in shareholder letters is a sign that companies are focused on executing strategy. For this reason, investors might expect to find employee commentary in all shareholder letters. However, among the 2001 shareholder letters, we found that an astonishing 40 percent of the companies failed to acknowledge employee contributions. And in 2010, only 21 percent of the survey companies recognized employees as being essential to producing desired business results.

INTEGRITY: TALKING THE WALK

"Integrity" is a value that is frequently cited in shareholder letters. It means an "adherence to moral and ethical principles; soundness of moral character; honesty." The derivation of *integrity* comes from the Latin word *integer*, meaning a whole number. This supports another definition: "the state of being whole, entire, or undiminished."

Consider that over the 10 years of the Rittenhouse Rankings Candor Surveys, the word *integrity* has been found 343 times in 249 shareholder letters. Yet neither FedEx nor Dominion used this word in its stories. Instead, each CEO described how corporate actions revealed corporate integrity. The executives' letters *embodied* integrity.

People act with integrity when their words and actions are aligned. Buffett stressed the importance of integrity in running a business when he wrote, "In looking for people to hire, you look for three qualities: integrity, intelligence, and energy. And if they don't have the first, the other two will kill you."[7]

Indeed, many of the thousands of people who travel to Omaha, Nebraska, each spring to attend the Berkshire Hathaway annual shareholder weekend do so to see if the company's actions support the words in Buffett's shareholder letters and how he answers investors' questions.

Buffett releases his shareholder letter over the Internet on a Saturday at the end of February, so that anyone in the world can read it simultaneously and no one investor gets an unfair advantage. Journalists and investors search the letter for insights into Berkshire's results and the state of the economy. They are also treated to a smorgasbord of the company's values. For example, Berkshire's letter from 2000 included 10 cultural values that were revealed in stories and performance reports:

1. Be Frugal and Multiply.
2. Your Word Is Your Bond.
3. Don't Over Promise, and Never Bet the Ranch.
4. Admit Mistakes and Learn from Them.
5. Pay for Performance.
6. Love What You Do and Build a Sense of Community.
7. Know Your Strengths and Limitations.
8. Never Sacrifice the Future for Short-Term Gain.
9. Be Accountable and Speak Candidly with Your Partners.
10. Be Fair to All Investors.

At the company's annual meeting, investors are treated to an unscripted six-hour Q&A session with CEO Buffett and Vice-chair Charlie Munger. These Q&A excerpts from the 2012 annual meeting were prepared from notes by Professor David Kass of the University of Maryland. They illustrate the company's underlying values.[8]

When Buffett was asked, "What types of investments should we avoid?" he revealed his appreciation for *Cultural Value 7: Know Your Strengths and Limitations* and responded:

We stay away from things we do not understand. [We need] to understand competitive position and earnings power 5–10 years into the future. If the price is too high, that eliminates another group of potential investments. Company size eliminates other investments. Berkshire has not bought an IPO in 30 years. The idea that a new issue is going to be the cheapest thing to buy among thousands of stocks is crazy.

When Buffett was asked, "Please explain why you target a minimum of $20 billion in cash on BRK's [Berkshire Hathaway's] balance sheet," he acknowledged the importance of *Cultural Value 9: Be Accountable and Speak Candidly with Your Partners* and replied:

There is no magic number. We think of the worst case and then add an extra margin for safety. We have 600,000 shareholders and members of my family have 80 percent of their net worth in BRK. We do not want to go broke because we took a chance and risked what they have and need for what they do not have and do not need. Accordingly, Berkshire's returns 99 out of 100 years will be less than they would otherwise have been. But we will survive that one year when no one else does. Life in financial markets has nothing to do with Sigmas and standard errors.

INTEGRITY AND CORPORATE PERFORMANCE

Can companies ranked high in integrity outperform companies that are not? Can they beat the market? Consider each of the companies just described for their exemplary corporate value systems. In all but 8 of the last 46 years of Buffett's leadership, Berkshire Hathaway's increase in book value has outperformed the S&P 500 Index—including dividends. From 2002 to 2012, Berkshire's "A" stock has more than doubled in value compared to the S&P 500.

In mid-2012, Wells Fargo traded up 35 percent over the prior year and beat the S&P 500's 17 percent gain. Over the 10-year period between 2001 and 2010, Rittenhouse Rankings found that Wells

Fargo's shareholder equity increased by $114 billion, and it outperformed three other major U.S. banks (JPMorgan, Bank of America, and Citigroup). The bank that began life as a stagecoach company is now the largest U.S. bank measured by market capitalization and the fourth largest in terms of assets.

Between 2001 and 2010, FedEx's share price grew 61 percent and Dominion's grew 69 percent. During this time, both companies outperformed the S&P 500 Index, which was up 29 percent. In contrast, Dominion's shareholder equity increased almost 40 percent during this period, and FedEx's shareholder equity almost tripled.

Could a relationship between sustainable and superior market performance and the integrity of cultural values be predictable or correlated? In 1987, two Harvard professors, John Kotter and James Heskett, decided to study the strength of this relationship.

CORPORATE CULTURE AND PERFORMANCE: THREE THEORIES

Kotter and Heskett knew that trying to discover a link between corporate culture and superior long-term economic performance was an audacious undertaking. How could something as subjective as corporate culture be measured? How could they show a connection between culture and reliable measures of long-term economic performance, such as market price, earnings and book value growth, or the net present values of cash flows? The researchers addressed each of these concerns and isolated three questions to guide their research:[9]

1. Did a relationship exist between culture and long-term economic performance?
2. If a relationship was shown to exist, why did it exist, and what was its nature?
3. Could corporate performance be improved by exploiting this relationship?

To answer these questions, the researchers framed three theories about corporate culture and tested these empirically. Their findings about the strengths and weaknesses of each theory were published in the 1992 book *Corporate Culture and Performance*. Their research affirmed some widely accepted assumptions about the importance of corporate culture and challenged others:

Theory 1: Companies with Strong Cultures Will Succeed Because Employees Share the Same Values

The advantages of strong cultures where almost everyone marched to the beat of the same drum seemed obvious. Widely shared values between managers and employees inspired everyone to perform at their best. Companies with strong cultures needed fewer bureaucratic controls. This allowed informal management systems to emerge organically from daily interactions which, in turn, drove higher levels of performance and satisfaction. The long-term economic success of companies such as Johnson & Johnson in the late 1980s was believed to have resulted from their having a strong, aligned culture.

This theory had supporters, but its detractors pointed out that shared values could also get a company into trouble. Serious problems could result when teams marched off together in lockstep—in the wrong direction. This was the fate of IBM's buttoned-down imperial culture in the years before CEO Lou Gerstner took charge and of GM's numbers-based culture in the 1980s. Finding a positive but modest statistical correlation, Kotter and Heskett concluded that Theory 1 was elegant, but incomplete. They turned to Theory 2.

Theory 2: Companies with Strong Cultures That Are "Strategically Appropriate" Will Show a Stronger Correlation with Economic Performance

This theory held that companies with different cultures, like FedEx, with its entrepreneurial culture, and Dominion, with its regulated culture, can both succeed when each company has developed *appropriate* strategies that are consistent with the corporate values. The shortcoming of this theory is that companies with strong and strategically appropriate cultures are more likely to dismiss customer and market information that challenges widely held strategic assumptions.

As a result, such companies were slow to adapt to change and to execute new strategies. Although they achieved superior economic performance over the short to medium term, Kotter and Heskett found this was not necessarily true over the longer term.

Theory 3: Companies with Adaptive Cultures Are More Likely to Succeed Financially over Time

In this phase of their research, Kotter and Heskett studied the values and attributes of companies described as having adaptive cultures. These values included confidence in managing change, a proactive and prudent assessment of risk taking, a collaborative approach to fact finding, and creating workable solutions to problems.

Companies with adaptive cultures were more likely to focus on meeting the needs of all three key stakeholder groups—employees, customers, and shareowners—not just investors.

This multistakeholder approach was expected to create greater long-term economic success because valued employees would be highly motivated to encourage customers to buy more products and services. In turn, loyal customers would increase company sales, cash flow, and profits, and this would satisfy investors.

Using this comprehensive stakeholder model as a guide, Rittenhouse Rankings began to search for commentary in CEO communications that revealed leaders who:

- Described the needs of the three stakeholder groups and how the company is meeting these needs
- Reported each year on the company's progress in meeting change goals
- Used vocabulary that reveals the CEO's passionate and personal engagement to advance change efforts

The letters written by GE CEO Jack Welch during the last six years of his 20-year tenure illustrate each of these qualities. In addition,

Welch's letters were entertaining. He used colorful vocabulary and imagined what his audience needed and wanted to know.

IMAGINING AN AUDIENCE AND REPORTING ON PROGRESS

Welch began his 1995 letter by describing the then-current fad in business to break up large companies and sell off businesses so the parent could become more nimble and competitive. Since GE was the world's largest conglomerate company, it was easy to imagine the question uppermost in the minds of its investors: Would Welch break up GE? He replied:

> [W]e're not. We've spent more than a decade getting bigger and faster and more competitive, and we intend to continue. . . . Breaking up is the right answer for some big companies. For us it is the wrong answer. "Why" is the subject of our letter to you this year.

Welch reminded readers of the audacious plan GE laid out well over a decade earlier:

> We set out to shape a global enterprise that preserved the classic big-company advantages—while eliminating the classic big-company drawbacks. What we wanted to build was a hybrid, an enterprise with the reach and resources of a big company—the body of a big company—but the thirst to learn, the compulsion to share and the bias for action—the soul—of a small company.

To reshape GE, Welch and his team had narrowed their focus on businesses that were, or could become, either number one or number two in their global markets. Those that failed this test would be fixed, sold, or closed. The company delivered on this mission. Throughout the 1980s, GE divested or sold $10 billion worth of marginal businesses and completed $19 billion of acquisitions that would strengthen its existing world-class businesses.

Welch, who had declared war on corporate bureaucracy, reported on his progress in the letter. During the prior decade, he wrote that

GE had eliminated "strategic planning apparatus, corporate staff empires, rituals, endless studies and briefings—all the classic machinery that makes big company operations smooth and predictable—but often glacially slow."

These actions changed GE's internal communications. Welch noted, "As the underbrush of bureaucracy was cleared away, we began to see and talk to each other more clearly and more directly." As the businesses were being strengthened, the company took on the job of changing employee behavior "and create in GE, the spirit and soul of a small company."

Welch wanted to cultivate an employee mindset throughout the company that he called "boundaryless behavior." He wanted GE employees to be open to "seeking and sharing new ideas, regardless of their source." This required that everyone in the company be involved in a program called "Work-Out." It was based on "the simple belief that people closest to the work would know more than anyone, how it could be done better." Welch explained:

> Across GE today, holding a Work-Out session is as natural an act as coming to work. People of disparate ranks and functions search for a better way, every day, gathering in a room for an hour, or eight, or three days, grappling with a problem or an opportunity, and dealing with it, usually on the spot—producing real change instead of memos and promises of further study. Everyone today has an opportunity to have a voice at GE, and everyone who uses that voice to help improve things is rewarded.

As the Work-Out philosophy spread throughout the company, he noted that meetings at GE "became interactive forums for disseminating new ideas and the sharing of experiences, instead of self-serving 'reports' and windy speeches."

Welch described important progress in "the demise of the 'Not-Invented-Here'" mindset. GE employees were now more open to improving their businesses and learning best practices from other companies. They adapted customer feedback techniques from Walmart; introduced new products from Toshiba, Chrysler, and Hewlett-Packard; and copied quality initiatives from AlliedSignal, Ford, and Xerox.

Welch described how investors benefited from these cultural initiatives. At the beginning of the 80s' decade, "GE returned to its share owners about $850 million a year in dividends." However, as "boundaryless" behavior began to change the culture in the early nineties, Welch boasted that GE had "returned to share owners about $2.3 billion a year in dividends and repurchased an additional $5.5 billion of our stock."

Underscoring the economic significance of this cultural change, Welch wrote that: "Moving from about a 1 billion dollars of share owner support in 1985 to $6 billion in 1995 says more than any of the words we've written about the new GE, and its new look to investors."

In this same letter, Welch reported how company change was affecting customers:

> Improving the profitability of our customers through technology upgrades of the enormous installed base of GE equipment— scores of thousands of jet engines, locomotives, turbines and CT scanners, for instance—is an enormous growth opportunity for us and a profit opportunity for our customers.

A dramatic and often ignored example of GE's adaptability was reported in Welch's last shareholder letter in 2000. He explained why GE no longer chose to be in businesses that ranked one or two in their markets:

> One of GE's long-standing management tenets has been the belief that businesses must be, or become, number one or number two in their marketplaces. We managed by that tenet for years, and enjoyed the business success that came, over time, from implementing it. But, once again, *insidious bureaucracy* crept into the definition of number one or number two and began to lead management teams *to define their markets more and more narrowly* to assure that their business would fit the one-or-two share definition.
>
>   It took a mid-level Company management training class reporting out to us in the spring of 1995 to point out, *without*

shyness or sugar-coating, that *our cherished management idea* had been *taken to nonsensical levels.* They told us we were missing opportunities, and limiting our growth horizons, by shrinking our definition of "the market" in order to satisfy the requirement to be number one or two. [author's emphasis]

After this 1995 revelation, GE leaders were asked to choose businesses having no more than a 10 percent share in their markets. He credited this change as a major factor in GE's ability to achieve double-digit revenue growth between 1995 and 2000. This underscored the importance of having a culture where everyone is encouraged to speak up and which breeds "an endless search for ideas that stand or fall on their merits rather than on the altitude of their originator."

In his 1998 letter, Welch warned against the danger of complacency, which means "never allowing a company to take itself too seriously, and reminding it constantly, in the face of any praise or good press, that yesterday's press clippings often wrap today's fish."

Welch's mastery of vocabulary made his letters fun to read and informative. Phrases such as "insidious bureaucracy," "without shyness or sugar-coating," "ideas that stand or fall on their merits," and "yesterday's press clippings often wrap today's fish" were just not found in other CEO letters.

Welch enjoyed playing with words. Toward the end of his 1995 letter, he referred back to his opening comment on the current business fad to spin off businesses. Would GE choose to be bigger or smaller? Welch replied that the "only answer to the trendy question—'What do you intend to spin off?'—is 'cash—and lots of it.'"

This 1995 communication ended with a story about ringing the New York Stock Exchange's opening bell to celebrate the one-hundredth anniversary of the Dow Jones Industrial Average. GE shared the podium with Dow Jones executives on this important occasion because it was the only company of the original Dow Jones Index that was still in business. Welch noted wryly: "We celebrated that occasion, but thought 'surviving' an anemic adjective, inadequate to the vibrancy of our Company and the promise of its future."

How many CEOs comment on adjectives? None of the executives in the Rittenhouse Rankings database of more than 1,000 shareholder letters has ever used this word. Yet Welch cared enough in his letter to question the adequacy of a word like *surviving*. He knew that vocabulary was a powerful weapon in the battle to change cultures.

Like Buffett, he understood that finding the *right* word means everything.

SUSTAINABILITY CULTURES

During Welch's tenure as CEO, GE reported 100 consecutive quarters of increased earnings per share from continuing operations. After he retired in 2001, GE was ranked as having the biggest market capitalization of any company, $590 billion. When Welch joined GE, the company was worth about $14 billion. This long-term performance secured his reputation as one of the most successful and respected CEOs in history.

However, after Welch left the company, it became apparent that the predictability and consistency of GE's past earnings growth had been based not just on tangible economic growth in its business units, but also on "confusing, but apparently legal [accounting] gimmicks."[10] While no other company has reported this kind of consistent upward earnings growth since 2001, a belief still persists that companies can achieve constantly growing or sustainable earnings.

As Figure 2.1 shows, the word *sustainability* began to show up in shareholder letters in 2001.

Over the decade of our study, however, the word *sustainability* has been used more frequently by CEOs to describe financial, not environmental and social, aspirations. By 2010, over one-fifth of the companies included this language, and 24 percent of these described sustainability solely in a financial context.

Communication, Culture Change, and Performance

Rittenhouse Rankings research shows that Kotter and Heskett's 1987 mission to find cultural attributes that supported long-term or

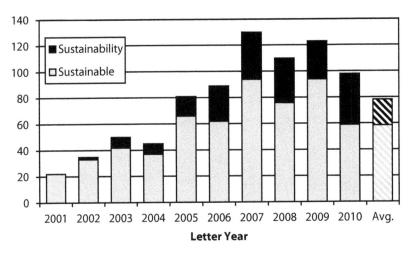

Figure 2.1 **Word Frequency of Sustainability and Sustainable**

sustainable economic performance has grown ever more important to executives.

Among their key findings, Kotter and Heskett declared that communication was essential in nurturing adaptive cultures. But not just any kind of communication would achieve the desired results. They concluded that respectful and questioning dialogue between three stakeholder groups was essential to promote strategic and constructive adaptation. Long-term economic performance was more likely to result when:

1. A company promoted meaningful and candid dialogue between employees, customers, and owners.
2. Employees engaged in dynamic two-way conversations with customers that allowed them to anticipate important changes in the competitive environment.
3. Leaders were empowered throughout the company to share this intelligence and propose strategies and actions to take advantage of change.

During the course of their study, Kotter and Heskett interviewed a large number of analysts and investors. They were surprised to find that many of these financial professionals based their investment recommendations on analyzing both the financial numbers and the quality of the corporate culture. Even quantitatively oriented analysts tended to favor companies that exhibited values such as "entrepreneurship, prudent risk taking, candid discussions, innovation, and flexibility." They also searched for less desirable traits, such as "bureaucratic" inefficiencies and an emphasis on "short-term results."[11]

When asked to name the stakeholders that corporate executives in companies cared about most, the analysts frequently cited, "themselves."

Once at an investor meeting, I asked a panel of financial analysts to describe their approach to corporate culture. All agreed that observing and analyzing cultural values and assumptions was one of the most important and difficult aspects of their jobs. They believed it took years of experience to determine if the values in a culture could be trusted.

As they spoke, it became clear to me that they lacked a disciplined approach to identify cultural values. They had no model to give them clear insight into understanding corporate systems that grew out of the culture and that led to outstanding or inadequate performance. They failed to see the link between executive communication and sustainable performance.

This was not surprising. It had taken Rittenhouse Rankings almost 10 years to develop a Model of a Sustainable Business that allowed us to see relationships between culture and performance. This model allows investors with little or no business training to gain informed insights on the quality of the culture. It helps CEOs and corporate managers to intuitively and quickly identify corporate strengths and weaknesses.

In 2003, I rolled out a poster-sized version of this model to Warren Buffett in his Omaha office. After reviewing it, he asked, "Where can I get copies?"

CHAPTER 3

Creating a Model of a Sustainable Business

Sustain, verb

1. To keep in existence; maintain.

2. To supply with necessities or nourishment; provide for.

3. To support from below; keep from falling or sinking; prop.

4. To support the spirits, vitality, or resolution of; encourage.

5. To bear up under; withstand: can't sustain the blistering heat.

6. To experience or suffer: sustained a fatal injury.

7. To affirm the validity of: The judge has sustained the prosecutor's objection.

8. To prove or corroborate; confirm.

9. To keep up (a joke or assumed role, for example) competently.

[Middle English *sustenen*, from Old French *sustenir*, from Latin *sustinēre* : *sub-*, from below; see *sub-* + *tenēre*, to hold; see *ten-* in Indo-European roots.][1]

The Rittenhouse Rankings Sustainable Business Model is based on operating principles, especially those related to Capital Stewardship, Accountability, and Candor. All three of these help to account for Berkshire Hathaway's long-term success.

Berkshire's vice chairman, Charlie Munger, believes that models are essential to decision making. Fond of quoting, "To the man with only a hammer, every problem looks like a nail," Munger admits to having a working memory of between 90 and 100 mental models. These allow him to factor in assumptions and permutations that elude others. Says Buffett, "Munger has the best 30-second mind in the world. He sees the essence of everything before you can even finish the sentence."[2]

In a 1994 speech at the University of Southern California, Munger imagined that students in the audience might be daunted by the prospect of managing up to 100 mental models. Not to worry, he assured them. Just a few can do most of the "heavy lifting."[3] These include arithmetic models such as compound interest, statistics, and high school algebra, as well as physics and engineering models such as critical mass and backup systems. He relies on a working knowledge of accounting to locate the gaps in financial statements that reveal corporate instability.

Understanding behavioral psychology is equally important. For instance, Munger was inspired by C. F. Braun, the founder of the CF Braun Engineering company, who believed that confusing and incomplete communications wasted time and led to costly mistakes. Braun made a rule that all written communications at the company had to state *who was going to do what, where, when, and why.* Employees who repeatedly forgot it were fired.

To make intelligent investing decisions, Munger advised students to hang "facts on a latticework of mental models." Simply remembering and repeating facts was not enough. They had to be filtered through these models. Applying the wisdom of philosophers throughout the ages allows Munger to focus on what is important in life and in investing. His insights show up on the Internet as explosive sound bites:

When any guy offers you a chance to earn lots of money without risk, don't listen to the rest of his sentence. Follow this, and you'll save yourself a lot of misery.

I think that one should recognize reality even when one doesn't like it; indeed, especially when one doesn't like it.

If you don't allow for self-serving bias in the conduct of others, you are, again, a fool.

A man does not deserve huge amounts of pay for creating tiny spreads on huge amounts of money. Any idiot can do it. . . .

People really thought that giving a predatory class of people the ability to do whatever they wanted was free-market enterprise. It wasn't. It was legalized armed robbery. And it was incredibly stupid.[4]

In 2002, Munger presided over the Wesco Financial Corporation's annual meeting. As the company's CEO, he opened the floor to questions after completing the business agenda. When a young man raised his hand and asked Munger to recommend stocks to buy, he refused. "I can't tell you this," he declared. "You need mental models—a checklist of procedures [to help you decide]. . . . If you're trying to analyze a company without an adequate checklist, you may make a very bad investment. . . ."[5]

Munger asked people in the audience to raise their hands if they used mental models to make decisions. He paused and noted, "Only one hand is raised." When he learned that this individual had graduated from "MIT," Munger was not surprised. The Massachusetts Institute of Technology's mathematical and science-based curriculum is steeped in mental models.

I was inspired by this story to take the Rittenhouse Rankings research and create a model of seven systems that define sustainable businesses. This model would allow business leaders to intuitively see and more clearly communicate their business strengths and weaknesses. It would permit investors to evaluate the integrity of the company's culture and leadership. And it would allow Rittenhouse Rankings to systematically code CEO language and identify balanced businesses with solid, sustainable foundations.

A CHECKLIST TO CODE CONTENT

To create a Sustainable Business Model, Rittenhouse Rankings first had to organize the over 130 performance-related topics we had discovered in reading over 1,000 shareholder letters. These included cash flow, competitive advantage, corporate purpose, paradox, strategic statements, financial and operating goals, and many others.

The next step required us to create rules or protocols for each topic. For example, the protocol for the topic "Business Opportunities" has three rules. The commentary has to (1) describe actions that generated revenues and sales; (2) name specific initiatives, such as launching new products, completing acquisitions, expanding existing markets, and many others; and (3) count only initiatives that are based in the present or expected in the future.

Table 3.1 presents a checklist to contrast the different Business Opportunities found in the 2003 and 2004 shareholder letters from Johnson & Johnson (J&J), Novartis, and Pfizer. These Business Opportunities included topics such as new products, acquisitions, and market expansions. Organizing this data in a checklist allowed us to see which companies cited the most and fewest opportunities in each year. As Table 3.1 shows, Johnson & Johnson reported the most business opportunities and Novartis the fewest.

"Positioning Actions" is another frequently mentioned topic and described company initiatives that support revenue growth. Unlike business opportunities, which bring cash into a business, positioning actions typically consume cash.

The protocol for Positioning Actions also has three rules. This commentary has to (1) describe actions that consume cash; (2) name specific initiatives, such as advertising, research and development, supply chain improvements, management changes, and many others; and (3) count only initiatives that are based in the present or expected in the future.

We created a checklist for Positioning Actions from the same six shareholder letters mentioned previously (see Table 3.2).

Table 3.1   **Comparing Business Opportunity Topics from the Johnson & Johnson, Pfizer, and Novartis 2003 and 2004 Shareholder Letters**

	JNJ		PFE		NVS	
Business Opportunities	'03	'04	'03	'04	'03	'04
1. New products	✓	✓	✓			
2. Acquisitions	✓	✓	✓		✓	✓
3. Licensing	✓				✓	
4. Commercialize new technology	✓	✓		✓	✓	✓
5. Product extensions	✓	✓	✓			
6. Geographic market expansion	✓	✓	✓	✓	✓	
7. Partnerships			✓	✓		✓
Total	**6**	**6**	**5**	**2**	**4**	**3**

Table 3.2   **Comparing Positioning Actions Topics from the Johnson & Johnson, Pfizer, and Novartis 2003 and 2004 Shareholder Letters**

	JNJ		PFE		NVS	
Positioning Actions	'03	'04	'03	'04	'03	'04
1. Management changes	✓			✓		
2. Productivity initiatives	✓					
3. Board changes	✓	✓			✓	
4. Arbitration rulings	✓					
5. R&D investments	✓	✓	✓	✓	✓	
6. New headquarters/research				✓	✓	✓
7. Divestitures				✓		
5. Preventing counterfeit drugs				✓		
6. Restructuring		✓		✓		✓
7. Sarbanes-Oxley						✓
Total	**5**	**3**	**4**	**3**	**3**	**3**

The checklist in Table 3.2 allowed Rittenhouse Rankings to see that J&J reported the greatest number of positioning actions and Novartis the fewest. Comparing total business opportunities and positioning actions for all three companies in both years, we noted that fewer positioning actions were reported than were business opportunities.

But when Rittenhouse Rankings compared these company topics to the ones in our Sustainable Business Model, we found that positioning actions such as advertising and marketing, hiring or downsizing, inventory management, distribution and supply chain systems, and safety programs, typically reported by other companies, were omitted by these three.

Our findings raised obvious questions: Why had Pfizer and Novartis neglected to report on productivity initiatives in 2003? What made J&J and Pfizer omit reports about their efforts to prepare for the new Sarbanes-Oxley disclosure regulations? Were these omissions deliberate or unintended oversights? The lists revealed gaps in CEO commentary, and as these added up, we grew less confident in management's ability to offer a balanced picture of company performance.

At the same time, the limitations of checklist analyses seemed obvious. They revealed nothing about the contextual details in reports on business opportunities and positioning actions. Checklists ignored meaningful facts and commentary that helped explain the significance of corporate actions and results. They could not record the breadth and depth of a CEO's vocabulary.

BEYOND CHECKLISTS: MEASURING CONTEXT

This connection between leadership and vocabulary was described by Ludwig Wittgenstein, the twentieth-century philosopher, who wrote, "The limits of my language are the limits of my world." He believed that words are powerful because they allow us to see and penetrate the world. When we name something, we can see it through our mind's eye.

Applying Wittgenstein's principle to executive communication, Rittenhouse Rankings has shown that CEOs with rich vocabularies gain competitive advantages. They are more alert to business opportunities and to dangers. They know how to engage and motivate their people to achieve desired results. Conversely, executives who lack a vocabulary advantage are handicapped in adapting to changing environments.

Vocabulary mastery shapes perceptions of CEO leadership, which in turn impacts the company's stock price. Coding executive communications allows Rittenhouse Rankings to find leaders who explain complex ideas simply, balance strategic actions with vision and aspirations, and can engage audiences with empathy and straight talk. These leaders care about finding the "right word." As Mark Twain famously observed, "The difference between the right word and the almost right word is like the difference between lightning and the lightning bug."

GAINING STRATEGIC ADVANTAGE: SCORING FOR CONTEXT

The checklists shown in Tables 3.1 and 3.2 revealed that Johnson & Johnson reported more business opportunities and positioning actions than did the other two companies. But when we analyzed the context in these commentaries and awarded points for meaningful details, we found that Novartis achieved higher scores than the other two companies.

A comparison of the research and development commentaries in each company's 2003 shareholder letter illustrates these contextual and scoring differences.

Johnson & Johnson

In the excerpt below, Johnson & Johnson CEO Bill Weldon described the R&D progress made in J&J's consumer business segment. (Note that each progress detail in this commentary is highlighted in italics.) First, Weldon described the "significant investment" made in 2003 and how this produced a "more robust [R&D] pipeline":

> Our *significant investment in research and development—over $4.6 billion in 2003*—has resulted in a solid stream of strong new can-

didates at every stage of the development process. Indeed, *our pharmaceutical pipeline is more robust than it has ever been in our history.* [author's emphasis]

He then reported that applying science and technology to create *new and differentiated* products enabled the consumer segment to post its best performance in nearly a decade: "Growth of 13.2 percent (with operational growth of 9.4 percent and a benefit from favorable currency of 3.8 percent) was led by the performance of our combined skin care businesses of NEUTROGENA®, AVEENO®, CLEAN & CLEAR®, and RoC®."

Weldon also wrote about the scientific and technological advances that made it possible to grow J&J's AVEENO line of skin care products:

> The AVEENO® line is *a great example of the increasing application of science and technology to consumer products.* Originally a line of colloidal oatmeal products, it is growing to become a full line of skin care products that use one or more natural ingredients in clinically proven, proprietary applications. [author's emphasis]

Pfizer

In his R&D reporting, Pfizer CEO Hank McKinnell described the purpose of Pfizer's R&D as "to sustain growth and serve more patients," and also listed the company's R&D resources:

> We continue to invest heavily in biomedical research and development to *sustain our growth and serve more patients.* Pfizer manages the world's largest pharmaceutical research effort: more than *13,000 scientists worldwide, supported by $7.1 billion in funding during 2003 and a projected $7.9 billion investment in 2004.* [author's emphasis]

McKinnell reported on R&D progress by naming the number of molecules and projects in Pfizer's development pipeline:

Our development pipeline *now includes approximately 130 new molecules and 95 projects to expand the use of our current medicines—an expertise in which we have no peer.* [author's emphasis]

But he failed to provide examples that explained the significance of these molecules and projects. Without supporting commentary, it was difficult to accept his claim that Pfizer's expertise in this area was peerless. Nevertheless, he did add details about three ongoing drug studies that could provide significant health benefits:

In 2003, three major studies—ASCOT, CARDS and REVERSAL—*demonstrated significant health benefits of therapy* with Lipitor, vastly expanding its potential reach. In June, Pfizer reported that our leading anti-infective, Zithromax, may improve the potency of first-line therapies against drug-resistant malaria. This potential breakthrough, now being tested in the field, may offer great hope for the millions of people—most of them children—who suffer, and too often die, from this age-old disease. [author's emphasis]

These examples helped to build confidence in Pfizer's growth prospects.

Novartis

CEO Daniel Vasella was the only executive among the three to link R&D investment with the company's corporate strategy and sustainable growth ambitions. He also praised the company's employees for their "commitment" to the successful execution of this "innovation-oriented strategy." In fact, Vasella was the only one of the three to use the word *strategy* in his 2003 letter:

We attribute *our success to our clear focus on sustainable growth, our corresponding, consistently innovation-oriented strategy,* and the capabilities and *commitment of our associates.* Accordingly, *we see our investments in Research and Development as being of primary importance.* [author's emphasis]

Novartis reported a 32 percent increase in R&D funding, which supported the company's purpose: to help patients: "Last year *we increased our investment in Research and Development by 32%*. In Pharmaceuticals alone, we invested more than USD 3 billion in 2003 to *discover and develop innovative medicines, and to improve treatments for patients*" [author's emphasis].

Vasella described the company's R&D investment in Cambridge, Massachusetts, telling readers that nearly 400 scientists were at work in the new labs.

> The first phase in the buildup of our new research center in Cambridge, Massachusetts was successfully completed. *Nearly 400 scientists are already working in the new laboratories. In 2004, we will continue the expansion.* [author's emphasis]

He also told investors that these "over-proportional investments will yield mid- to long-term returns." In other words, he warned investors that these investments would not produce a short-term payback. Meaningful details were also offered to describe the quality and productivity of the company's R&D pipeline. Vasella named diseases that Novartis's new compounds would target: diabetes, hypertension, and cancer, among others. He reminded readers that Novartis's new medicines would improve patient treatments and also demonstrate "attractive commercial potential."

The Rittenhouse Rankings coding system revealed that Vasella's commentary included more indicators of progress than did the other two companies. And while J&J and Pfizer also reported on their progress, they failed to meaningfully connect these details to the overall corporate strategy. Are these communication differences reflected in market prices?

Consider that from 2002 to 2012, Pfizer's stock fell 32 percent and J&J's stock increased 28 percent. In contrast, Novartis's long-term shareholders saw their stock grow 42 percent. Novartis was the only company among the three to outperform the S&P 500, up 38 percent over the same period.

EXPLAIN COMPLEX IDEAS SIMPLY

Results like these help to explain why Warren Buffett works countless hours writing and rewriting his shareholder letters to present complex ideas simply. He expects that candid and clear explanations will support the execution of Berkshire's strategies, which in turn will lead to increased shareowner wealth.

Buffett's communications are noteworthy for their consistency. He and Munger repeatedly have stated that they will invest only in what they know. Recall that in 2000 Buffett was dismissed as irrelevant and out of step with the market. He refused to buy technology and dot-com companies that were turning founders and early investors into overnight paper millionaires. From March 1999 to March 2000, Berkshire's "A" stock fell from $80,000 a share to just over $40,000. Buffett lost his ranking as second richest man in the world.

At the 2000 Berkshire Hathaway shareholder meeting, one irate investor took the microphone and suggested that Buffett and Munger receive "lashes with a wet noodle" for missing the technology boom. He asked, "Isn't there enough left in your brainpower to look into technology? I made over 100% in technology mutual funds."[6]

Buffett replied sharply, "Lots of people say they know how to invest in technology. Why would you have us invest in it for you?" He invited those in the audience wanting to invest in technology to seek out this shareholder.

After this meeting, I asked Buffett if it was harder to write his letter when Berkshire's stock was heading south. He confessed that he liked the challenge of writing about a bad year. In fact, his 1999 letter (published in 2000) anticipated many investor questions about the company's subpar performance. No excuses were offered.

In the next year's shareholder letter, Buffett offered a parable about speculation. He used the story of Cinderella to warn investors about the thin line dividing investment discipline and the "sedation" produced by "effortless money."

> Now, speculation—in which the focus is not on what an asset will produce but rather on what the next fellow will pay for it—is

neither illegal, immoral nor un-American. But it is not a game in which Charlie and I wish to play. We bring nothing to the party, so why should we expect to take anything home?

The line separating investment and speculation, which is never bright and clear, becomes blurred still further when most market participants have recently enjoyed triumphs. Nothing sedates rationality like large doses of effortless money. After a heady experience of that kind, normally sensible people drift into behavior akin to that of Cinderella at the ball. They know that overstaying the festivities—that is, continuing to speculate in companies that have gigantic valuations relative to the cash they are likely to generate in the future—will eventually bring on pumpkins and mice. But they nevertheless hate to miss a single minute of what is one helluva party. Therefore, the giddy participants all plan to leave just seconds before midnight. There's a problem, though: They are dancing in a room in which the clocks have no hands.

Ironically, on March 10, 2000, just weeks after the publication of his letter, the Nasdaq Composite index, where many technology and dot-com stocks trade, reached its all-time high of 5,048. That same day, Berkshire Hathaway's stock closed at $41,300. By year-end, however, the Nasdaq had lost more than half its value and closed at 2,471. Berkshire's A stock, in contrast, was up 72 percent and ended the year at $71,000.

MODELS TO FORETELL THE FUTURE

Buffett sees the future more clearly than others thanks to models and principles that keep him focused on what is most important. This foresight has benefited Berkshire's owners for over 40 years. In his 2002 letter, Buffett warned investors about "the burgeoning quantities of long-term derivative contracts and … uncollateralized receivables." He coined the term "financial weapons of mass destruction":

Charlie and I believe Berkshire should be a fortress of financial strength—for the sake of our owners, creditors, policyholders and employees. We try to be alert to any sort of megacatastrophe risk, and that posture may make us unduly apprehensive about the burgeoning quantities of long-term derivatives contracts and the massive amount of uncollateralized receivables that are growing alongside. *In our view, however, derivatives are financial weapons of mass destruction, carrying dangers that, while now latent, are potentially lethal.* [author's emphasis]

Only six years later, Buffett's prophecy was realized: a cascading daisy chain of defaults in derivatives and derivative-based securities triggered a global financial meltdown. In his 2008 shareholder letter, Buffett commented on the continuing dangers of derivatives:

Derivatives are dangerous. They have dramatically increased the leverage and risks in our financial system. They have made it almost impossible for investors to understand and analyze our largest commercial banks and investment banks. They allowed Fannie Mae and Freddie Mac to engage in massive misstatements of earnings for years. So indecipherable were Freddie and Fannie that their federal regulator, OFHEO [Office of Federal Housing Enterprise Oversight], whose more than 100 employees had no job except the oversight of these two institutions, totally missed their cooking of the books. . . .

Improved "transparency"—a favorite remedy of politicians, commentators and financial regulators for averting future train wrecks—won't cure the problems that derivatives pose. I know of no reporting mechanism that would come close to describing and measuring the risks in a huge and complex portfolio of derivatives. Auditors can't audit these contracts, and regulators can't regulate them. When I read the pages of "disclosure" in 10-Ks of companies that are entangled with these instruments, all I end up knowing is that I don't know what is going on in their portfolios (and then I reach for some aspirin).

In this same letter, after admitting that derivatives are virtually impossible to understand and regulate, Buffett described the 251 derivatives that Berkshire had on its books; he explained that each contract was "mispriced at inception, sometimes dramatically so." To date, Buffett is the only CEO we have found who has been able to explain the nature of the derivative contracts the company holds and also promises to inform investors each year about their status. (Keeping his promise, he has reported on these positions in his 2009, 2010, and 2011 letters.) As Berkshire's largest shareholder, he will share the pain with his owner-partners if these bets go wrong.

Each of the previous excerpts illustrates how Buffett draws upon left-brain logical, deductive, and rational capabilities *and* right-brain creative, intuitive, nonlinear, and emotional capabilities. He mixes math with metaphor and enlightenment with entertainment. Like great leaders in politics, science, and education, he is both strategic and visionary. He inspires others to do the same.

GAINING ADVANTAGE THROUGH STRATEGIC AND VISIONARY LEADERSHIP

Over the years, I have interviewed CEOs and asked them to name the leaders they most admire. Abraham Lincoln and Winston Churchill are mentioned most frequently. Both are renowned for their inspired leadership during wartime and their mastery of language.

Lincoln grew up memorizing long passages from the Bible and Shakespeare. He spoke and wrote in the cadences of these works. His most memorable speech is also his shortest, the 270-word-long Gettysburg Address:

> Four score and seven years ago our fathers brought forth on this continent, a new nation, conceived in Liberty, and dedicated to the proposition that all men are created equal.
>
> Now we are engaged in a great civil war, testing whether that nation, or any nation so conceived and so dedicated, can long endure. We are met on a great battle-field of that war. We

have come to dedicate a portion of that field, as a final resting place for those who here gave their lives that that nation might live. It is altogether fitting and proper that we should do this.

But, in a larger sense, we can not dedicate—we can not consecrate—we can not hallow—this ground. The brave men, living and dead, who struggled here, have consecrated it, far above our poor power to add or detract. . . . [F]rom these honored dead we take increased devotion to that cause for which they gave the last full measure of devotion—that we here highly resolve that these dead shall not have died in vain—that this nation, under God, shall have a new birth of freedom—and that government of the people, by the people, for the people, shall not perish from the earth.

This speech is strategic and visionary. Garry Wills, historian and author of *Lincoln at Gettysburg: The Words That Remade America*, notes that it changed the meaning and purpose of the war. Instead of preserving an economic system, the Gettysburg Address consecrated the battlefield and reframed the war as a fight to the death for the equality and freedom of all people. It linked the sacrifice of both Union and Confederate soldiers to a truth enshrined in the Declaration of Independence: that all men are created equal.[7]

Lincoln supported his words with action. Vowing that he would fight for these principles "until successful or till I die, or am conquered or my term expires, or Congress or the country forsakes me,"[8] he persevered despite crushing setbacks and defeats. He lived long enough to see the surrender of the Army of the South. His words and actions, however, have endured long after his assassination. They inspired the civil rights movement in the 1960s and strengthened the resolve of people fighting for democracy in the 2011 Arab Spring uprisings.

FIGHTING A WAR WITH WORDS

Churchill became prime minister of England on May 10, 1940, the same day that the Germans invaded France and the Low Countries. Britain was woefully unprepared for war. The nation lacked weapons, planes, supply chains, trained soldiers, officers, and a strategy. In September, Hitler's air force began bombing the citizens in London and other large British cities. Fearing a possible Nazi invasion, Churchill drew upon the only weapon he had to rally his people: his words. He used them expertly in this June 4, 1940, speech broadcast on the BBC:

> Even though large tracts of Europe and many old and famous States have fallen or may fall into the grip of the Gestapo and all the odious apparatus of Nazi rule, we shall not flag or fail. We shall go on to the end, we shall fight in France, we shall fight on the seas and oceans, we shall fight with growing confidence and growing strength in the air, we shall defend our Island, whatever the cost may be, we shall fight on the beaches, we shall fight on the landing grounds, we shall fight in the fields and in the streets, we shall fight in the hills; we shall never surrender. . . .

Churchill's actions supported his words. As bombs rained down upon the city, he, his wife, and key government and military leaders moved into underground bunkers not far from his Downing Street office. Churchill's presence in the city during the darkest days of the Blitz helped sustain the courage of the British people. It inspired resistance efforts throughout Europe.

Consider that business for many corporate executives is like war. CEOs want to win customers and demolish their competitors. They launch campaigns to introduce new products and increase sales and revenues. They develop patents and secret technologies to gain competitive advantage. It stands to reason that leaders who care about language will be stronger commanders and win more battles.

But can any CEO rise to this level of eloquence? Except for Warren Buffett, few other CEOs are remembered for their writings. The 1995 shareholder letter written by Coca-Cola CEO Roberto Goizueta, however, ought to be remembered. It is a powerful demonstration of an ability to communicate from the right and left brains, to mix strategy and vision.

ONCE YOU LOSE EVERYTHING

Roberto Goizueta served as Coca-Cola's CEO from 1981 to 1996. Born into a wealthy Cuban family, he graduated from Yale in 1953 with a degree in chemical engineering and returned to Cuba, where he joined Coca-Cola. After just a few years, Goizueta was named the chief engineer for the company's five Cuban bottling plants. But when Fidel Castro seized power, Goizueta and his family left Cuba in 1960, arriving in the United States with about $40 and 100 shares of Coca-Cola stock.

Later in life Goizueta said, "Once you lose everything, what's the worst that's going to happen to you? You develop a self assurance."[9] He continued to work for Coke in Miami and relocated to Atlanta four years later. In 1966 he was promoted to vice president, the youngest VP in the company's history. In 1980 he was named chairman of the board and CEO.

Goizueta's life experiences made him realize that "what has always been will not necessarily always be forever." He was a risk taker and made tough decisions to improve Coke's competitive position by expanding global operations. His actions transformed the company's conservative culture. These leadership qualities were evident in Goizueta's 1995 shareholder letter, which began with a story about Coca-Cola's "virtually infinite opportunity for growth":

Dear fellow share owners:

The other day, after I spoke to a group of engineering students at my alma mater, one of them asked me a simple question: "Which area of the world offers The Coca-Cola Company its greatest growth potential?" Without hesitation, I replied, "Southern California." They all laughed, thinking I was trying to be funny.

So to drive home the point, I shared with them one very interesting fact. The per capita consumption of bottles and cans of Coca-Cola is actually lower in the southern part of California than it is in Hungary, a country which is one of our supposedly "emerging" markets, while the U.S. is supposedly a "matured" soft drink market.

The students went silent for several seconds. I'm sure they had never before pondered our virtually infinite opportunity for growth.

But, as you might guess from the opening of this annual report, we have. So has one of our best bottlers, which is hard at work seizing that opportunity in California.

This story illustrates Goizueta's talent to inspire and motivate investors and employees. He urged Yale students to think about Coke's markets not just as geographies or percentage of share, but as per capita consumption. He imagined new profit possibilities by thinking differently about opportunity. His letter offered commentary about the Corporate Strategy and Vision, as well as evidence of Accountability, Capital Stewardship, and the quality of Stakeholder Relationships. It demonstrated his Candor and Leadership.

Visionary and Strategic Framing

Goizueta's power to motivate was evident in the way he described Coke's universal appeal and accessibility that "meets the fundamental, frequently recurring human need for refreshment." He defined these terms:

By universal appeal, I mean we sell a product with physical attributes that the human palate enjoys, no matter what the culture or demographic status. Five or six decades ago, we stopped listening to those who said that Coca-Cola simply would not be accepted in certain societies, where centuries-old beverage consumption habits would surely lock us out. *But, just as consumption of Coca-Cola surpassed the combined consumption of the two leading teas in Great Britain some time ago, so will the per capita consumption of Coca-Cola surpass that of the leading bottled water in France this year, two milestones most people said would never come to pass.* [author's emphasis]

Goizueta debunked the notion that Coke lacked appeal in different cultures and demographics by citing these consumption statistics from Great Britain and France.

He added that Coke's success depended on strategies to create profitable distribution systems that made its products accessible in markets around the world at affordable prices:

> [T]he "delicious and refreshing" nature of . . . Coca-Cola [is] of great importance, but so is the *universal accessibility of Coca-Cola. Not only does Coca-Cola satisfy a basic human need, it is also highly affordable to an overwhelming majority of people worldwide.* [author's emphasis]

Accountability and Capital Stewardship

Goizueta linked visionary, strategic, and financial fundamentals in his shareholder letter commentary. He underscored Coke's long-term investment appeal when he invoked "the grandfather test":

> Having a powerful brand can make for good financials. But having a powerful brand attached to a highly accessible and universally appealing product distributed through an unmatched business system can make for outstanding financials. . . . *That's one of the key reasons I have never heard anybody say, "I sure am glad my grandfather sold his Coca-Cola stock."* [author's emphasis]

He reported on the company's average return on capital ("more than triple our average cost of capital") to show how Coca-Cola stewards capital. To support these capital stewardship metrics, Goizueta described the company's 1995 results:

> Underpinned by 7 percent growth in our oldest market, the United States, our worldwide unit case volume increased 8 percent, to 12.7 billion unit cases. *And Coca-Cola, that 110-year-"young" brand,* grew by more than 425 million additional cases last year. As we have said before, volume growth is our key to

generating economic profit, and economic profit is the key to driving the value of your investment. [author's emphasis]

Goizueta explained that volume growth is vital to generating economic as opposed to accounting profit. He reminded readers that Coke, "a 110-year–'young' brand," is a family stock holding passed along from generation to generation.

Stakeholders

Goizueta wanted investors to understand that the company's success depended on making sure that all stakeholders got value from buying, consuming, making, delivering, and investing in Coke. In particular, he noted that the contributions of Coke's bottlers, retail distributors, and consumers were essential to the company's success:

> We know we can create superior value for you only when we're able to create superior value for our bottling partners, our customers and, ultimately, the people who buy and drink our products. We believe everybody should sell Coca-Cola, and everybody should get value from it. We've worked hard to make sure we operate in partnership with some of the world's very best business persons, and today we have the best of the best....
>
> We continue to work long and hard to help make our customers successful. For instance, some quick-service restaurants in the United States must sell as many as three regular hamburgers to generate the same profit that they generate by selling one large serving of Coca-Cola. Looking forward, we have committed ourselves to becoming even better skilled at contributing to the profitability of our customers.

Goizueta recognized employee contributions when he described the company mindset as "seeing where Coca-Cola is not":

> With my own eyes, I have seen my colleagues all over the world identify with their own eyes the growth opportunities that nobody else knew existed. *When these people walk into any envi-*

ronment, they don't see Coca-Cola; they see where Coca-Cola is not. They see an infinite universe, and they see those 64 daily ounces of opportunity.

As a result, we have found some of our best opportunities right under our own noses. In the United States, for example, we accounted for 80 percent of the soft drink industry's growth last year. One of the main reasons was that we were able to generate significant unit case sales volume through venues where we had never set foot before.

The truth is, however, that we are only just now really focusing on developing this skill—the skill of seeing new opportunities—as a true strategic capability. "Seeing where Coca-Cola is not" has to be more than just a knack that some people have and some people don't. It must be a required, self-sharpening skill. [author's emphasis]

Goizeuta's candid and inspiring commentary revealed his credible and potent leadership.

Leadership and Candor

Goizueta warned readers that no one, including himself, would take success for granted. He asked rhetorically how the company could perpetuate this mindset of seeing where Coke is not and replied it would happen when Coke became a company with a global learning culture. He envisioned a time when the company would be able to "institutionalize the process of rapidly learning from every aspect of our environment: our consumers, our customers, our partners, our competitors, seemingly unrelated organizations, and, yes, our own mistakes."

Anticipating skeptics who would write off this "learning culture as just another flavor-of-the-month business fad," he declared that this "commitment to a 'learning culture' should extend to every one of our people worldwide [who would be] personally responsible for driving their own learning." He reminded readers that he too would be accountable. He wrote, "I'm proud to say that I learned more in 1995 than any year before, but not as much as I will this year."

CREATING A MODEL OF
A SUSTAINABLE BUSINESS

Analyzing Goizueta's letter from these perspectives of Vision, Strategy, Accountability, Capital Stewardship, Stakeholders, Leadership, and Candor reveals the depth and breadth of his commentary. However, it was possible to see these distinctions only in hindsight. In 1995 we lacked a Sustainable Business Model.

In 2003, Rittenhouse Rankings organized the 130 topics we had found in shareholder letters into seven primary systems: Capital Stewardship, Strategy, Accountability, Vision, Leadership, Stakeholder Relationships, and Candor, to create a Model of a Sustainable Business. We diagrammed the interrelationships of these systems as a hub-and-spoke graphic, with six of the systems orbiting around one central system.

The placement of the systems was deliberate. They revealed how each system checked and balanced the others. The model showed companies what was needed to create a resilient and adaptive business that could thrive in boom and bust markets.

The Left-Brain System

The left-brain part of the Rittenhouse Rankings model is made up of the *Strategy* and *Accountability systems*. Both draw upon the capabilities of deductive logic, rationality, and objective analysis. We include topics under "Strategy" to code a company's business opportunities and positioning actions as well as strategic statements, competitive advantages, and market awareness.

This Strategy system is balanced by a system of Accountability that includes topics to code factors such as linking goals with results, reporting on financial results, and the company's outlook. A strong system of Accountability supports the execution of Strategy. Lacking Accountability, a company is likely to squander investor capital. These two systems are connected via the upper-left and lower-right quadrants of the model (see Figure 3.1).

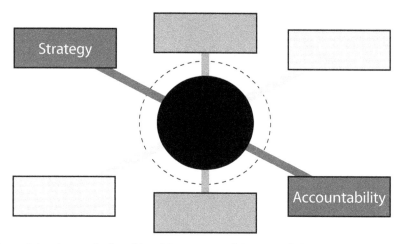

Figure 3.1   **Interrelationship of Strategy and Accountability**

The Right-Brain System

The right-brain part of the model is composed of *Vision* and *Leadership*. The Vision system is placed in the upper-right quadrant of the model (see Figure 3.2) and includes capabilities that reside in our right brains: inductive reasoning, emotional intelligence, and intuition. Vision is

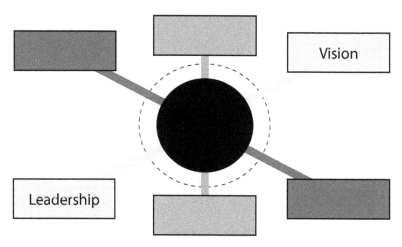

Figure 3.2   **Interrelationship of Vision and Leadership**

revealed in topics that code corporate purpose, innovative practices and ideas, original vocabulary, and emotional intelligence.

The Vision system is balanced by a system of strong Leadership, found in the lower left-hand quadrant. Strong leadership is needed to support a substantive corporate vision. Without strong leadership, a company is likely to have a diffuse and unoriginal vision that can waste shareholder equity. Topical clues that code the elements of Leadership are investor education, corporate problems and mistakes, and a world-view of risks and opportunities.

The Spinal System

The *Stakeholder Relationships* and *Candor* systems make up the backbone of the model (see Figure 3.3). Topics in the Stakeholder Relationships system define how broadly or narrowly a company imagines its stake-holders and how it anticipates and meets their needs. Topical clues that code the elements in the Stakeholder Relationships system include balancing stakeholder needs, empathy, reporting on what customers want, and descriptions of corporate culture.

The Stakeholder Relationships system is balanced by a system of Candor, which ensures that stakeholder relationships are built on trust.

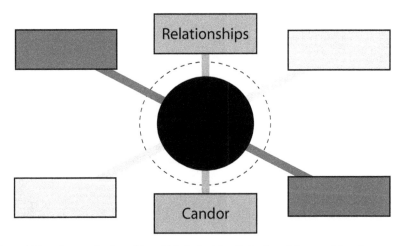

Figure 3.3   **Interrelationship of Stakeholder Relationships and Candor**

Without Candor, trust cannot grow and flourish. A company in which leaders set an example of consistent candid communication is more likely to foster customer loyalty, inspire employee accountability, and reduce investor turnover.

The hub of this model is *Capital Stewardship* (see Figure 3.4). Commentary connected to Capital Stewardship reveals whether a CEO's actions are based on attitudes of being *entrusted with* or *entitled to* investor capital. CEOs like Buffett, Dick Kovacevich of Wells Fargo, and Costco founder James Sinegal have solid reputations built on attitudes of entrustment. Conversely, CEOs like Enron's Jeff Skilling and Tyco's Dennis Kozlowski are still serving time for practicing entitlement.

This hub is defined by topical clues that code for a CEO's commitment to financial practices, especially cash and cash flow reporting, balance sheet management, capital discipline, financial and operating goals, and metrics and risk awareness.

In 2003, I showed the Rittenhouse Rankings model to Jack Bogle, the founder of the Vanguard Group, the second largest mutual fund investment company in the world. A passionate advocate of fiscal responsibility, Bogle founded Vanguard in 1974 to offer investors the lowest prices for the safest returns. He has long criticized managers who played accounting games by promoting short-term over long-term gains.

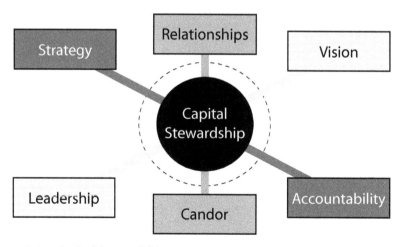

Figure 3.4 **Capital Stewardship**

I met Bogle at a church, where he had agreed to speak on business ethics with financial reporter Consuelo Mack. Rolling out a two-by-three-foot-sized poster of the Model of a Sustainable Business, I told him how it had been developed over the years. Bogle examined the graphic carefully and listened as I described the checks and balances among the seven systems. He asked a few questions and then looked at the model again, zeroing in on the central placement of Capital Stewardship.

Half jokingly and half seriously, he suddenly declared, "Copernicus-like, it shows the true position of the sun!"

CHAPTER 4

Capital Stewardship

Steward, noun

1. A person who manages the property or affairs for another entity.

2. A ship's officer who is in charge of making dining arrangements and provisions.

3. A flight attendant, especially but not exclusively a male flight attendant. Often as "air steward," "airline steward," etc.

4. A union member who is selected as a representative for fellow workers in negotiating terms with management. [syn: shop steward]

5. A person who has charge of buildings and/or grounds and/or animals. [syn: custodian, keeper]

6. In IT, somebody who is responsible for managing a set of projects, products, or technologies and how they affect the IT organization to which they belong.

[From Middle English, from Old English *stīweard*, *stīġweard* ("steward, housekeeper, one who has the superintendence of household affairs, guardian"), from *stīġ* in the sense house, hall + *weard* ("ward, guard, guardian, keeper").][1]

ack Bogle founded The Vanguard Group in 1974 with a clear mission: to steward investor capital. He created the investment industry's first index fund that was geared just for individual investors. The strategy was simple: offer investors the best risk-adjusted returns at the lowest cost. It worked. At year-end 2011, The Vanguard Group had $1.6 trillion under management. It was ranked as the largest mutual fund in the world.[2]

In a 2009 interview with *Forbes* magazine, Bogle discussed the impact of the global financial crisis. He called the U.S. investment system "deeply troubled." "Our system costs too much," he told the reporter, "and does not provide enough value. The more you pay, the less you get. If the market gives an 8% return, and it costs 2.5%, you get 5.5%. That is what is called the relentless rules of humble arithmetic. There is too much cost in the system and not enough value."[3]

He continued: "There is too much speculation and not enough investment. The turnover in the market is two-and-a-half times what it was in 1929. Speculation is in the driver's seat and investment has been put aside."

Bogle's principal beef was with managers who focused on salesmanship rather than stewardship. He complained, "People create new products—I hope you are sitting down—to make *themselves* wealthier, not their clients."[4]

Looking at the Rittenhouse Rankings Sustainable Business Model, Bogle might have envisioned a new financial order. It is a blueprint for companies that put attitudes of stewardship—not entitlement—in the center of their organizations. Like the hub of a wheel, capital stewardship keeps the outer systems connected and moving together.

Bogle has long championed the need for a new financial order. Hearing him compare the Rittenhouse Rankings capital stewardship–centered model to the theories of sixteenth-century Polish astronomer Nicholaus Copernicus was thrilling. In 1543, Copernicus published a book that challenged the prevailing belief in an Earth-centered universe.[5] However, his bold theory about the possibility of a heliocentric universe was largely ignored. It was not until 1687, when Isaac Newton worked out the laws of gravity and mechanics to explain how planets revolved in elliptical orbits around the sun, that Copernicus's theory was fully accepted.[6] A century later, philosopher Immanuel Kant suggested that Copernicus's methods of discovery were "revolutionary." Other philosophers took this to heart and coined the term "Copernican Revolution."[7]

History reminds us that as scientists are often champions of new ideas, they are also accustomed to taking a long-term view. They are like CEOs who persist in realizing the fundamental long-term value of their businesses, despite markets that are governed by short-term results.

SCORING CONTENT IN SHAREHOLDER LETTERS

In order to measure the breadth and depth of authentic CEO disclosure, Rittenhouse Rankings developed a methodology to score over 1,000 shareholder letters and created a database showing trends in executive communication. Communication scores allowed us to rank-order companies based on their having the most or least meaningful disclosure.

To calculate these scores, each of the 130 topics in the Rittenhouse Rankings Sustainable Business Model was assigned a value that ranged from 1 to 20 points. Values were selected based on corporate finance principles and investment banking experience. They weighed the relative importance of each topic to business success.

For example, 5 points were awarded for reports of qualitative goals such as, "Our goal is to increase return on equity." But if goal statements included a quantitative standard such as, "Our goal is to grow earnings 4 to 6 percent over the next two years," then 10 points were awarded. In other words, a company that reported three qualitative goals would earn 15 points for goal commentary, but another describing three quantitative goals would get a total of 30 points.

Companies that used the words *cash* and *cash flow* got 3 points for each citation. Three additional points were added for each detail about cash and cash flow. For example, a company that reported—our (+3) operating (+3) cash flow totaled (+3) $3.0 billion at year-end—earned a total of 9 points for each detail.

Imposing this quantitative rigor allowed us to objectively measure content. Rittenhouse Rankings assumed that companies with high scores that ranked consistently in the top of our survey would qualify as long-term holdings in stock portfolios. They would earn superior returns over time because they focused on stewarding investor capital and practicing candor. To find such companies, investors can search for clues in shareholder letters and other executive communications related to these topics: (1) cash and cash flow, (2) operating and financial goals, (3) capital discipline metrics, (4) balance sheet measures, and (5) risk awareness.

CLUE 1: CASH AND CASH FLOW

Cash and *cash flow* are the lifeblood of a business. When companies run out of cash, they die. To understand the fundamentals of cash flow, consider how it ebbs and flows in a business. It comes into a company when decisions are made to:

1. Generate sales, revenues, and profits
2. Sell assets or parts of a business
3. Borrow debt or issue preferred stock
4. Offer shares of company stock to public or private buyers

Cash leaves a business when it is used to:

1. Purchase equipment and materials to manufacture products and cover other operating costs such as salaries, vendor services, interest on debt, and taxes
2. Acquire businesses or significant assets
3. Pay dividends to shareholders
4. Repurchase stock in the market

When cash remains after all these payments are made, it is reinvested back into the business.

Cash flow is defined in a number of different ways: operating cash flow, net cash flow, and net pretax cash flow. As former Johnson & Johnson (J&J) CEO Ralph Larsen wrote in his 2001 shareholder letter, "Its virtue is its clarity. You either generate cash or you don't."

CEOs use two different terms to describe cash flow: *operating cash flow* and *free cash flow*:

- *Operating cash flow* is calculated by taking the company's net income (total revenues minus total expenses) and adding back the depreciation and amortization expenses, which are noncash expenses.
- *Free cash flow* is calculated by taking the operating cash flow number and deducting capital expenditures, dividends paid to shareholders, and cash paid to repurchase company stock in the marketplace.

Free cash flow is the sign of a healthy business. It tells investors how much money remains for reinvestment after outlays for operating and interest expenses, taxes, capital expenditures, and dividends. Strong recurring free cash flow can be used to grow future earnings. It means that a company is largely self-sufficient and does not need to rely on outside funding to grow.

Given its importance, investors might expect every shareholder letter to include commentary on operating and free cash flow. They would be wrong. Over one-third of the shareholder letters written in 2001 and more than one-quarter of the letters written in 2010 failed to report on this topic. Some companies, like J&J and IBM, have excelled in writing about cash flow.

IBM and Johnson & Johnson's 2001 Shareholder Letters

Both IBM and J&J have grown their businesses for over a century because they steward their brands, cash, and reputations for long-term success. Table 4.1 shows how many times each company used the words *cash* and *cash flow* in its 2001 and 2010 shareholder letters.

Table 4.1   **Contrasting Cash Flow Citations in J&J's and IBM's 2001 and 2010 Letters**

	2001		2010	
Cash Flow	**J&J**	**IBM**	**J&J**	**IBM**
1. Cash flow (operating)	✓	✓	✓	✓
2. $ free cash flow in year	✓	✓	✓	✓
3. Free cash flow	✓		✓	✓
4. $ free cash flow 10 years before	✓			✓
5. $ free cash flow 5 years before	✓			
6. $ free cash flow in year before				✓
7. $ future cash flow				✓
8. Cumulative cash flow over 10 years				✓
9. Defines free cash flow	✓			
Total	**6**	**2**	**3**	**7**

It shows that in 2001, J&J used the words *cash flow* and *cash* six times and IBM two times in their respective letters. In 2010, IBM used the words seven times and J&J three times. However, when we applied our point-scoring system to measure the words and also added points for context, we found a greater discrepancy. In 2001, IBM scored 30 points for cash and cash flow, and J&J scored 42 points. In 2010, IBM scored 69 points and J&J scored only 12. The differences in these point scores will illustrate the Rittenhouse Rankings methodology for scoring and measuring content and context in executive communications.

For instance, former J&J CEO Larsen offered this exemplary commentary on cash flow in his 2001 letter:

> *Yet another measure of financial performance* which we have focused on is [1] ***cash flow*** *from operations.* [2] *"Free **cash flow"*** [3] *(defined as **cash remaining** after making the capital expendi-*

tures required to support the growth of our business) is, in fact, [4] one of the very best measures of how a company is performing. [5] *Its virtue is its clarity. [6] You either generate* **cash** *or you don't.* [7] It is not subject to many varying interpretations or accounting changes. We are pleased to report that [8] *Johnson & Johnson's* [9] **"free cash flow"** *reached an impressive [10] $7.1 billion in 2001—a* record—up from [11] *$2.6 billion just five years ago and [12] $700 million a decade ago.* [author's emphasis]

In the next paragraph, Larsen linked cash flow to the company's strong balance sheet and its ability to repurchase company stock and also maintain a "triple A" credit rating:

[Y]our Company is growing in both sales and earnings and [13] *generating substantial levels of* **cash flow**. The net result is that *our balance sheet is exceptionally strong.* Our excellent financial standing is demonstrated by our ability to implement the *recently announced repurchase of up to $5 billion of the Company's stock* while *maintaining our "triple A" credit rating—a rating few companies have achieved.* [author's emphasis]

With six references to "cash" and "cash flow" and seven details about cash and cash flow in these two paragraphs, J&J CEO Larsen earned 39 points (13 × 3 points) for this commentary.

In contrast, the excerpt below from IBM CEO Sam Palmisano's 2001 shareholder letter contained fewer references to cash and cash flow:

Earnings declined from 2000 levels, yet we delivered very strong profitability—net income of $7.7 billion for the year and *more than* [1] *$14 billion of* [2] **cash from operations**.

Our [3] *continued* **strong cash flow** *gave us* [4] the flexibility to make investments in our future—[5] *$5.8 billion in research and development,* [6] *$5.7 billion in capital expenditures,* and [7] *$1.1 billion for strategic acquisitions to strengthen our portfolio.* The bulk of our acquisition investment was used to acquire the database assets of Informix Corp., which improved our share position and growth potential in the battle for database software leadership. After making all those investments, we used our [8] **strong cash position** *further to increase shareholder value by* [9] *raising our common stock dividend 8 percent and by repurchasing $5.3 billion in IBM common shares.* We ended the year with [10] a **cash balance** of [11] *$6.4 billion.* [author's emphasis]

In this excerpt, we counted four citations of "cash" and "cash flow" and seven details. IBM earned 33 points (11 × 3 points) for this commentary compared to J&J's 39 points.

IBM and J&J's 2010 Shareholder Letters

IBM CEO Palmisano offered even more detailed cash and cash flow commentary in his 2010 letter. To explain why the company's 2010 cash flow performance was noteworthy, he began:

[The company earned [1] *"record **free cash flow**"* in 2010.] Since 2002, we have added $14 billion to IBM's pre-tax profit base, increased our pre-tax income 3.4 times, our earnings per share 4.7 times and our [2] **free cash flow** [3] *2.8 times. Cumulatively, we have generated about* [4] *$96 billion of* [5] **free cash flow**.

[6] **Cash flow:** *IBM has consistently generated* [7] **strong cash flow,** [8] *a key indicator of real business performance.* In 2010 our [9] **free cash flow,** [10] *excluding the year-to-year change in Global Financing receivables, was* [11] *$16.3 billion, an* [12] *increase of $1.2 billion from 2009. IBM ended 2010 with* [13] *$11.7 billion of cash and marketable securities.*

Investment and return to shareholders: Our [14] *superior* **cash flow** *has enabled us to invest in the business and to generate substantial returns to investors. Our 2010* [15] **cash** *investment was* [16] *$6 billion for 17 acquisitions—13 of them in key areas of software. After investing* [17] *$6 billion in R&D and* [18] *$4 billion in net capital expenditures, we were able to return more than* [19] *$18 billion to you—$15.4 billion through share repurchases and $3.2 billion through dividends.* [author's emphasis]

After reporting on the year's cash flow performance, Palmisano looked back 10 years and then confidently reported IBM's five-year cash outlook:

> Over the last 10 years, we have nearly tripled our EPS, [20] *added $109 billion in* [21] **free cash flow**, returned $107 billion to you, tripled our software profits and increased the share of our revenue from growth markets from 11 to 21 percent, excluding divested PCs and printers. Over the next five years, we expect to grow our operating (non-GAAP) earnings to at least $20 per share, *to generate another* [22] *$100 billion in* [23] **free cash flow**, to return an additional $70 billion to you, to grow our software profit to about half of total segment profit and to increase growth markets' contribution to our revenue to nearly 30 percent. [author's emphasis]

Identifying these 23 references to cash flow and applying our point system, we calculated that CEO Palmisano scored 69 points for this commentary. In contrast, J&J CEO William Weldon's 2010 cash flow report was brief:

> *We generated* [1] **free cash flow** *of approximately* [2] *$14 billion* and held our AAA credit rating. We also executed a $1.1 billion debt offering at the lowest interest rate for long-term corporate debt in history.

J&J was awarded 6 points for this cash flow commentary.

Is a score differential of 69 versus 6 points reflected in market performance? Consider that over the past decade, IBM's stock has been up 172 percent, besting a 38 percent increase in the S&P. During this same period, J&J gained 29 percent.

How reliable is this cash and cash flow point-scoring system? We considered the possibility that other analysts might assign different weightings to the topics. For instance, some might award 5 points for each mention of cash and cash flow and 3 points for each detail. Following this method, J&J would have scored 54 points for its 2001 commentary and 18 points for its 2010 commentary.

The beauty of the Rittenhouse Rankings measurement system is that it allows for different scoring protocols. What matters most is the systematic application of these points. This scoring discipline can allow analysts to rigorously compare the amount of disclosure in all executive communications.

Shareholder letter readers who choose to dig deeper can look at a company's balance sheet and cash flow financial statements to see if the cash flow numbers listed in those financial statements match the numbers in the communication. These financial statements are typically found in annual reports and in a company's 10-K filing with the Securities and Exchange Commission (SEC).

When you try to match these numbers, remember that counting cash is difficult. It is like trying to "keep a wave upon the sand," a description used by Rodgers and Hammerstein in *The Sound of Music* to describe unruly behavior. Accountants, therefore, choose a date, typically at the end of a quarter or year, and report the amount of cash in the business at that moment on the company's balance sheet.

CLUE 2: BALANCE SHEET STRENGTH

A balance sheet does just that: it balances two values in a business: the assets and liabilities plus equity. The asset side of a balance sheet lists the dollar value of items such as cash, marketable securities, plant and equipment, inventories, and accounts receivable (money that customers owe but that has not yet been received or recorded). The liability side reports items such as short-term debt, accounts payable (money owed to suppliers and others but not yet paid out), long-term debt, and deferred taxes (taxes not yet paid out but owed). Luca Pacioli, an Italian mathematician known as "the Father of Accounting," invented the double-entry method of bookkeeping in 1494. While it is not a perfect system, it is the best we've got and has not changed much since the fifteenth century.[8]

Every time a company completes a business transaction, entries are made on each side of the balance sheet. For example, a company that borrows $1 million for five years from a bank will record an increase in "long-term debt" (on the liability side) and an increase in "cash" (on the asset side). How would a company report $20 million received from its customers for goods sold? The accountants would record this payment by reducing "Accounts receivable" by $20 million and then adding $20 million to the company's "Cash" account.

Liquidity as a Measure of Balance Sheet Strength

A highly liquid business is a strong business, because it can pay its debts without difficulty. To get a true picture of *business liquidity*, compare the amount of "cash and cash equivalents" (i.e., cash invested in securities that can be quickly turned into cash) in the Assets column on the balance sheet with the amount of "short-term debt and liabilities" in the Liabilities column. If the amount of short-term borrowing and liabilities is significantly greater than the amount of cash and other short-term assets, a business may be heading for problems.

Over the period of the Rittenhouse Rankings Culture and Candor survey, only about one-third of all the companies have included balance sheet reporting in their shareholder letters. Among these companies, Capital One Financial Corporation has regularly offered in-depth balance sheet reporting. In his 2008 shareholder letter, CEO Richard Fairbanks reminded investors about the company's "deep heritage of disciplined balance sheet management." He described four steps that Capital One had taken before the 2008 financial meltdown to protect the company's balance sheet:

1. We largely avoided mortgages, except for portfolios we inherited through banking acquisitions.
2. We chose to focus on credit cards and auto finance which, although they had high loss rates, proved to be the most resilient consumer loans during the recession.
3. We also managed our securities portfolio with a focus on liquidity, avoiding exposure to risky investments such as collateralized debt obligations and structured investment vehicles, which led to massive write-downs at many other banks.

4. We raised over $5 billion in private capital, including $1.5 billion in common equity and an additional $2 billion of Tier 1
capital, bolstering our already strong balance sheet.

Because of these actions, Capital One was able to meet government stress tests of capital strength during 2009—"one of only four
lending banks to do so." In addition, the company was able to maintain
*"healthy capital ratios both before and after [it] redeemed the government's
TARP preferred shares. [It was] one of the first banks to repay TARP
and, unlike most other large banks, [it] never relied on any government
funding program."* [author's emphasis]

How has this balance sheet discipline paid off? Figure 4.1 shows
that from 2009 through 2012, Capital One's stock increased 64 percent
compared to Wells Fargo's 12 percent, Citigroup's 62 percent decline,
and Bank of America's 43 percent drop. In fact, Capital One was the
only one of the four banks to beat the S&P 500's 46 percent increase
during this period.

Balance Sheet Management and the Perils of Leverage

Credit agencies such as Standard & Poor's, Moody's, and Fitch evaluate the strength of leverage ratios, book values, cash flow, and earn-

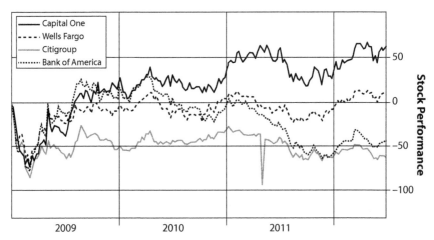

Figure 4.1   **Capital One and Competitors' Market Performance 2009–2012**

ings quality and assign credit ratings to companies that range from triple-A to low investment-grade or even junk ratings. These measures assess the probability that debt investors will recover their principal and receive interest payments over time. Companies that have taken on excessive debt are assigned low credit ratings.

While liquidity risk refers to relative cash positions, leverage risk in a business refers to the overall debt/equity ratio. This ratio is calculated by dividing the total dollar value of a company's liabilities by its total assets. Debt investors in highly levered companies with low credit ratings are less likely to recover their principal and receive interest payments over time when credit becomes tight and market liquidity dries up.

It is important to remember that the word *credit* comes from the French word *credere*, which means "to believe." This linguistic fact sheds light on a fundamental economic paradox. While the value of markets is reported in hard numbers, the behavior of these markets is determined by emotional reactions to news, gossip, and sentiments that cannot be controlled or quantified.

In his 2010 letter, Buffett commented on the perils of excessive leverage. He described emotional truths about borrowed money that are frequently ignored by chief executives and investors:

> Unquestionably, some people have become very rich through the use of borrowed money. However, that's also been a way to get very poor. When leverage works, it magnifies your gains. Your spouse thinks you're clever, and your neighbors get envious. But leverage is addictive. Once having profited from its wonders, very few people retreat to more conservative practices. And as we all learned in third grade—and some relearned in 2008—any series of positive numbers, however impressive the numbers may be, evaporates when multiplied by a single zero. History tells us that leverage all too often produces zeroes, even when it is employed by very smart people.
>
> Leverage, of course, can be lethal to businesses as well. Companies with large debts often assume that these obligations can be refinanced as they mature. That assumption is usually

valid. Occasionally, though, either because of company-specific problems or a worldwide shortage of credit, maturities must actually be met by payment. For that, only cash will do the job.

Borrowers then learn that credit is like oxygen. When either is abundant, its presence goes unnoticed. When either is missing, that's *all* that is noticed. Even a short absence of credit can bring a company to its knees. In September 2008, in fact, its overnight disappearance in many sectors of the economy came dangerously close to bringing our entire country to its knees.

He explained Berkshire's cash-holding philosophy, based on ideas that Rittenhouse Rankings has found neither before nor since in our research:

> At Berkshire, we . . . have pledged that we *will hold at least $10 billion of cash*, excluding that held at our regulated utility and railroad businesses. Because of that commitment, we customarily *keep at least $20 billion on hand* so that we can both withstand unprecedented insurance losses (our largest to date having been about $3 billion from Katrina, the insurance industry's most expensive catastrophe) and quickly seize acquisition or investment opportunities, even during times of financial turmoil.
>
> By being so cautious in respect to leverage, *we penalize our returns by a minor amount*. Having loads of liquidity, though, lets us sleep well. Moreover, during the episodes of financial chaos that occasionally erupt in our economy, we will be equipped both financially and emotionally to play offense while others scramble for survival. That's what allowed us to invest *$15.6 billion in 25 days of panic* following the Lehman bankruptcy in 2008. [author's emphasis]

Thanks to Buffett's conservative cash-holding policy, Berkshire became the banker of last resort to highly-rated Goldman Sachs and GE when they got caught in the 2008 liquidity crunch and desperately needed cash. Buffet's strict capital discipline practices have benefited his investors for over four decades.

CLUE 3: CAPITAL DISCIPLINE

CEOs who steward investor capital will typically offer commentary about "returns on investment (ROI)," "returns on invested capital (ROIC)," or "returns on assets (ROA)." Each metric reveals how efficiently a company is investing its capital to grow the business.

When investors learn what a company expects to earn on a new venture, they compare this return to the blended cost of the company's debt and equity capital also called its "cost of capital." Companies that earn returns higher than their cost of capital are disciplined investors.

The strength or weakness of a CEO's capital discipline is also expressed in commentary about "book or market value." Book value refers to what an investor owns in a business after subtracting all the liabilities and the shareholder equity.

Market value is calculated by multiplying the number of company shares outstanding by the current market price. Savvy investors will calculate the market-to-book ratio of a business to see how much the market is willing to pay for the company's net assets. In fact, instead of relying on constantly changing market values, Buffett uses book value as his preferred standard to measure Berkshire Hathaway's long-term performance.

ConocoPhillips: Returns on Capital Employed

ConocoPhillips has historically been a top scorer in reporting on capital discipline. In his 2009 letter, former CEO James Mulva explained how capital discipline guides the company's capital allocations and is woven into the company's strategy. He described the year's notable financial highlights, which included earnings of $4.9 billion, a 13 percent reduction in "controllable costs," and a "7 percent return on capital employed."

The company faced numerous difficulties that year: "weak energy demand," "commodity price volatility," "the global recession," "financial turbulence," and "regulatory uncertainty" in the United States. But despite these challenges, ConocoPhillips continued to invest in long-term strategies like exploring for oil in areas that "can potentially *yield attractive returns*, as opposed to service fees" [author's emphasis].

Mulva reported that the company funded its $11 billion exploration program with operating cash flow and met its strategic objectives by reallocating capital. For instance, ConocoPhillips sold noncore assets to support "a smaller capital program" and reduced capital that was used to support the less profitable downstream or refinery businesses. Mulva explained what these decisions would mean to shareholders:

> If market conditions improve or sale proceeds exceed expectations, we expect to consider a balanced approach that could include *limited expansion of our capital program*, additional debt reduction and share repurchases. These measures would not change our expectation of continued annual dividend increases. [author's emphasis]

Finally, Mulva told investors to expect not only *"higher returns on capital employed,"* but also *"a gradual reduction of our debt-to-capital ratio from today's 31 percent to a target of 20 percent"* [author's emphasis]. Offering this measure of accountability demonstrated Mulva's stewardship discipline.

CLUE 4: RIGOROUS FINANCIAL AND OPERATING GOALS

Goal statements are important indicators of capital stewardship. In addition to searching for the word *goal*, Rittenhouse Rankings also looks and scores for the words *objective*, *target*, and *aim*. Meaningful financial goal statements indicate that a CEO is serious about stewarding capital.

Goal statements tend to fall into three categories: motherhood, serious, and superior goals:

1. *Motherhood goals* are often stated as platitudes, such as "our goal is to delight all our customers." For example, AOL Time Warner offered this generic objective in its 2001 letter:

When the Company completed the merger, we said that our *goal was nothing less than to be the most respected and most valued company in the world.* We will strive to deliver superior and sustainable growth for our shareholders. [author's emphasis]

2. *Serious goal* statements combine corporate intentions with quantifiable outcomes, such as, "Our stretch goal is to increase sales next year by 20 percent" or, "We set a goal to increase customer referrals by 15 percent." For example, in its 2001 letter, Dow Chemical reported on a goal to increase earnings by applying Six Sigma cost-cutting disciplines:

Our people are embracing not only the tools associated with Six Sigma, but also the mindset—approaching their work with an ever-greater intolerance for waste. As a result, we are halfway toward *our Six Sigma goal of creating $1.5 billion in cumulative earnings* before interest and taxes by the end of 2003. [author's emphasis]

3. *Superior goals* wrap meaningful context around goal statements. These are the rarest of all statements. This annotated excerpt from Warren Buffett's 2000 letter illustrates the number of contextual points he provided to create meaningful disclosure:

Charlie and I continue to *aim* at [1] *increasing Berkshire's per-share value* at a rate that, over time, [2] will modestly exceed the gain from owning the S&P 500. . . . To reach our goal [3] we will need [4] to add a few good businesses to Berkshire's stable each year, [5] have the businesses we own generally gain in value, and [6] avoid any material increase in our outstanding shares. [7] We are confident about meeting the last two objectives; the first will require some luck. [author's emphasis]

In these four sentences, Buffett offered:

1. A performance metric—"per-share value" (per-share book value) or "per-share intrinsic value," each referring to a cash or balance sheet measure of performance instead of the more traditional measure of per-share stock price
2. A specific performance benchmark: to "modestly exceed the gain from owning the S&P 500"
3. The three things Berkshire must accomplish to meet this goal—add a few good businesses, grow existing businesses, and avoid issuing new shares
4. His candid assessment of attaining this goal, including the importance of luck in finding attractive businesses to buy

Each detail turns his paragraph into an "excellence goal." Receiving 5 points for each detail, this goal excerpt scored 35 points.

Goal setting instills corporate discipline that enforces accountability and boosts execution. So why doesn't every CEO report on his or her goals in shareholder letters?

Our research shows that only 31 percent of the letters written in 2001 and only 37 percent of the letters in 2010 reported on meaningful financial goals.

Top-Scoring Dow Chemical (2001) and FedEx (2010)

In 2001, the Dow Chemical Company scored highest in candor for its detailed financial goal reporting. In the excerpt below, former CEO Michael Parker listed the objectives the company intended to meet throughout his industry's boom and bust cycle:

> Our sights are set on creating value growth at rates that exceed our industry's average.... Our focus on becoming ever better and bigger is *defined by our tough slate of financial objectives across the cycle which drive us to*: [author's emphasis]
>
> Generate a return on equity of 20 percent.

Return 3 percent above our cost of capital.

Earn our cost of capital at the trough.

Grow earnings per share by 10 percent per year.

Dow even reported on a goal it could not meet in 2001:

> Despite the difficulties of 2001, *we continue to close in on achieving all but the toughest of these—earning the cost of capital at the trough—a goal made impossible by the challenge of integrating Union Carbide and our other acquisitions in severe trough conditions.* [author's emphasis]

FedEx's 2010 letter was one of the top scorers in reporting on operating goals in the Rittenhouse Rankings 2011 Culture and Candor Survey. CEO Fred Smith wrote that the company's long-term goals were to be a market leader and the most profitable carrier in the industry. He reported that meeting the company's "LTL (less-than-truckload)" goal was particularly challenging in 2010. The continuing economic downturn had reduced customer inventories, so that demand for LTL capacity was also depressed. This reduced the company's prices and profits.

To mitigate these pressures, Smith combined the Freight Sales and Customer Service units with FedEx Services to lower costs and increase efficiencies. As a result, FedEx improved productivity in its pickup and delivery and line-haul operations.

Smith described two metrics by which the company measured progress in meeting its goals: (1) reducing aircraft cost and emissions per unit transported, and (2) reducing direct operating costs per vehicle mile.

1.   Here is what he reported on reducing "cost and emissions per unit transported":

> Under the right circumstances, FedEx would like to have at least twenty-two [more fuel-efficient] 777Fs in service by 2014 and another 16 by 2020. The 777Fs fly farther on less fuel, and they carry nearly 14,000 more pounds of freight

than the MD-11s they replace. Put those things together, and they create a meaningful advantage for FedEx: a steep reduction in *cost and emissions per unit transported*. [author's emphasis]

2. This is what he reported on "reducing direct operating costs per vehicle mile":

We've worked with Modec and Navistar to develop a new all-electric commercial delivery truck that we're now using in London and Los Angeles. These electric delivery vehicles are particularly well suited for densely populated, moderate-climate urban areas, *where they cut our direct operating costs by 60-80 percent per vehicle mile*. As the capital costs of these electric vehicles come down—and their battery capacity and range go up—we'll be able to convert more of our fleet. [author's emphasis]

In a shareholder letter "first," Smith credited director Judy Estrin, the CEO of JLabs LLC, for helping the company meet its *"far-reaching goals"* [author's emphasis]. He recognized her "deep knowledge of science, information technology, and innovation [that] made her counsel extremely valuable to our company."

CEOs who publish meaningful financial and operating goals and focus on capital discipline, cash flow, and balance sheet management demonstrate a healthy respect for risk, another measure of stewardship.

CLUE 5: RISK AWARENESS

One of the most important jobs of a CEO is to manage risk/reward trade-offs. Investors could rightly expect to find the word *risk* in virtually all shareholder letters. Our research shows, however, that 41 percent of CEOs in our survey used the word *risk* in their 2007 letters. Among the letters written in 2008, only 32 percent of CEOs cited "risk."

The *Free Online Dictionary* defines *risk* as "the possibility of suffering harm or loss; danger." It also has specific financial meanings: (1) "the danger or probability of loss to an insurer," (2) "the variability of returns from an investment," and (3) "the chance of nonpayment of a debt." Twenty-seven percent of the letters written in 2001 after the terrorist attacks in New York City and Washington, D.C., cited "risk"—the fewest number in the past decade. Only one company, AIG, mentioned "terrorism risk" in 2001. Rittenhouse Rankings research showed that 40 percent of the companies on average used the word *risk* in their letters between 2005 and 2007, a sign of the looming financial crisis. In the 2010 survey letters, however, this number dropped to 30 percent. Of these, the following CEOs offered exemplary risk reporting:

- Citigroup CEO Vikram Pandit described how the company's "*risk management* and operations and technology functions were turning into sources of competitive advantage." [author's emphasis]
- Fiat CEO Sergio Marchionne reported on a corporate reorganization that gave each business "a well-defined operating profile, enabling it to *fully demonstrate an intrinsic value that risked being only partially realized in their conglomerate form.*" [author's emphasis]
- ConAgra CEO Gary M. Rodkin described "*risk management* services and tools that leverage grain market intelligence *to help customers navigate the volatile commodities landscape to better manage their costs.*" [author's emphasis]

Case Study: Travelers Insurance Company

Travelers Insurance Company CEO Jay Fishman, however, provided the most extensive commentary on financial risk of all the letters in the Rittenhouse Rankings survey. The word *risk* was used 14 times in various contexts in his 2010 letter, including:

1. Risk/reward trade-off:

   Our financial goal is to achieve a mid-teens return on equity over time. This goal motivates us to deliver industry-leading results over the long term by *thoughtfully managing the risks we take and only assuming risks* for which we believe we are appropriately compensated. . . . We believe that *this goal is consistent with our careful balance of risk and reward and encourages a long-term perspective.* [author's emphasis]

2. Competitive advantage:

   Despite the various challenges in the economy and faced by our industry over the last several years, our consistent top-tier performance demonstrates *a fundamental competitive advantage that we have in assessing risk and reward on both the asset and liability sides of our balance sheet.* [author's emphasis]

3. Customer products:

   [I]n National Accounts, we meet the needs of our largest customers by offering flexible program design and *risk management services* to better manage their total cost of risk. [author's emphasis]

4. Risk and corporate purpose:

   CEO Fishman is the only CEO in our decade-long survey to link business risk to the company's corporate purpose:

   [O]ur everyday business *is absorbing the risks* that individuals and businesses cannot afford to retain on their own, and risks can take many forms with wide-ranging consequences. . . . As our iconic red umbrella conveys, we are committed to providing our customers with sound property and casualty insurance protection from the *ever-changing risks they face.* [author's emphasis]

From a historical perspective, Fishman's focus on risk was ironic. In the late 1990s, former Travelers CEO Sandy Weill successfully lobbied the U.S. Congress to repeal the Glass-Steagall Act and allow the company to merge with Citibank. This legislation had been in place since 1933, when it was passed by Congress to prevent future speculative bubbles, such as those that had led to the Great Depression. In April 1998, Citicorp and Travelers Group announced their merger to create the first mega-diversified financial services firm in the United States. The repeal of the Glass-Steagall Act in November 1999 legitimized the merger.

Looking back, financial experts in 2012 now credit this historic combination as having set the stage for the 2008 catastrophic global financial collapse. Even the architects of this 1998 merger, former Travelers CEO Sandy Weill and former Citibank CEO John Reed, publicly declared in 2012 that the repeal of Glass-Steagall was "a big mistake." They and other critics advocate for greater separation between the conservative cultures of deposit-handling financial businesses and the highly speculative cultures of investment banking businesses.

Could the shareholder letters written by Weill before the merger have offered insights into his ability to assess future risk/reward trade-offs? Compare the 14 citations of risk awareness in Travelers' 2010 letter with the letters Weill signed as Travelers' CEO in the years leading up to the repeal of Glass-Steagall mentioned the word *risk* only once. In his 1997 letter, Weill described how a strong base of stable recurring profits would allow the bank *"to absorb risks" so it could generate better than average returns over the long term* [author's emphasis]. He obviously could not envision the risk that, 10 years later, American taxpayers would be required to absorb losses at his newly created financial supermarket.

An Undeclared Business Risk: Communication Risk

Investopedia.com, one of the Internet's largest sites devoted to investing education, cites numerous factors in its definition of *business risk*:

[T]he possibility that a company will have lower than anticipated profits, or that it will experience a loss rather than a profit.
Business risk is influenced by numerous factors, including sales
volume, per-unit price, input costs, competition, overall economic climate and government regulations.

One significant omission in this definition is "communication
risk," the smoking gun we discovered in analyzing Weill's shareholder
letters and finding only one report on business risk. When companies
publish incomplete or inaccurate and potentially deceptive communications, they create communication risk. Leaders who choose to spin
the facts or omit important details in their reports are exposed to the
extreme risk that by attempting to mislead others, they eventually mislead themselves.

Rittenhouse Rankings has found over the years that transparency
and candor are effective antidotes to mitigate communication risk. We
found that shareholder letters written in 2002 reflected the lessons
learned from Enron's collapse. That year, 26 percent of the companies commented on the importance of transparent financial disclosure.
They anticipated the impact of the Sarbanes-Oxley legislation passed
by the U.S. Congress that would become effective in 2003 and impose
significant financial and criminal penalties for inaccurate disclosures.

In his 2003 letter, then-Novartis CEO Daniel Vasella reset expectations about the impact of Sarbanes-Oxley. Assuring investors that the
company would comply with every part of the act, Vasella cautioned,
more realistically, that it was unlikely "given our 78 000 associates that
we will be successful everywhere at all times." Consider that in 2003,
only 7 percent of the CEOs in our survey reported on transparency.

In 2002, 19 percent of the companies in the Rittenhouse Rankings
Culture and Candor Survey reported on financial transparency, compared to 6 percent in 2007 and 1 percent in 2009. By 2010, no companies
reported on this indicator of capital stewardship and risk mitigation.

Each year, we search for executives who aren't afraid to report
on company problems and missteps; who anticipate and address tough
investor questions. We look for leaders who offer substantive, original,

and authentic communications. We score executive communications for transparency and, more importantly, for candor. Over the years we have seen that Candor scores are the key determinant in finding trustworthy companies that can out execute and outperform competitors in the market.

CHAPTER 5

Candor and Communication Risk

Candor, noun

1. Whiteness, brilliance; obsolete: unstained purity.

2. Freedom from prejudice or malice: fairness.

3. Archaic: kindliness.

4. Unreserved, honest, or sincere expression: forthrightness.[1]

The quality of being honest and straightforward in attitude and speech.

Ability to make judgments free from discrimination or dishonesty.

[French and Latin; French *candeur*, from Latin *candor*, from *candēre*, to illuminate. First known use: 14th century.][2]

The word *candor*, like the word *candle*, is derived from *candere*, a Latin word meaning "to illuminate." Candor is defined as "the quality of being honest and straightforward in attitude and speech and the ability to make judgments free from discrimination or dishonesty."

If transparency is concerned with appearances and clarity, then candor is defined as honest behavior and making "judgments free from discrimination." Leaders who adopt a candor standard choose to shine light into dark places. They choose to trust and be trusted. They run sustainable companies.

Candor and Stewardship are hallmarks of Berkshire Hathaway's corporate governance and culture. Buffett stewards his words and principles as fiercely as he counts his cash. When a shareholder at the company's 2012 annual meeting asked if it was appropriate for Buffett, as CEO, to speak out publicly on tax reform and other political and social issues, Buffett snapped back, "When Charlie and I took this job we did not agree to put our citizenship in a blind trust."[3] Some shareholders grumbled, but others cheered.

Principle 12 of the Berkshire Hathaway *Owner's Manual* sets out Warren Buffett's candor commitment to his owners:

> *We will be candid in our reporting to you, emphasizing the pluses and minuses important in appraising business value. Our guideline is to tell you the business facts that we would want to know if our positions were reversed. We owe you no less. Moreover, as a company with a major communications business, it would be inexcusable for us to apply lesser standards of accuracy, balance and incisiveness when reporting on ourselves than we would expect our news people to apply when reporting on others. We also believe candor benefits us as managers: The CEO who misleads others in public may eventually mislead himself in private. [italics theirs]*

This is Buffett's Golden Rule of investor communications: communicate with your investors as you would wish them to communicate with you. Candid communication is an antidote to the risk of self-deception. Candor is the language that builds trust.

GLOBAL TRUST SURVEY

Each year since 2000, the Edelman public relations firm has published a survey on global trust, interviewing thousands of college-educated respondents from 25 countries around the world.

In its 2012 Trust Barometer survey, Edelman researchers found that just 38 percent of the respondents trusted information from a CEO, a drop of 12 percent from 2011 and the largest since the survey began.[4] In fact, the survey showed that only government officials and regulators were found to be less trustworthy than business leaders.

The Rittenhouse Rankings Culture and Candor Surveys show a similar downward trend in trust and candor. Since 2003, we have found that about 40 percent of the CEOs we survey publish letters that are ranked high or medium in candor, while 60 percent publish letters that are ranked low or seriously deficient in candor. Rittenhouse Rankings has also observed that companies ranked high in candor are more stable and reliable than low-ranked companies. They offer more consistent returns and outperform in market downturns, compared to companies ranked low in candor.

STEWARDSHIP, CANDOR, TRUST, AND LIES

In July 2012, Rittenhouse Rankings conducted a Google search for "stewardship and candor." The first result was a link to *Buffett's Bites*, my 2010 guide to Buffett's shareholder letters. The second cited environmental stewardship; the third, church stewardship; the fourth, family stewardship. The fifth and sixth results again invited visitors to *Buffett's Bites* and the Rittenhouse Rankings blog, *Investing Between the Lines*. That day, Google showed Rittenhouse Rankings to be top-ranked in "stewardship and candor." A similar search conducted in October 2012 showed that Rittenhouse Rankings was again listed among the top four results for "stewardship and candor."

Numerous academic and consulting studies recommend candor practices as essential to the smart execution of strategy. When management consultant Keith Ferrazzi and his team rated candor among executives at six top banks, they found that the teams scoring lowest in candor reported "the poorest financial returns of the six during the global economic crisis."[5]

Conversely, "groups that candidly communicated about risky securities, lending practices and other problems" were able to preserve shareholder value. Studying over 50 large companies from 2008 to

2011, Ferrazzi determined that "observable candor" was the best predictor of high-performing teams.

You might well ask: if candor is so critical to building trust and strengthening performance, then why don't more businesses promote it? Rittenhouse Rankings blames the "elephant in the room." Companies that ignore highly visible, troublesome problems are likely to be candor laggards. Candor champions, on the other hand, are more likely to confront these elephants. Leaders in such companies tackle conflicts, knowing that unresolved issues will erode performance.

Candor is not easy to measure and score because it has two faces: its absence and its presence. Smart executives will recognize both faces, even though the lack of candor is more frequently cited than its presence. In July 2012, a Google search produced 918 results for the "presence of candor." But a search for results related to the "absence of candor" turned up over 19,000 hits. In other words, that day the absence of candor trumped the presence of candor by a factor of 21 to 1. A similar search conducted in October 2012 produced 999 results for the presence of candor and 21,900 for its absence, a ratio of 22 to 1.

In other words, the Internet reveals that people, including executives, are more likely to deny and obfuscate their problems than to discuss and resolve them. Given this inclination, it is reasonable to ask: Why would a CEO choose to work with an advisor such as Rittenhouse Rankings, which counsels candid disclosure and problem resolution? The good news, from our perspective, is that many prominent companies have sought our counsel precisely because we have alerted them to company blind spots.

The old joke, "How can you tell if a politician is lying?" usually gets a laugh: "Watch his lips move." It speaks to a fundamental truth: that everyone lies. But it ignores an equally important principle: that different kinds of lies have different consequences. And these can vary considerably. Why? Because some lies are benign and others are toxic.

Polite and white lies are benign. They are told to smooth over difficult social situations and can do more good than harm. Deliberate omissions of facts or statements, however, can be toxic. Whether the motivation comes from fear or a desire to avoid conflict, it is important in all instances to consider the significance of the information that is left out and the consequences for doing so. The more significant the information is to understanding truth and consequences, the more toxic the lie.

When we state that something is true even when we know it to be false, we are telling outright lies. These are more toxic and can create bigger problems than the ones they try to avoid. Deliberately deceptive lies tend to smooth over situations in the short term. However, as Shakespeare famously observed, "truth will out."

Then there are the lies of self-deception, the ones we tell about ourselves. These are the most toxic, because they create dangers we cannot see. Why? Telling them blinds us to uncomfortable truths about who we are and how we see the world.

Sincerity and Candor

In 1793, the philosopher Immanuel Kant defined candor as always speaking "the whole truth which [we] know."[6] He concluded that it was not realistically possible for humans to meet this standard. In fact, Kant might have enjoyed watching the 2009 movie *The Invention of Lying*, which was cowritten and codirected by featured actor Ricky Gervais.[7] It dramatizes a world in which people tell the truth, or rather say out loud exactly what is on their minds—all the time. In this full-disclosure world, advertising copy changes dramatically. For example, this is how a spokesman for Coca-Cola pitched his product in the movie:

> Hi, I'm Bob. . . . I'm here today to ask you to continue buying Coke. Sure it's a drink you've been drinking for years, and if you still enjoy it, I'd like to remind you to buy it again sometime soon. It's basically just brown sugar water, we haven't changed the ingredients much lately, so there's nothing new I can tell you about that. We changed the can around a little bit though. See, the colors here are different there, and we added a polar bear so the kids like us. Coke is very high in sugar and like any high calorie

soda it can lead to obesity in children and adults who don't sustain a very healthy diet. So that's it, it's Coke. It's very famous, everyone knows it.[8]

Kant understood that humans could never approach this level of candor. Instead, he proposed a more realistic standard: *sincerity.*[9] Sincere people, he believed, would strive to be "truthful" in everything they said. This passage from Coca-Cola CEO Roberto Goizueta's 1995 shareholder letter would have met Kant's sincerity test:

> We sell a product that not only has universal appeal and accessibility, but also meets the fundamental, frequently recurring human need for refreshment.
>
> By universal appeal, I mean we sell a product with physical attributes that the human palate enjoys, no matter what the culture or demographic status. Five or six decades ago, we stopped listening to those who said that Coca-Cola simply would not be accepted in certain societies, where centuries-old beverage consumption habits would surely lock us out. But, just as consumption of Coca-Cola surpassed the combined consumption of the two leading teas in Great Britain some time ago, so will the per capita consumption of Coca-Cola surpass that of the leading bottled water in France this year, two milestones most people said would never come to pass.
>
> Yet, such milestones do come to pass, and one of the primary reasons is the "delicious and refreshing" nature of the product that comes in a bottle, can, glass or cup of Coca-Cola.
>
> That's of great importance, but so is the universal accessibility of Coca-Cola. Not only does Coca-Cola satisfy a basic human need, it is also highly affordable to an overwhelming majority of people worldwide.

Nothing Goizueta wrote could be described as insincere, although he could have bolstered his claims by citing third-party validation for the consumption trends reported in the passage. Goizueta doesn't say that everyone finds Cola-Cola to be "delicious and refreshing."

Instead, he creates an impression that this experience is "universal." Importantly, he omits clichés and jargon that would have diluted his message.

Now consider this passage from Coca-Cola's 2010 shareholder letter:

> This past year, I had the privilege of visiting our Coca-Cola operations in 17 countries on four continents. During my travels with our associates around the world, we opened new bottling plants, visited research and development centers, worked with retail customers, met with consumers and suppliers, and collaborated with an assortment of amazing leaders from business, government and civil society. From the bustling cities of China to the remote villages of South Africa, I walked away with one overriding impression of the Coca-Cola Company. What I saw and continue to see in the second decade of the 21st century is *a company that is steadily and strategically advancing its momentum all around the world.* [author's emphasis]

Current Coca-Cola CEO Muhtar Kent's description of his travels during the year is sincere, truthful, and personal. At the end, however, he stumbles when he reflects on the significance of these experiences and reports, "[Coca-Cola] is *a company that is steadily and strategically advancing its momentum all around the world*" [author's emphasis].

How is it possible for Coke or any company to "steadily and strategically [advance] its momentum"? This description doesn't qualify as a lie. Instead, it is meaningless, the kind of doublespeak or nonsense that George Orwell portrayed in his classic novel *1984.* In our model, such commentary triggers negative points. It shows that that the writer has temporarily lost touch with the real world.

A Simple Candor Test

Just about anyone can measure the absence of candor in an executive communication. When Rittenhouse Rankings analyzes a shareholder letter, we start reading with a red pencil or pen in hand and use it to underline clichés such as "employees are our greatest assets," "our future is bright," "advancing momentum," and "we aim to create shareholder value." This kind of meaningless jargon and platitudes diminishes our understanding of the business and our trust in the leadership.

When we finish coding a communication, we look back at the pages. If we see more red than black ink on the pages, we put a company on probation. We dig further to examine the company's accounting and its marketplace claims. This was certainly true of Enron, whose 2000 shareholder letter offered the following linguistic anesthesia:

> Our *talented people, global presence, financial strength and massive market knowledge* have created our sustainable and unique businesses. EnronOnline will accelerate their growth. We plan to *leverage all of these competitive advantages to create significant value for our shareholders.* [author's emphasis]

In one short paragraph, Enron introduced six popular CEO clichés:

Talented people
Global presence
Market knowledge
Financial strength
Leverage competitive advantages
Significant value for our shareholders

Each "competitive advantage" is an important business concept, but so many generalities are meaningless to the reader. Not only do these clichés fail to inspire trust, but they should cause a prudent investor to wonder what the company might be hiding.

Investors who read between the lines and look for the absence of candor can spot companies like this that may be headed for trouble. A letter with more negative than positive candor is a sign that either the CEO has failed to engage meaningfully in the letter-writing process or that the culture is candor-blind or candor-phobic.

Without a commitment to candor from the top, lawyers and communications consultants will do their best to dilute the CEO's message and keep readers confused. Investors who find a fogged-over communication need to ask: does the CEO not understand the business, or does he or she not want owners to understand it?

A CEO decides what he wants to communicate and how. The stakes are high. Communication choices made by a CEO can determine the success of his leadership and the value of the company's stock.

SCORING FOR FOG

Rittenhouse Rankings coined an acronym for the absence of candor: "FOG." It stands for "**f**act-deficient, **o**bfuscating **g**eneralities." While the other systems in the Rittenhouse model, like Capital Stewardship, are awarded positive points, statements that are coded as FOG earn point deductions. For example, each cliché in a letter is awarded a 3-point deduction, and Orwellian or nonsensical statements trigger 5-point deductions. The 26-points deduction scored in the Enron excerpt are illustrated below:

> Our [–3] talented people, [–3] global presence, [–3] financial strength and [–3, hyperbole] massive market knowledge have created our [–3] sustainable and unique businesses. EnronOnline will accelerate their growth [Orwellian, –5]. We plan to [–3] leverage all of these competitive advantages to create [–3] significant value for our shareholders [–3].

Overused words such as *solid*, *momentum*, and *enhanced* also trigger point deductions. Rittenhouse Rankings calls these "weasel words." Why is this term appropriate? It refers to what happens when weasels invade farms to steal chicken eggs. After making a small hole in the egg, they suck out the yolk and discard the shell. A short story by Stewart Chaplin published in 1900 compared this weasel behavior to "words that suck the life out of the words next to them."[10] The term stuck.

Weasel words, clichés, jargon, and hyperbole are easy to spot. But some FOG codes require readers to dig more deeply. How can you detect when a CEO is writing about an uncomfortable subject? Look for incomplete explanations or awkward grammar. See if important facts are omitted about a strategic initiative. Whether consciously or not, this omission is evidence of FOG. When you find nonsense masquerading as common sense, be warned.

To calculate the "presence of candor score" in an executive communication, Rittenhouse Rankings totals all the positive points awarded for cash and cash flow, business opportunities, risk assessment, and other topics and then subtracts all the FOG points. In the Rittenhouse Rankings 2010 Culture and Candor Survey, the "presence of candor scores" ranged widely from only 15 percent FOG to over 300 percent. This latter score, in which negative candor points far exceed positive candor points, signals that a company is in serious trouble or could be headed for it. For example, AIG's 2005 and 2007 shareholder letters were highly transparent, but lacked candor. They indicated blue sea, a nautical term for troubled waters ahead.

Case Study: AIG Candor Alert

On March 15, 2005, Martin Sullivan, a career AIG manager, replaced CEO Hank Greenberg, who had served the company for 38 years. Over this time, Greenberg had built AIG into the largest insurer in the world. He resigned on March 14, 2005, after a highly public investigation into a complex transaction the company had entered into four years earlier. Regulators believed this had improperly reported AIG's earnings. Because of this ongoing investigation, AIG's 2004 shareholder letter was not published until June 10, 2005. Newly named CEO Sullivan began with an introduction:

> As only the third Chief Executive Officer in AIG's 86-year history, I am well aware of the tremendous opportunities and responsibilities of leading this great company. The opportunities throughout our markets are enormous, and we have the talent, resources

and focused strategies to capitalize on them. *Among our most important responsibilities is maintaining our entrepreneurial focus while serving customers efficiently and responsively, and fostering the highest professional and ethical standards.* [author's emphasis]

Sullivan's statement that one of the company's "most important responsibilities" was maintaining "our entrepreneurial focus" was a transparent admission, but from a candor perspective, Rittenhouse Rankings questioned this focus. Specifically, why would an insurance company whose success depends on prudent risk/reward analysis want to be known for having an entrepreneurial culture? Entrepreneurs are risk takers. They take on ventures with highly uncertain outcomes. Wouldn't investors prefer insurance companies where executives nurtured cautious cultures that prized conservative cash-holding policies?

More to the point, why did Sullivan believe AIG had a "responsibility" to be entrepreneurial? Would this entrepreneurial orientation compromise the company's commitment to "fostering the highest professional and ethical standards"? Rittenhouse Rankings coded this statement as "strategic dissonance" and deducted 10 points.

To his credit, Sullivan commented on the ongoing accounting investigation in his letter. He wrote:

This is a challenging time for AIG, but we are confronting the issues before us honestly and forcefully. We have met with the New York State Attorney General's office, the Securities and Exchange Commission, the Office of Thrift Supervision and several state insurance commissioners. We have communicated our commitment to cooperate fully with all investigations of accounting, brokerage commissions, sales practices and other matters. . . .

He offered his personal commitment that AIG would implement needed reforms:

Under my leadership, AIG will step up and take an active role implementing the reforms necessary at AIG and throughout the insurance industry. We are working to ensure that every employee in our organization upholds the highest standards. . . .

Sullivan also described steps he was taking to improve AIG's compliance practices:

> We have also strengthened our compliance function. Employees who have compliance questions or concerns, or have a violation to report, can contact a Compliance Help Line. Translators are available in more than 70 languages for those employees who need assistance. Employees who wish to remain anonymous may do so. We have augmented our ethics education program on a worldwide basis to reinforce the standards set forth in our Code of Conduct.

He explained that AIG would consolidate risk management into one Enterprise Risk Management department: "To enhance risk management throughout the organization, we have brought together our credit, market and operational risk management capabilities into one Enterprise Risk Management department, which is led by Bob Lewis, who brings nearly 30 years of financial services industry experience to the function."

In fact, a special committee had been formed at AIG called the "Complex Structured Finance Transaction Committee." It included senior executives from the business groups as well as from finance, legal, and claims operations, and it reported regularly to AIG's board of directors and to Sullivan. The purpose of this committee was to make certain that all business units had established policies and procedures to comply with the directives of this Committee.

Curiously, Sullivan added that one of the business units, AIG Financial Products Corporation (AIGFP), had its own separate Transaction Review Committee:

> Since April 2004, AIG Financial Products Corp. also has had its own Transaction Review Committee. All of our business units have established policies and procedures to comply with the directives of the Complex Structured Finance Transaction Committee.

This sentence prompted several questions: Why did AIGFP require its own Transaction Review Committee? What were these "Complex Structured Finance Transactions"? What did the committee monitor? Rittenhouse Rankings grew even more curious about AIGFP when we compared the ways that Sullivan reported the operating income results at AIGFP with those of the other business segments. For instance:

1. Operating income for the entire Financial Products group was reported as "$2.61 billion, compared to $1.23 billion in 2003."
2. International Lease Finance Corporation (ILFC), the largest operating lessor of advanced new aircraft to airlines around the world, had "operating income of $712.2 million in 2004, compared to $776.9 million a year earlier."
3. The Consumer Finance business reported that "operating income increased 29.6 percent in 2004 to $808.1 million."
4. The Capital Markets operations, which represent the integrated operations of AIG Financial Products Corp. and AIG Trading Group Inc., reported "operating income of $1.03 billion."

We wondered: Why did only three of the four business units report their 2004 operating income in relation to 2003 results? Why did only the Capital Markets group fail to offer a comparative measure? Had the group's 2004 operating income increased or decreased? We duly noted these questions and continued reading. The letter ended with an emotional description of AIG's culture:

> Generations of families have worked for AIG. Similarly, we have customers and agents around the world whose parents, grandparents and great-grandparents have been our customers and agents. We look forward to serving their children and grandchildren too.

> For 86 years, we have succeeded by making positive contri-
> butions to the consumers and companies we serve and the coun-
> tries where we do business. Our customers choose us because
> they know we stand behind them. We must always live up to that
> promise and earn their trust. As I have emphasized repeatedly,
> my success, and the success of AIG's management, will be mea-
> sured in large part on how well we address those issues.

All in all, the presence of candor in the 2004 letter outweighed
its absence. That 2004 letter ranked 40th in the Rittenhouse Rankings
survey, AIG's strongest showing in over four years. Would the company improve its candor rankings in future years? It did not. In fact,
the rankings continued to decline.

Three years later, Sullivan began his 2007 communication by
describing the year's promising start and its "disappointing conclusion,
both in terms of our results and share price performance."

> The U.S. credit crisis, recession fears and record-high oil prices
> caused economic disruption and uncertainty. In addition, some
> of our businesses did not meet expectations. *Nevertheless, the
> fundamental strength of our core operations is intact, and we made
> important advances in key markets.* We remain *confident in our
> strategy to leverage our financial strength and global franchise* to
> continue our growth in both emerging and developed markets.
> [author's emphasis]

The end of this passage raised questions: If the core businesses
were fundamentally strong and the noncore businesses were not, was
the company planning to exit these noncore businesses? We also wondered: What were these "important advances in key markets"?

To his credit, Sullivan did not hide AIG's disappointing financial
results. He reported that net income had dropped to $6.20 billion from
$14.05 billion. Also, diluted earnings per share had fallen to $2.39 from
$5.36. Sullivan's detailed commentary explained what had triggered
these losses. Rittenhouse Rankings was not surprised to find they were
linked to the AIGFP business:

Included in 2007 net income and adjusted net income was a charge of $11.47 billion pretax ($7.46 billion after tax) for *unrealized market valuation losses* related to the AIG Financial Products Corp. (AIGFP) *super senior credit default swap portfolio*. [author's emphasis]

Reading this passage, we asked, "What would cause this 'unrealized loss' to be realized? Would it show up in the income statement at some future time?"

Sullivan introduced a new term in his letter that had never before appeared in the Rittenhouse Rankings survey: "super senior credit default swap portfolio." While he never explained what this was, we knew it was important: these securities had triggered a $7.46 billion loss.

In the following paragraph, Sullivan attempted to answer the question we anticipated, what would happen if the "unrealized loss" was realized?

Based upon its most current analysis, AIG believes *any losses that are realized over time on the super senior credit default swap portfolio of AIGFP will not be material* to AIG's overall financial condition, although *it is possible that realized losses could be material to AIG's consolidated results of operations for an individual reporting period*. [author's emphasis]

Reading this paragraph numerous times produced mental whiplash. Such an awkwardly constructed sentence, "any losses that are realized over time . . . will not be material to AIG's overall financial condition, although it is possible that realized losses could be material to AIG's consolidated results of operations for an individual reporting period," signaled extreme discomfort. It seemed time for investors to prepare for turbulence ahead.

Still, Sullivan tried to put on his game face:

We continue to believe that AIGFP will not realize significant losses from this derivative business, which insures against the default of certain securities. Since its creation, AIGFP has been a strong performer and is an important component of AIG's diverse portfolio of businesses.

In the end, the negative candor points in AIG's 2007 letter counted by Rittenhouse Rankings were almost two times greater than the positive candor points. In the 2008 Culture and Candor survey, AIG's 90th place ranking signaled a potentially dangerous loss of trust between the company and its stakeholders.

On September 16, 2008, just six months after the 2007 shareholder letter was published, AIG was granted an $85 billion bailout from the U.S. Treasury. *Time* magazine reported that AIG "was deemed too huge (its assets top $1 trillion), too global and too interconnected to fail."[11] Reporter Justin Fox offered a revealing report on AIG's "super senior credit default swap portfolio." He simply described the significance of these complex securities:

> [AIG FP is] a huge player in the new and *mysterious business of credit-default swaps*: derivative securities that allow banks, hedge funds and other financial players to insure against loans gone bad.... AIG generally sells credit-default swaps, thereby promising to insure others against defaults. *It's a great business when defaults are low; when they rise it can turn toxic.... AIG FP lost more than $10 billion in 2007 and $14.7 billion in the first six months of this year. That, along with losses in other investment portfolios, has cut deeply into the parent company's capital reserves.* [author's emphasis]

Rittenhouse Rankings could only wonder why Sullivan had never provided such a clear explanation about the risks of this complex business. Fox tried to explain why government officials and regulators never raised questions that were readily apparent from reading the company's communications:

> While the company's insurance subsidiaries are regulated by New York insurance superintendent Eric Dinallo, it is overseen at the holding company level by the federal Office of Thrift Supervision,

which mostly regulates the savings and loan industry. Plus, it was awfully hard for outsiders—and even insiders—to understand the gravity of the company's problems. "You can read through every financial statement in the world and have absolutely no clue as to the risks they are taking," says Leo Tilman, a former Bear Stearns strategist who now runs the advisory firm L.M. Tilman & Co.

Rittenhouse Rankings disagreed with Mr. Tilman's assessment. Our reading of the 2007 shareholder letter revealed plenty of clues that signaled the need for extreme caution.

In his article, reporter Fox faulted AIG for providing "a mere paragraph on AIGFP" in its annual report:

> The particular risks that brought the company to the brink of bankruptcy seem to lie not with its core insurance businesses but with its derivatives-trading subsidiary *AIG Financial Products. AIG FP, as it's called, merits a mere paragraph* in the nine-page description of the company's businesses in its *most recent annual report.* [author's emphasis]

However, Rittenhouse Rankings had readily found two alarming paragraphs about AIGFP in Sullivan's shareholder letter that pointed to potentially serious problems.

When Sullivan's 2007 letter was published on March 14, 2008, AIG's stock was trading at about $41. Had investors read this alarming statement and prudently sold their AIG stock, they would have avoided the material drop in its value to $1.57 at year-end. In other words, transparency and candor lapses provided clear indications of trouble before they were recognized by the market. So why were so many investors, regulators, and customers blindsided by this impending disaster? We offer three explanations:

1. *Avoidance.* It is human nature, and therefore investor nature, to deny problems as long as possible and hope they go away.

2. *Doubting the power of words.* Investors rely on accounting numbers and ignore the power of words to reveal, predict, and create the future.

3. *Mistrusting common sense.* Investors chose to believe the financial media, company analysts, and credit agencies rather than trust their own common sense and good judgment.

Goldman Sachs and AIG

In 2010, a brilliant lawyer I know asked me to review tortuous language in the Goldman Sachs 2009 shareholder letter. He had circled a 935-word passage that attempted to explain whether Goldman had been financially exposed to an AIG default. It seemed to deflect accusations that Goldman had received preferential treatment in the U.S. government's decision to bail out AIG. Accounting for 40 percent of the shareholder letter commentary, this explanation began with a clear statement of facts:

> Since the mid-1990s, Goldman Sachs has had a trading relationship with AIG. Our business with them spanned a number of their entities, including many of their insurance subsidiaries. And it included multiple activities, such as stock lending, foreign exchange, fixed income, futures and mortgage trading.
>
> AIG was an AAA-rated company, one of the largest and considered one of the most sophisticated trading counterparts in the world. We established credit terms with them commensurate with those extended to other major counterparts, including a willingness to do substantial trading volumes but subject to collateral arrangements that were tightly managed.

Then, abruptly, the FOG rolled in. The next paragraphs offered dazzling displays of obfuscation. The italicized words below highlight business jargon and tortured phrases that raised important questions:

> As we do with most other counterparty relationships, we limited our overall credit exposure to AIG through *a combination of col-*

lateral and market hedges in order to protect ourselves against *the potential inability of AIG to make good* on its commitments. We established *a pre-determined hedging program*, which provided that *if aggregate exposure* moved above a certain threshold, credit default swaps (CDS) and other credit hedges would be obtained. This hedging was designed to keep our overall risk to manageable levels.

As part of our trading with AIG, we purchased from them *protection on super senior collateralized debt obligation (CDO) risk. This protection was designed to hedge equivalent transactions executed with clients taking the other side of the same trades. In so doing, we served as an intermediary in assisting our clients to express a defined view on the market.* The net risk we were exposed to *was consistent with our role as a market intermediary rather than a proprietary market participant.* [author's emphasis]

The contrast between this commentary and the earlier paragraphs in the letter was stark. When I asked the lawyer why he could not see this difference, he replied, "I thought I wasn't smart enough to understand what they were saying."

I have heard this justification many times. And each time I wonder: Why is it comparatively easy to deny and ignore rather than to trust our own good judgment and common sense? Is it because we fear our vulnerability in relation to leaders whom we must trust? To imagine that they would injure us to advance their self-interest is disturbing, even frightening. Instead, we choose to doubt ourselves. We become like the adults in Hans Christian Andersen's fairy tale *The Emperor's New Clothes*. We praise the splendor of the emperor's invisible new robes and deny what our eyes tell us to be true—he is as naked as a jaybird.

THE PREDICTIVE VALUE OF CANDOR AND EXECUTION: HEWLETT-PACKARD AND DELL

In July 1999, Carly Fiorina was chosen to be CEO of Hewlett-Packard, becoming the first female chief executive officer of a Fortune 20 corporation in the history of U.S. business. When Rittenhouse Rankings compared the beginning of Fiorina's first shareholder letter, published in December 1999, with the opening of CEO Michael Dell's shareholder letter for Dell Inc., we gained valuable insights into Fiorina's leadership style.

Fiorina addressed her letter to "HP Shareowners" and began by offering her impressions of HP after just six months on the job. She described how impressed she was with "the soul, spirit and character of HP," but failed to mention the qualities that defined HP's "soul and spirit":

> When I came to HP—in July 1999—I was impressed with the people I met, impressed by the soul, the spirit, the character of HP. I continue to be impressed. It is a privilege to lead this great company, a company that has invented so much in the 20th century and has so much to offer in the 21st.

In contrast, Michael Dell imagined a broader audience. He addressed his 1999 shareholder letter to "Our Customers, Stockholders, Suppliers, and Employees." His opening statement described Dell as "the most successful company in our industry" and reported on the company's accomplishments:

> Dell entered the 21st century as the most successful company in our industry. We are the No. 1 computer-systems company in the United States and No. 2 worldwide, rising from No. 25 a decade earlier. Ours was the No. 1 performing stock in the Standard & Poor's 500 in the 1990s. These accomplishments are a great source of pride for our employees, and the result of our continued ability to win the confidence and business of customers around the globe.

Both CEOs next reported on their companies' earnings. In contrast to HP's low-key "solid start to the year" and "slim revenue growth," Dell exuberantly reported that the company "grew at twice or more the industry rate in every product category, every customer segment, and every regional market, and faster than any major competitor.

Our direct business model remains the industry's standard for growth, flexibility and profitability."

While HP reported that it had "improved our execution and the competitiveness of our product portfolios," Dell boasted that "our consistently industry-leading operating results *are achieved* because of *a zealous focus on our customers*, together with *crisp execution*" [author's emphasis]. HP announced it was developing a "plan to generate profitable growth and consistency of financial results," but Dell described a dynamic pioneering direct business model based on "our deep understanding of their needs [that] enables us to effectively and efficiently develop and deliver relevant products and services, and a superior customer experience." In other words, Dell's active, customer-focused reporting made it sound like the rabbit to HP's tortoise.

Two years later, Carly Fiorina showed that she had grown into her CEO role. Her 2001 shareholder letter was confident and visionary. It imagined how HP would capitalize on the power of an interconnected world made possible by advances in computing power and the growth of the Internet:

> In 2001, we witnessed a heightened acceleration away from the era of pure products and toward a new era of interconnected, networked solutions. We are now entering a period of computing that defies all limits and crosses all borders, in which everything works with everything else, everywhere, all the time.
>
> Since I arrived at HP, we've taken aim at the heart of this transformation, and set a goal to reinvent this great company: to restructure and revitalize ourselves to recapture the spirit of invention that is our birthright, and apply it to meeting customer needs.
>
> Our ambition is simple and clear. We believe that HP has a unique opportunity and unique capabilities to transform markets by being at the center of the emerging technology landscape: connected, intelligent devices and environments; a new generation of Web-based applications and services—e-services; and the Internet infrastructure that keeps the entire system up and running, always.

Her letter started with a story about HP's founding values. She reminded investors that founders Bill Hewlett and Dave Packard regarded growth "as a requirement for survival." To address this mandate, Fiorina announced on September 6, 2001, that Hewlett-Packard would merge with the Compaq Computer Company. Capping a two-year search among various acquisition candidates, Fiorina wrote that both the HP directors and management were convinced this merger was "the single best way to create shareowner value and return HP to industry leadership."

Reading between the lines, Rittenhouse Rankings asked, "Why was a merger with Compaq needed to 'return HP to industry leadership'?" And why was there no mention of the merger's strategic advantages? Instead, Fiorina addressed an important investor question: Could HP successfully execute the merger and achieve the intended synergies and savings? To build investor confidence, Fiorina offered a story at the end of her letter about founder Dave Packard:

> When Dave Packard took his first professional job at General Electric in 1935, he was given a challenge—quality control of mercury-vapor rectifier tubes. They were made in batches of 20, and every tube in the last batch had failed before Dave was given the job.
>
> He began by learning everything he could about why the process might have failed in the past. Working with the factory people to conduct tests and identify every possible cause of failure, Dave ensured that every single tube in his batch of 20 passed its final test perfectly.
>
> I think of this story when I hear the critics predict that the integration of two large companies will fail. Just like Dave Packard, we have done our due diligence. We have addressed the critical factors for successful merger execution—including defining governance for the new company, ensuring an unyielding focus on customers throughout the pre- and post-integration process, developing clear product roadmaps, preparing ourselves for Day One of the new HP across every level of the company, ensuring that we have rigorous plans for capturing the

cost-savings we have identified and staying in constant communication with employees and stakeholders.

We have studied scores of mergers to identify possible stumbling blocks. We are leveraging our experiences with the Agilent spin-off and with Compaq's merger with Digital Equipment. Our dedicated merger integration team of more than 450 people is applying a rigorous methodology to oversee and execute a thorough pre-close integration plan to prepare the new HP for success on Day One—and beyond.

We know, as Bill and Dave did, that if you believe in people, if you let them make full use of their talents, they can accomplish great things.

That has always been the power of the HP Way—and it always will be.

After reading this story, we wondered: why would Fiorina compare the complex merger of two multibillion-dollar corporations with vastly different cultures to Packard's controlled laboratory success? Her story was one of the oddest we had ever encountered. Fiorina clearly wanted to convince readers that HP would persevere in its quest to realize merger synergies. However, she failed to show an appreciation for the complexity of merging different corporate cultures and different systems, policies, and practices. Lacking such a focus, the story raised doubts in our minds that the merger could be executed successfully.

In fact, the merger proved to be Fiorina's undoing. A bruising proxy fight with the son of one of HP's founders erupted soon after the announcement. He and other board members questioned the merger's benefits. In the end, Fiorina won the proxy battle, and Compaq was acquired. But questions persisted about the wisdom of the merger. The board asked Fiorina to leave the company in February 2005.

Candor and Execution

The HP story underscores the strategic link between candor and execution. Jack Welch and others have noted that the absence of candor in a workplace can be a significant deterrent to success. As we noted in Chapter 2, Welch feared that bureaucratic cultures discouraged people from candidly speaking their minds. He advocated that companies develop corporate cultures to encourage "honest feedback." He explained, "If you reward candor, you'll get it."[12]

Management consultant Lynn Harris has similarly championed the importance of authentic and honest internal communications that lead to "better, faster decisions and actions." In an article titled, "Truth-Telling: Confronting the Reality of the Lack of Candor Inside Organizations,"[13] she described the need to build trusting and collaborative cultures where "opposing views are debated and more effective solutions and innovations are created." At the same time, she admitted that finding such attitudes in companies was far from the norm. She wrote that most organizations feared truth-telling:

> I'm not talking about malevolent dishonesty. No one goes to work thinking "I'm going to hinder my own and my company's performance by withholding the truth from my colleagues." I'm talking about the many moments each day where we think one thing, but say something different; where we have an idea that may be of value, but we hold back and say nothing; where we are called upon to give an honest opinion, but decide to say what is easier or what we think others want to hear.

Alan Mulally, who was named CEO of Ford Motor Company in September 2006, held similarly strong views on the strategic value of collaborative and open cultures. In fact, changing bureaucratic attitudes at Ford was the centerpiece of his turnaround strategy.

APPLAUDING CANDOR

At year-end 2006, Ford Motor Company reported its largest-ever operating loss—a whopping $18 billion. It posted negative earnings per share of $6.72, down from positive earnings of $0.78 in 2005.

In his 2006 letter to shareholders, written just months after joining the company, Mulally wrote that he met once a week in half-day sessions with his senior management team to review progress and address roadblocks. "Problems and concerns are discussed candidly," he wrote in his letter. Reading this, I wondered, *how* is that happening?

The *how* was revealed in *American Icon*, Bryce Hoffman's 2012 page-turning history of Mulally's rescue of Ford.[14] It offered a front-row seat into these weekly senior management meetings. The first was held on September 26, just 21 days after Mulally started at the company. As the managers filed into the room, they discovered that the rules for the meeting were written on large sheets of paper posted on the wall: "Respect, listen, help and appreciate each other." However, these managers had a different agenda. They would size up this new CEO and figure out what he wanted to hear.

Mulally told the group he expected candid discussion of problems. Instead, he got happy talk. Each week he listened respectfully as business heads described their problem-free operations. Over the next several weeks, Mulally grew increasingly frustrated with such a one-sided view of company operations. In the meeting on October 26, 2006, he asked, "We're going to lose billions of dollars this year. Is there anything that's not going well here?"

The answer to his question was deafening silence. No one in the room trusted that Mulally would keep his word, that straight talk would go unpunished.

One executive, Mark Fields, the head of North American operations, decided he would test Mulally's promise. His people had just told him the North American launch of the new Ford Edge was in trouble. Strange sounds were coming from the suspension system, and it appeared the launch would have to be postponed. Fields decided to announce this news at the next weekly performance meeting. He had nothing to lose. He expected to be fired after reporting the launch delay.

In that morning's presentation, Fields put up a PowerPoint slide. It showed the Edge launch coded in red—a sign of danger. He declared, "We're holding the launch."

No one spoke. All eyes were on the CEO.

Suddenly Mulally put his hands together and began to clap loudly. "Mark," he exclaimed, "this is great visibility. Who can help him with this?" Two hands shot up and offers were made to send quality experts to the production plant.

This candor breakthrough was the moment Mulally had waited for. But at the next meeting, Fields continued to be the only leader to discuss business problems. Nevertheless, his presence sent a message: He was not a "dead man walking." He had not been fired. The managers saw that Mulally was true to his word: honesty would not be punished.

At the next performance meeting, every executive showed up with slides coded in red. Mulally later would call this meeting "the defining moment in Ford's turnaround."

Now the company could execute the strategy that Mulally had laid out.

"Strategy" is the third system in the Rittenhouse Rankings Sustainable Business Model. When we read executive communications, we look for strategic plans, actions, and results.

CHAPTER 6

Strategy

Strategy, noun

1a. The science and art of using all the forces of a nation to execute approved plans as effectively as possible during peace or war.

 b. The science and art of military command as applied to the overall planning and conduct of large-scale combat operations.

2. A plan of action resulting from strategy or intended to accomplish a specific goal.

3. The art or skill of using stratagems in endeavors such as politics and business.

[French *stratégie*, from Greek *stratēgiā*, office of a general, from *stratēgos*, general; Greek *stratēgia*, generalship, from *stratēgos*. First known use: 1810.][1]

earning that the word *strategy* is derived from a Greek word meaning "office of a general" got me thinking about what CEOs have in common with high-ranking officers. Both leaders create winning and losing strategies. They size up the strengths and weaknesses of their competitors (enemies). They decide how to allocate resources (artillery), map out product development and marketing plans (battlefields), and motivate teams of employees (soldiers). Successful CEOs create straightforward strategies based on reliable information and sound analysis that inspire people to action.

CASE STUDY: FORD MOTOR COMPANY'S ONE TEAM, ONE PLAN, AND ONE GOAL

Simplicity and reliability were the hallmarks of CEO Alan Mulally's communications after he was named Ford Motor Company's CEO in 2006. The company's turnaround strategy included just three elements: *One Team, One Plan, and One Goal.* These were described in his shareholder letter, released just six months after joining Ford:

One Team

In any successful enterprise, people come first. A skilled and motivated team working together can accomplish incredible things. The principles and practices we have put in place at Ford to run our business are unlocking the full potential of the people who work here.

Everyone with a stake in the outcome is included in the decision making process. Together, we developed a single plan for our entire global enterprise, with clear performance goals. Although we work as a team, individuals are given responsibility and authority, and held accountable for delivering results. Achievements are measured by facts and data, not anecdotes and opinions.

One Plan

In the past, Ford's regional operations were run as largely autonomous business units. Many of them were highly successful operating this way, but in today's intensely competitive global market this system has too many inefficiencies to create sustained success. We are moving quickly to change it.

Mulally described a new unified operating structure in his letter and laid out four key priorities that would align and guide the actions of the entire global team:

1. Aggressively restructuring our company to be profitable at a lower volume and changed product mix
2. Accelerating product development while achieving manufacturing excellence through reduced complexity and improved quality
3. Obtaining financing to complete our plans
4. Working together with teamwork and accountability

Then he described Ford's "One Goal":

Our goal is simple—to build more of the products that people really want and value. Exciting new products that reflect the needs of today's and tomorrow's customers, with striking designs that are safer, more fuel efficient and offer even greater value. That includes an expanded commitment to small cars, more crossovers, and more capable and fuel efficient trucks.

Look for strategic statements like these when you read an executive communication. Pay attention to how a company intends to meet the needs of its customers and employees. Look for leaders who match their words with actions.

It takes considerable effort to explain complex strategies and opportunities simply. CEOs must sort and prioritize their disclosures. And investors must be on the lookout for communications overloaded with unnecessary information. This can reveal leaders lacking in strategic confidence. It's a balancing act. As Albert Einstein remarked, "Things should be made as simple as possible, but no simpler."

To find strategically confident and competent leaders, Rittenhouse Rankings looks for seven clues. These include executive actions to:

1. Distill complex strategies
2. Set performance milestones

3. Link strategy and capital discipline
4. Prioritize positioning actions
5. Communicate efficiently
6. Build broad-based agreement through strategic repetition
7. Disclose unique competitive advantages

Each is described below.

CLUE 1: STATE COMPLEX STRATEGIES SIMPLY

Case Study: Toyota's Strategic Principles

Like those of Ford's Mulally, then-Toyota CEO Katsuaki Watanabe's strategies were clear and direct. He reported on two key principles in his 2006 shareholder letter: (1) to "[provide] clean and safe products and [enhance] the quality of life everywhere through all our activities" and (2) "to create and develop advanced technologies and provide outstanding products and services that fulfill the needs of customers worldwide."

These were captured in a one-sentence description of the automaker's strategy:

> *Our key strategies for growth* are *enhancing technology development capabilities* centered on *environmental technology* and *increasing production through the advancement of localization.* [author's emphasis]

Toyota's early leadership in manufacturing and selling hybrid automobiles revealed the success of this strategy, which advanced technology to meet consumers' environmental and quality-of-life goals. In 2006, then-President Jim Press of Toyota's North American operations commented on the company's intention to put gasoline-electric technology in more U.S. vehicles. "Hybrid isn't an alternative," he said. "It will be the heart of most of everything we drive. There will be diesel hybrids, advanced gasoline hybrids, fuel-cell hybrids, [and] ethanol hybrids."[2] At that time Toyota accounted for 72 percent of the U.S. hybrid market. With gasoline prices at record levels, total hybrid sales in the United States rose 28 percent in the first five months of 2006.[3]

Toyota's second growth strategy in 2006, "advancement of localization," described a goal to build cars closer to its customers and expand manufacturing plants overseas. Plants then under construction in China and Texas would increase Toyota's annual production capacity by 300,000 vehicles. New manufacturing plants planned for Thailand, China, Russia, and Canada were expected to boost annual capacity by another 700,000 units.[4]

Case Study: General Motors

In contrast to the action-oriented statements in Watanabe's and Mulally's 2006 shareholder letters, General Motors CEO Rick Wagoner presented a strategy that explained what the company did, but it looked backward, not forward:

> . . . *we have a very straightforward strategy: great cars and trucks that build strong brands, supported by industry-leading technology.* Students of GM and the industry know this is not a new strategy. It's the one that made GM number one more than 75 years ago; now, it's re-making GM all over again, all over the world. [author's emphasis]

Wagoner's fundamental goal for the company was to structure it for sustained profitability and growth. This was vitally important. Consider that GM had been losing money ever since 2004. But who would enact these needed changes? Employees and customers were curiously absent from Wagoner's strategic statement.

Unlike Mulally, who based Ford's turnaround strategy on the principle that people come first "in any successful enterprise," the only people mentioned in Wagoner's strategy statement were "students of GM and the industry." Instead of mentioning the employees who would make the company's cars and trucks, Wagoner stated that these *vehicles* (author's italics) would "build strong brands supported by industry-leading technology."

Wagoner reminded readers that this was "not a new strategy." It had made GM the number one automaker for more than 75 years. But maintaining a first-place sales ranking in 2006 was proving to be unprofitable given the company's high legacy costs. That year, GM's automotive business alone lost $3.2 billion. Wagoner's focus on the past raised an obvious question: What drove him to continue pursuing a strategy gushing red ink?

Toward the end of this letter, Wagoner broadened the company's strategy to include global positioning:

> Our goal is to fundamentally transform GM, into a globally integrated automaker that creates great cars and trucks, with outstanding design and the best technology, building strong brands—*a company that is truly global, not just in terms of where we build and sell, but in our mindset.* [author's emphasis]

Wagoner's desire to build a company with a global "mindset" recognized the rapid growth in consumer spending in Asia and other emerging nations. But what were the qualities that defined this global mindset? Because Wagoner never described them, it was impossible for investors to gauge how a new "mindset" would change the company's performance. Investors who followed the company probably guessed that the motivation for adopting this global perspective was prompted by the success of non-U.S. automakers like Toyota, which were capturing more of GM's U.S. market share every year.

Wagoner had reasons to fear Toyota's growing dominance based on product quality and competitively low labor costs. In 2003, Toyota surpassed Ford as the world's number two automaker[5] and was looking to replace GM as number one. In 2006, a leaked document from Toyota's global master plan reported a goal to control 15 percent of the world car market by 2010. However, rather than combat this threat by investing in innovative new technologies to raise fuel efficiencies and reduce costs as Toyota was doing, Wagoner was focused on changing attitudes and minds.

Each of the letters authored by Wagoner, Watanabe, and Mulally offered different strategies. But how could investors determine which CEO would be most successful in executing them?

CLUE 2: SET PERFORMANCE MILESTONES

To evaluate a CEO's execution advantage, Rittenhouse Rankings looks for performance milestones. Here is what Mulally wrote in his 2006 shareholder letter:

> Our most immediate concern is fixing our business in North America. We are taking the painful but necessary steps [1] to achieve a $5 billion reduction in our annual operating costs by 2008 compared to 2005. And we are accelerating our new product development. [2] By the end of 2008, 70 percent of our Ford, Lincoln and Mercury lineup by volume in North America will be all-new or significantly freshened compared with 2006 models. [3] *We also will speed up the time it takes us to get new products to market by 30 to 50 percent.* In 2009 and beyond, the pace of new product introductions will accelerate even further. [4] *Our plan is to return our North American Automotive operations to profitability by 2009.* [author's emphasis]

In one paragraph, Mulally clearly laid out four measures to achieve Ford's One Goal. The company would (1) reduce operating costs by $5 billion in 2008; (2) increase the number of new models in the Ford, Lincoln, and Mercury lines by 70 percent; (3) shrink by 30 to 50 percent the time that it takes to get new products to market; and (4) report profits in the North American business by 2009.

GM's Wagoner omitted performance milestones in his 2006 shareholder letter. Instead, he described the results of cost-cutting initiatives in GM's North American automotive operations:

> We cut $9 billion in structural costs on a running rate basis by the end of 2006—$2 billion above the target I discussed in my

letter to you last year, and $4 billion above our initial target. *We realized $6.8 billion of these savings in our 2006 financials, and plan to realize the full $9 billion in 2007.* [author's emphasis]

Rittenhouse Rankings read this paragraph several times. At first it seemed that Wagoner was setting a milestone to realize the full savings in 2007. Parsing through this confusion, however, it appeared that GM would realize only $6.8 billion of these cuts in the 2006 time frame and would report the remainder in 2007. Instead of setting milestones, Wagoner was explaining accounting differences. Similarly, he described actions that were intended to improve performance, but again neglected to report quantitative progress metrics:

Major actions included reducing our salaried and hourly workforce, revising U.S. salaried and hourly retiree health care benefits, restructuring our U.S. salaried employee pension plan, decreasing our executive and board of directors' compensation, and aggressively pursuing structural-cost reductions throughout the company.

Then Wagoner made a confident prediction about future success. He declared that GM would continue to increase spending on new products, "despite [the company's] financial challenges":

The most important element of our future success will always be great cars and trucks. To support that, and despite our financial challenges, we continue to raise spending on new products. *In 2007 and 2008, we plan to spend $8.5 billion to $9 billion on capital investments, an increase of nearly $1 billion from 2005 and 2006.* Last year, nearly 30 percent of our U.S. retail sales volume came from newly launched products, up from about 20 percent in 2005. In 2007, that number will grow. [author's emphasis]

GM's strategy would require spending more money on new products. But how would this spending stem the tide of red ink? Furthermore, how would GM fund its ambitious new product initiatives? This was not mentioned. Instead, Wagoner continued his litany about GM's great products and described new launches planned for 2007 and beyond:

> In North America, we'll launch a number of important new vehicles, including the 2008 Chevrolet Malibu family sedan and second-generation Cadillac CTS luxury sedan. Both won widespread praise at this year's Detroit auto show for their compelling exterior designs, well-crafted interiors, improved fuel efficiency and innovative features.
>
> Of course, we'll launch many other exciting cars and trucks throughout the world this year, including the Opel GT and Cadillac BLS wagon in Europe, the new Buick Park Avenue in China, the Chevrolet Matiz in India, the Chevrolet Captiva throughout our Latin America, Africa and Middle East region, and the Chevrolet HHR, which will be expanded into Europe and throughout the Asia Pacific region.
>
> Only by introducing stylish, segment-leading cars and trucks will we improve the image and value of our brands and stand out among the many choices in the marketplace. That's why we're committed to ensuring that GM cars and trucks are design leaders, inside and out—cars like the Chevy Camaro convertible.

Rittenhouse Rankings also noted that Wagoner failed to mention customers in this commentary. In fact, the word *customer* was found only once in his 2006 letter. In contrast, Toyota mentioned customers eight times and Ford five times.

At the end of his launch commentary, Wagoner described the benefits of GM's global product development system. These were "increasingly evident" in "crisper product execution, shorter life cycles, better quality, lower cost and a real focus on making GM, once again, a design-driven company."

But this commentary failed to build our confidence. What were the quantitative metrics GM used to determine that product execution was "crisper" and "better quality"? How was the company measuring returns on investment and its cost of capital? Other than describing cash flow and liquidity management, Wagoner's letter omitted reports on GM's capital discipline practices.

CLUE 3: LINK STRATEGY AND CAPITAL DISCIPLINE

Investors who follow Berkshire Hathaway know that CEO Buffett is singularly focused on intelligently allocating capital. He invests in businesses that take a dollar of invested capital and turn it into more than a dollar of profit.

Rittenhouse Rankings looks for CEOs who link their strategies with capital discipline. Here is how Toyota's executive vice-president for finance, Mitsuo Kinoshita, described the company's liquidity practices in his 2006 annual report letter:

> Toyota maintains a solid financial base by ensuring sufficient liquidity and stable shareholders' equity. [1] *At fiscal 2006 year-end, liquid assets* were approximately ¥3.8 trillion while shareholders' equity stood at roughly ¥10.5 trillion.* Toyota's sound financial position enables the Company [2] *to continue flexible, forward-looking investment—even during sharp fluctuations in operating and market condition* and [3] *underpins the high credit ratings that give access to low-cost, stable financing.* Given the expected growth in automotive markets worldwide, I believe that [4] *maintaining adequate liquid funds is essential for the implementation of forward-looking investment to enhance products, develop next-generation technology, and establish production and sales systems in Japan and overseas for the global expansion of operations.* [author's emphasis]

In the passage above, Kinoshita offered four elements that define Toyota's plan to ensure "sufficient liquidity and stable shareholders' equity." Specifically, he:

1. Measured the ratio of liquidity to shareholders' equity

---

* Excluding finance subsidiaries.

2. Emphasized the importance of maintaining consistent investment throughout economic cycles
3. Reminded investors that strong liquidity leads to strong credit ratings, which in turn lead to stable, low-cost financing
4. Linked liquidity maintenance to strategic goals that will enhance products, develop new technology, and expand production and sales systems globally

This commentary shows that Toyota is focused on capital discipline.

To his credit, CEO Wagoner also reported on how GM was managing its liquidity (the amount of cash and securities that could easily be converted to cash). He described the actions the company was taking to boost its cash position. These were critically important. In 2006, GM's automotive operations had posted a $3.8 billion cash shortfall.

To boost liquidity, GM expected to raise $2.3 billion in cash by selling "all or part of our equity stakes in Isuzu Motors Ltd. and Suzuki Motor Corp." The company also sold a 51 percent stake in General Motors Acceptance Corporation (GMAC), its credit and financing business. These actions were expected to raise $13 billion over three years. By year-end 2006, GM's liquidity position had substantially improved to more than $26 billion. Wagoner stated in his letter that, "Moving the business to positive operating cash flow is a top priority."

Ford's capital discipline report in the 2006 letter was linked to the third point in Mulally's four-point strategic plan: to obtain "financing to complete our plans." He reported that Ford had completed $23.5 billion in new funding to finance the company's restructuring. Preparing for tough times ahead, the company had mortgaged almost all its assets.[6] This brought the company's total automotive liquidity to $46 billion at year-end.

To measure the relative importance of these reports, Rittenhouse Rankings checked GM and Ford's liquidity statements against the numbers reported on their 2006 balance sheets (cash and securities that could easily be converted to cash). When we divided each company's

Table 6.1   **Cash and Cash Equivalents as a Percentage of Sales (Year-End 2006)**

1. Ford Motor	35.1%
2. General Motors	13.8
3. Toyota	12.6
4. Berkshire Hathaway	38.5
Average	**25.0%**

total liquidity by total automotive sales, we found that GM's liquidity-to-sales ratio was only 13.8 percent compared to Ford's 35.1 percent (see Table 6.1). Ford was going all out to maximize liquidity to support its auto sales and operations, but GM was tinkering. In fact, Ford's ratio almost matched Berkshire Hathaway's ratio of 38.5 percent.

CLUE 4: PRIORITIZE POSITIONING ACTIONS

The protocols used by Rittenhouse Rankings to code positioning actions and business opportunities in executive communications were described in Chapter 3. We code these initiatives as: *pricing, advertising and marketing, brand, safety practices, team, products, global markets*, and *customers*.

Pricing describes initiatives to set prices and boost sales. Other positioning actions include *advertising and marketing* and *brand-building* campaigns, as well as raising money in capital markets to fund new ventures or to strengthen the balance sheet. *Safety practices* can position companies to build caring, responsible corporate cultures and increase operating efficiencies.

Products and *global markets* guide Rittenhouse Rankings to find *business opportunities* that generate top-line revenues. We search for descriptions of new and existing products and also plans for geographic expansion to create new loyal *customers*.

Figure 6.1 shows the frequency of these key words in the shareholder letters of these three automakers from 2005 to 2007 and 2010. (After declaring bankruptcy in 2009, GM did not publish annual reports for 2008 and 2009.)

Rittenhouse Rankings believes that word choices reveal CEO's consciousness, what is top of mind when they think about plans and actions. Applying this principle, we made the following observations about what each company was most focused on in developing its positioning actions and seizing the most important business opportunities:

1. GM was most alert to brand issues; while Toyota was the least.
2. GM was most focused on its global positioning, while Ford offered the fewest global statements.
3. GM used the word *pricing* the most; Ford used it least.
4. Ford was most focused on products; Toyota was the least focused.

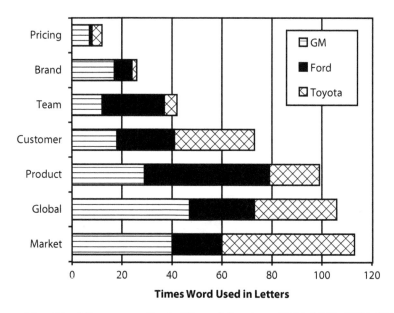

Figure 6.1   Word Frequency: Ford, GM, and Toyota—2005, 2006, 2007, 2010*

* GM did not publish annual reports in 2008 and 2009.

5. Ford used the word *team* most often; GM used it least.
6. Toyota was most focused on markets; Ford was the least focused.
7. Toyota was the most focused on customers, using the word 2.1 times more than GM, which mentioned them least.

How did these 2007 observations play out in 2012? Consider that Ford was still trying to increase its global sales and footprint, particularly in China and Europe. In 2011, GM regained its number one sales ranking after the Great East Japan Earthquake disrupted Toyota's supplies and manufacturing. However, by July 2012, Toyota again passed GM as the world's top automotive seller.[7]

And as he did before, Mullaly still wrote the most efficient shareholder letter, as evidenced by the Rittenhouse Rankings surveys from 2009 to 2011. We believe this is an indicator of respectful communications but also operational efficiency. Companies that communicate more content with fewer words are more likely to rally and align their employees. This allows them to execute strategies more precisely.

CLUE 5: COMMUNICATE EFFICIENTLY

Table 6.2 shows the efficiency scores for Ford, GM, and Toyota in the Rittenhouse Rankings Culture and Candor surveys from 2007 to 2011.

Table 6.2   **Efficiency Scores for Ford, GM, and Toyota**

Survey Year	2007	2008	2009	2010	2011
Ford Motor	(6.6)	(9.3)	22.7	34.4	33.4
Toyota Motor	29.1	14.5	5.8	12.9	5.7
General Motors	18.5	(0.6)	N/A*	N/A*	(1.1)

* Did not publish annual report.

To calculate these scores, Rittenhouse Rankings divided the net candor points in each shareholder letter (totaling all positive and negative candor points) by the number of words in the letter. The resulting metric represents how many units of meaningful information are delivered per word in the communication. In other words, Ford's 2008 shareholder letter delivered 22.7 units of candor per word compared to Toyota's 5.8 units of candor.

Why is communication efficiency important to execution? Consider that company employees are also shareholders. Wearing two stakeholder hats, they are more likely than others to read the annual report. A CEO who writes a letter noted for efficient, straight talk and principled engagement builds a culture in which decisions can be made quickly. People in the company are empowered to act because they trust the leader and have confidence in the direction of the enterprise. They are encouraged to work collaboratively to achieve common goals.

Conversely, employees who read rambling, meaningless executive messages will be discouraged from taking initiative and working together. Educator Parker Palmer described what happens when leaders choose words and actions that are not aligned:

> I know from my experience inside corporations and large-scale organizations that everybody is busy sizing up the leader and asking, "Is this a divided person or a person of integrity? Is what we see what we get? Is he or she the same on the inside as on the outside?" Students ask this about teachers in the classroom. Employees ask it about their bosses. Citizens ask it about their politicians. When the answer is, "No, what we're seeing on the outside is not the same as who they are on the inside," then everything starts to fall apart. That's because I have just described an unsafe situation: When leaders with the power to call the tune and shape the dance are perceived as lacking congruence or integrity, they create unsafe situations. And what do people do in unsafe situations? They start hiding out. They start faking it. They start giving less than what they have to give. They start playing it close to the vest. They start shielding themselves.

An organization simply cannot function at anywhere near full effectiveness when that kind of thing is going on—and there is a lot of that going on.[8]

In addition to efficiency, Rittenhouse Rankings examines executive communications to find if leaders have set out a plan and can stick to it. We compare letter commentary each year to determine the consistency of strategic intentions, plans, and results.

CLUE 6: BUILD WIDESPREAD AGREEMENT THROUGH STRATEGIC REPETITION

Irish playwright George Bernard Shaw once said, "The problem with communication is the illusion that it has occurred." He described a universal experience—we want people to remember what we say, but this often does not happen.

Effective speakers know this. They follow the adage: "tell them what you're going to tell them, tell them, and then tell them what you've told them." In the Digital Age, this advice is more relevant than ever. Each day we are assaulted with so much information we must filter out messages that do not interest us or that conflict with our beliefs.

How can executives break through this data deluge and introduce new ideas? It takes patience and strategic repetition. A study of communications between bosses and employees published in the June 2011 *Harvard Business Review* confirmed the importance of repetitive messaging:[9]

> Researchers discovered that one of every seven communications by the managers was completely redundant with a previous communication using a different technology. They also saw that the managers who were deliberately redundant moved their projects forward faster and more smoothly.

How effectively did the three automotive CEOs follow the adage of repeating important messages? Did they reiterate important messages to emphasize strategic consistency?

Toyota

In his 2007 letter, Toyota President Katsuaki Watanabe repeated the automaker's 2006 strategic goal to invest in research and development, but omitted the strategy of "localization." Was this no longer important to Toyota? Also, we noticed that Watanabe had added three new strategic goals: (1) to improve in *quality*, (2) *cost competitiveness*, and (3) *personnel training*. He declared these necessary to secure a "solid foundation for sustainable growth."

An investor might reasonably ask: Why were these added? Was Toyota having quality, cost, and personnel problems? News reports confirmed this to be true. On May 31, 2006, *USA Today* reported that Toyota was recalling almost one million vehicles around the world, including "nearly two-thirds of the Prius gas-electric hybrid cars sold in the United States."[10] The automaker suspected problems in the Prius steering shaft assembly.

In January 2007, Toyota recalled half a million pickup trucks and sport-utility vehicles because of another steering problem. *Bloomberg* reported growing concerns that in its effort to replace GM as the world's top-selling vehicle company, Toyota might have been sacrificing its reputation for producing quality vehicles.[11]

General Motors

In GM's 2006 letter, CEO Rick Wagoner reported on GM's progress in its North American turnaround strategy. But even as global sales and liquidity improved, the company continued to lose money. In 2007, GM posted a $38.7 billion drop in earnings. Wagoner tried to boost investor confidence in that year's letter:

> While these results are disappointing, in many respects the bigger story for GM in 2007 is what went on behind the numbers— under the hood, if you will. Look under the hood, and we see that *2007 was a "tipping point" for GM* in terms of structuring the *company and building the product and technology momen-*

tum necessary to **position us for sustained profitability and growth in the rapidly changing global auto industr**y. [author's emphasis]

But Rittenhouse Rankings noticed that Wagoner continued to use the same kind of business jargon as in prior letters—"building momentum" for "sustained profitability and growth." He chose weasel words rather than straightforward and credible ones. Latter events confirmed our concerns. That 2007 shareholder letter proved to be Wagoner's last as General Motors CEO.

On December 19, 2008, Wagoner secured a $17.4 billion taxpayer loan for the company, "under terms that would require the firm to radically restructure and show they [could] become profitable soon.[12] On March 29, 2009, under pressure from the Obama administration, which was reluctant to give the company more aid, Wagoner was replaced by GM's president and chief operating officer, Arthur "Fritz" Henderson. GM was given 60 days to come up with a restructuring plan.[13] The final plan required GM to declare bankruptcy so it could qualify for another $30 billion of taxpayer money. On June 8, 2009, the 101-year-old company, which had symbolized American prosperity around the world, sought protection from the bankruptcy court.[14]

Ford

In contrast to the two other CEOs, Alan Mulally began his 2007 shareholder letter the same way he started his 2006 letter: "one team, One Plan and one goal." Then he added a new element, "One Ford." He described the company's progress on each aspect of this turnaround plan.

At the end of 2008, the GM, Chrysler, and Ford CEOs were summoned to report on their troubled businesses before Congress. Ford was the only company that had declined a taxpayer handout. In 2009, while the global economy gasped for air, Ford proudly announced it had ended the year profitably. Mulally reported that this was "the strongest proof yet that our ONE Ford plan is working":

We reported full year 2009 net income of $2.7 billion, which was the company's first full year of positive net income since 2005 and a $17.5 billion improvement over the previous year. We achieved a pre-tax operating profit, excluding special items, of $472 million in 2009, which was a $7.3 billion improvement over 2008. . . . We still face significant challenges, but by following the ONE Ford plan we put in place three and a half years ago we are forging a path toward profitable growth. Our plan remains unchanged.

Mulally repeated the four strategic priorities that he had laid out in 2006, including the following:

- Aggressively restructure to operate profitably at the current lower demand and the changing model mix
- Accelerate the development of high-quality, fuel-efficient, safe new products that customers want and value
- Finance our plan and improve our balance sheet
- Work together as one team, leveraging our global assets

In his letters from 2006 to 2010, Mulally focused on how Ford would become more globally integrated and competitive. Always inclusive, he expected Ford to leverage global resources for "the greater good of the entire company." His consistent messaging gave Ford a competitive advantage in executing its strategy.

This and other indicators of competitive advantage are important clues to finding CEOs who can execute effectively.

CLUE 7: COMPETITIVE ADVANTAGE

Between the 2002 and 2011 Rittenhouse Rankings Surveys, Ford used the word *competitive* six times in its letters, and GM five times. But the company that cited *competitive* more than any other was Hewlett-Packard.

On March 29, 2005, HP's board of directors announced that Mark Hurd would become HP's new CEO and president, replacing interim CEO Robert Wayman, who had replaced Carly Fiorina earlier that year. Hurd's success at turning around NCR Corporation, a company smaller than HP but almost as complex, caught the board's attention. Board chair Patricia Dunn praised Hurd's ability to "develop internal talent while reaching outside for new skills, his understanding of the role of culture in a company's success and his personal integrity."[15]

Hurd's first shareholder letter explained his plan to turn HP around. He began by assessing the company's problems from the perspective of key stakeholders:

> Customers and partners told us they like HP and want to see us win. They told us the company has great technology and talented people, but *we were difficult to do business with and too complex.*
>
> From an employee perspective, *morale was mixed.* Although the company had been through a turbulent period, it was encouraging to find many of our people have a strong desire to improve perceptions of the company and to fight and win in the marketplace.
>
> Operationally, HP was a highly matrixed organization. . . . In a few cases, there were nine layers of management between the CEO and a customer. And some business divisions had less than 30 percent of their budgets directly under their control because of the way costs were allocated. *When this kind of organizational design is applied to a company of HP's scale, it represents the underpinnings of slow decision-making and confusion in terms of accountability.* [author's emphasis]

Hurd's priorities were clear: he wanted to build confidence in the company's success. He would make it easier for customers to do business with HP and be accountable to them and to all stakeholders. He laid out his strategic plans and linked these to existing and desired competitive advantages:

1. Advantage 1—Blended business model:

    Some would say that *being a "blend" company with a number of different business models reduces our focus and ability to achieve best-in-class cost structures. We actually see it as a* competitive advantage. The real opportunity is to build cost structures that best align to our most competitive businesses. In this way, the other businesses can gain competitive advantage and benefit from HP's scale along several dimensions—pricing, operating expenses and cost of goods sold, among others. [author's emphasis]

2. Advantage 2—Competitive cost structure:

   [While] the company's revenue growth for fiscal 2005 was impressive, increasing $6.8 billion, [Hurd noted] *"this growth was driven by lower-end products, which resulted in gross margin erosion.* Our cost structure was not competitive, *leaving significant room for improvement around spending discipline."* [author's emphasis]

3. Advantage 3—Scale to grow and compete:

   Our intention is *to engineer HP IT to be the world's best showcase for the company's technology.* It is also an example of how we can invest money to save money and, at the same time, build a capability in the business that allows us to scale, grow and compete in the marketplace. [author's emphasis]

Between 2005 and 2008, "competitive advantages" were mentioned 21 times in the letters authored by Mark Hurd, compared to three times in the period from 2001 to 2004. He clearly understood the strategic importance of understanding and leveraging a company's competitive advantages.

Case Study: Berkshire Hathaway and Enduring Moats

Finding companies with "enduring competitive advantages" has been the cornerstone of Warren Buffett's investment strategy. In his 1995 shareholder letter, he wrote about businesses with enduring, "unbreachable moats" as "economic castles." Such companies are expected to earn positive returns on capital over long periods of time. Buffett described auto insurer GEICO's "rock-bottom operating costs" as being "unbreachable." The concept was further developed in his 2007 letter:

The dynamics of capitalism guarantee that competitors will repeatedly assault any business "castle" that is earning high returns. Therefore a formidable barrier such as a company's being the low cost producer (GEICO, Costco) or possessing a powerful world-wide brand (Coca-Cola, Gillette, American Express) is essential for sustained success. Business history is filled with "Roman Candles," companies whose moats proved illusory and were soon crossed.

Our criteria of "enduring" causes us to rule out companies in industries prone to rapid and continuous change. Though capitalism's "creative destruction" is highly beneficial for society, it precludes investment certainty. A moat that must be continuously rebuilt will eventually be no moat at all.

Buffett searches for companies that work hard to protect and widen their moats through actions "to delight customers, eliminate unnecessary costs and improve products and services." In his 2005 letter, he reported on the challenge facing executives who want to protect their moat and must also meet short-term financial goals:

When short-term and long-term conflict, widening the moat must take precedence. If a management makes bad decisions in order to hit short-term earnings targets, and consequently gets behind the eight-ball in terms of costs, customer satisfaction or brand strength, no amount of subsequent brilliance will overcome the damage that has been inflicted.

Keeping a company focused on the long term in an increasingly short-term-oriented world requires strong, enduring, and consistent leadership.

Case Study: Hewlett-Packard's Leadership

Former Hewlett-Packard CEO Mark Hurd's letters between 2005 and 2008 demonstrated his ability to highlight immediate and longer-term problems. He crisply stated what needed to be done "to achieve a higher

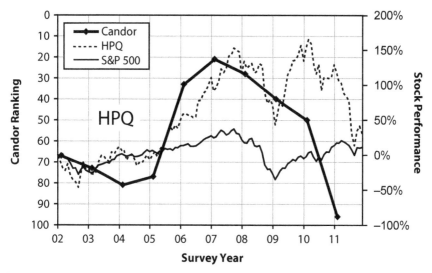

Figure 6.2   Hewlett-Packard Culture and Candor Rankings and Performance 2002–2011

growth rate" for the company. During this period HP's stock climbed 134 percent, the S&P grew 17 percent, and Dell dropped 49 percent.

As Figure 6.2 shows, the market applauded Hurd's leadership, particularly his management of the company's competitive strengths.

On April 23, 2010, HP's stock reached an all-time high of $53.90. Rittenhouse Rankings, however, did not support this optimistic outlook. We had seen Hurd's survey rankings fall between 2008 and 2009. They dropped even further in 2010. Instead of crisp declarative sentences, there was increasing evidence of FOG. For example, critically read this two-sentence excerpt from Hurd's 2009 shareholder letter:

> In 2009, *the global economy experienced* the worst recession in a generation. At HP, all of our work to reduce our cost base and to make it more variable proved immensely valuable. Beginning in our first fiscal quarter, *we had to address a rapidly deteriorating demand environment* across our product portfolio.

This passage raised questions: How could a global economy "experience" a recession as if it were an animate being? Why was numerical support omitted for the statement that reducing the "cost base" proved to be "immensely valuable"? And what did it mean "to address a rapidly deteriorating demand environment"?

These and other questions undermined Rittenhouse Rankings' confidence in Hurd's leadership. Based on our analysis of his 2005 and 2006 letters, we would have expected to find streamlined commentary such the following (author's paraphrase):

> Our prior work to reduce and prioritize costs as either essential or discretionary paid off. As the global recession spread, we were able to adjust costs in line with reduced demand for our products."

On August 9, 2010, just months after Hurd's 2009 letter was released, he was fired by the company's board of directors for misrepresenting a relationship with a company consultant. But as Figure 6.2 also shows, neither HP's candor rankings nor its stock price has improved since Hurd's departure. Such a pattern of language and market performance suggests that the company's problems may be strategic and cultural, not just leadership-based.

In 2007, Robert Burgelman, professor of management at Stanford University, published a progress report on the wisdom of HP's merger with Compaq. Despite initial doubts about the merger's success, Burgelman concluded it had been a sound strategic move. Carly Fiorina's vision of growth in the information technology industry had been validated. At the same time, he noted the difficulty of executing the merger:

> Where Fiorina failed—and where Hurd excels—was in educating HP managers and employees on how to realize the cost and operational efficiencies and translate those into higher margins for each business. This set the stage of achieving a higher growth rate. By getting HP's leaders to do a better job of exploiting the possibilities of the merger and thus the capabilities of the combined company, Hurd accomplished what Fiorina couldn't.[16]

Of course, this was written in 2007. What happened after 2007 to Hurd's demonstrated execution abilities? Why did his candor rankings fall? Could Hurd's straight talk have ruffled feathers? He had chutz-pah. I recall seeing him sitting on a dais at an investor meeting some years ago, answering questions from the floor instead of reading from a carefully worded script. He even acknowledged the discomfort this created in his investor relations team.

What precipitated his conflict with the board and subsequent dismissal? Much has been written about Hurd's departure, but to my mind, none of it adds up.

Writing in his *Forbes* blog in July 2011, John Kotter, former Harvard Business School professor and coauthor of *Corporate Culture and Performance*, offered a model that sheds light on this relationship between leadership and strategic execution. It described two types of executive behavior: "change management" and "change leadership."[17] The former refers "to a set of basic tools or structures intended to keep any change effort under control." The latter term, "change leadership," is broader and more dynamic. It includes "forces, visions and processes that fuel large-scale transformation."

Kotter observed that change management is often preferred by executives because it is more orderly. It tries to avoid problems associated with bold change initiatives, such as "rebellion among the ranks, [and] bleeding of cash." Its executive sponsors advocate gradual, incremental changes.

But how is it possible to "push things along" while at the same time minimizing "disruptions"? Kotter described how this tension plays out. Sometimes consultants trained in this field are brought in to deflect potential conflicts. Also, change management is focused on being efficient. Its sponsors try to stay within budgets.

But change leadership, he wrote, is "fundamentally different." It is about "big visions" and turbocharged urgency. It is designed to empower "masses of people who want to make something happen." It is risky. When executives choose game-shifting change over gradual, incremental change, then events can get out of control.

Change leadership that becomes disorderly may lose executive and board support. Nevertheless, Kotter believes this initiative is needed now more than ever to take advantage of "windows of opportunity" that are coming at us faster and closing more rapidly than in the past. It is more effective in deflecting or transforming approaching "hazards and bullets." It means taking "larger leaps at a faster speed." Kotter concluded, "Change leadership is going to be the big challenge in the future and the fact that nobody is very good at it—it's obviously a big deal."

His model of adaptive corporate change calls upon both right- and left-brain leadership capabilities. We search for clues in CEO letters for evidence of these capabilities. "Leadership" is the fifth system in the Rittenhouse Rankings Sustainable Business Model.

CHAPTER 7

Leadership

Lead, verb (used with object)

1. To go before or with to show the way; conduct or escort.

2. To conduct by holding and guiding.

3. To influence or induce.

4. To guide in direction, course, action, opinion, etc.

[Origin: before 900; Middle English *leden*, Old English *lædan* (causative of *līthan*, to go, travel).][1]

Not long ago, I met a smart and respected financial analyst at a midtown restaurant for lunch. He was at the bar when I arrived, holding his head in his hands as if he were in pain. Greeting him, I asked, "What's wrong?" He groaned and pointed to charts from an investor presentation made by one of the large companies he followed. "This company has over 10 operating subsidiaries," he exclaimed. "It's so complex. How can I keep track of them?" Then he wondered out loud, "How does management?"

As companies grow bigger, go global, and expand their reach, analyzing and tracking corporate performance is increasingly difficult.

Investors must trust executives to manage complexity. They must also determine if a CEO has the aptitude and skills to be both a manager and a leader.

Dictionary.com defines "leader" as someone who goes ahead and "shows the way." Leaders "influence" events and "induce" others to take actions. Managers, on the other hand, are expected to "take charge" or "dominate situations." They exert "control" to "bring about results and accomplish goals." Both kinds of behaviors are needed to create successful businesses. But of the two, leadership is harder to observe and measure.

To find executives who are both leaders and managers, Rittenhouse Rankings searches and codes commentary in executive communications that shows how a CEO:

1. Educates readers
2. Offers meaningful context
3. Reports on problems
4. Thinks dualistically
5. Articulates a dynamic worldview

CLUE 1: EDUCATES READERS

Case Study: Berkshire Hathaway and Insurance Float

For over 25 years, Warren Buffett has described the importance of "float" in valuing insurance businesses in his shareholder letters. In fact, no other insurance company followed by Rittenhouse Rankings has ever mentioned the word *float* in its letters. Because this informed and educated investors about an important business principle, we coded his commentary as, "valuation education." With this knowledge, investors can better estimate Berkshire's future cash flows and determine how well-prepared the company is to thrive in volatile markets.

Buffett educates and entertains readers. In his 2002 letter, he warned investors about derivatives, calling them "financial weapons of mass destruction." This commentary was often quoted in the media, but the risks he described were ignored by financiers around the world. In 2006 and 2007, billions of dollars of derivative securities backed by worthless promises were tucked away in global investment portfolios. Like ticking time bombs, they were harmless as long as investors in the derivative daisy chain never asked to trade in their securities for cash.

In his 2008 shareholder letter, Buffett explained in detail what made derivatives lethal. He started by describing the hopelessness of fully understanding derivative risks. This mini-seminar, excerpted below, was classic valuation education:

> Derivatives are dangerous. They have dramatically increased the leverage and risks in our financial system. They have made it almost impossible for investors to understand and analyze our largest commercial banks and investment banks. . . . Improved "transparency"—a favorite remedy of politicians, commentators and financial regulators for averting future train wrecks—won't cure the problems that derivatives pose. I know of no reporting mechanism that would come close to describing and measuring the risks in a huge and complex portfolio of derivatives. Auditors can't audit these contracts, and regulators can't regulate them. When I read the pages of "disclosure" in 10-Ks of companies that are entangled with these instruments, all I end up knowing is that I don't know what is going on in their portfolios (and then I reach for some aspirin).

Buffett then explained counterparty risk and how it created important "too big to fail" situations:

> The Bear Stearns collapse highlights the counterparty problem embedded in derivatives transactions, a time bomb I first discussed in Berkshire's 2002 report. On April 3, 2008, Tim Geithner, then the able president of the New York Fed, explained the need for a rescue: "The sudden discovery by Bear's derivative counterparties that important financial positions they had put in place to

protect themselves from financial risk were no longer operative would have triggered substantial further dislocation in markets. This would have precipitated a rush by Bear's counterparties to liquidate the collateral they held against those positions and to attempt to replicate those positions in already very fragile markets." This is Fedspeak for "We stepped in to avoid a financial chain reaction of unpredictable magnitude." In my opinion, the Fed was right to do so.

He continued on to describe how counterparty risk is linked to settlement risk:

A normal stock or bond trade is completed in a few days with one party getting its cash, the other its securities. Counterparty risk therefore quickly disappears, which means credit problems can't accumulate. This rapid settlement process is key to maintaining the integrity of markets. That, in fact, is a reason for NYSE and NASDAQ shortening the settlement period from five days to three days in 1995.

He explained how the "long-tail" settlement risk of derivatives is difficult to estimate because there are so many unknown counterparties included in the chain. Buffett compared this exposure to the risk of contracting venereal disease:

Derivatives contracts, in contrast, often go unsettled for years, or even decades, with counterparties building up huge claims against each other. "Paper" assets and liabilities—often hard to quantify—become important parts of financial statements though these items will not be validated for many years. Additionally, a frightening web of mutual dependence develops among huge financial institutions. Receivables and payables by the billions become concentrated in the hands of a few large dealers who are apt to be highly-leveraged in other ways as well. Participants seeking to dodge troubles face the same problem as someone seeking to avoid venereal disease: It's not just whom you sleep with, but also whom they are sleeping with.

Buffett concluded: derivatives produce "mindboggling screw-ups."

> Sleeping around, to continue our metaphor, can actually be use-
> ful for large derivatives dealers because it assures them govern-
> ment aid if trouble hits. In other words, only companies having
> problems that can infect the entire neighborhood—I won't men-
> tion names—are certain to become a concern of the state (an
> outcome, I'm sad to say, that is proper). From this irritating reality
> comes The First Law of Corporate Survival for ambitious CEOs
> who pile on leverage and run large and unfathomable deriva-
> tives books: Modest incompetence simply won't do; it's mind-
> boggling screw-ups that are required.

Then Buffett explained how he personally managed the derivatives in Berkshire's investment portfolio.

Finding detailed CEO explanations in shareholder letters such
as this is rare. However, former GM CEO Rick Wagoner's effort to
candidly educate investors about GM's legacy challenges in the midst
of falling sales and profits was also noteworthy.

Case Study: Most Difficult Year in GM's 98-Year History

In his 2005 letter, Wagoner described the year as "one of the most difficult" in GM's 98-year history. The challenges facing the company
included "global overcapacity, falling prices, rising health-care costs,
higher fuel prices, [and] global competition." All these had "significantly weakened" the company's financial results. That year GM lost
$3.4 billion, excluding special items; when these items were included,
the company had lost $10.6 billion. Wagoner declared this situation
"unsustainable."

GM's 2005 losses stemmed from two fundamental weaknesses: the
company's huge legacy cost burden in the U.S. market and its inability
to reduce operating costs in line with falling revenue. Wagoner educated readers about both problems:

> GM has been in business for nearly a century, and in the last four
> decades, our business has undergone tremendous structural

change. Vastly improved productivity, greater reliance on suppliers, and large growth in the number of competitors in our largest
market have all had an impact. But while GM today is a far leaner,
more productive automaker, we still carry a significant financial
burden of the past.

Consider that in 1962, we employed 605,000 people around
the world. Of those, 464,000 were in the United States, where we
sold 4.2 million cars and trucks. With only two major competitors, GM reached a record U.S. market share of 51 percent.

Fast-forward to 2005, GM employed 335,000 employees
worldwide. Of those, 141,000 were in the United States, where
we sold 4.5 million cars and trucks. While last year we competed
against 11 major automakers from around the world, GM still led
the market with a 26 percent share.

Over those 43 years, new technologies and downsizing
resulted in a much leaner GM, producing more vehicles with
far fewer employees. But the growth of our retiree population
exploded in those decades, leaving GM today with the financial
weight of outsized "legacy costs" for health care and pensions.
The chart below illustrates the scope of this obligation.

	1962	2005
U.S. Employees	464,000	141,000
Hourly Pension Plan*	31,351	337,588
Salaried Pension Plan*	8,885	115,762
Total Health Plan Recipients**	1,360,000	1,075,000

 * Number of U.S. retirees and surviving spouses who received pension plan benefits
** Estimated number of U.S. employees, dependents, retirees, and surviving spouses
    covered by health benefits

Wagoner offered a stark statistic: "for every active GM employee
in the United States last year, GM supported 3.2 retirees and surviving spouses. Back in 1962, the employee/retiree ratio was reverse:

GM had 11.5 active employees for every retiree or surviving spouse in our pension plans . . . GM's health-care bill in 2005—for every U.S. employee, dependent, retiree, and surviving spouse—totaled $5.3 billion."

He wrote that "no other company in the world has that kind of health-care obligation." Furthermore, the governments of GM's foreign-owned competitors covered "much of their employee and retiree health-care and pension costs."

A 2005 industry report confirmed Wagoner's analysis, estimating that the healthcare cost per GM vehicle was $1,525, while the healthcare cost per Toyota vehicle made in the United States was $201.[2] This disparity was reflected in the 2005 sales results: "GM's U.S. sales were down 4.3 percent while Toyota's sales were up 10.1. Because of its legacy costs, GM lost $2,331 on every vehicle it made while Toyota earned a profit of $1,488. GM's plants were running at 85 percent capacity, while Toyota's were running at 107 percent.[3]

Wagoner's exemplary reporting on this competitive disadvantage, however, was weakened by FOG. For instance, he described GM's "significant progress" in developing a commercial fuel-cell vehicle that promised to reduce carbon emissions and improve fuel economy. But there was no tangible evidence presented of what constituted this "significant progress."

Wagoner wrote that the company's turnaround in "the tough European market was on track" and described how "GM Europe cut its losses significantly based on good consumer acceptance of our new vehicles and strong progress on [its] cost-restructuring initiatives." But he never disclosed how costs were being restructured and whether those changes could be sustained. Without supporting information, it was difficult to share his confidence about company progress.

More cracks surfaced in GM's rocky foundation when accounting errors were discovered in the company's prior financial statements. On March 16, 2006, GM announced it would delay filing its annual report.[4] According to the *Wall Street Journal*, issues had been raised about the company's classification of cash flow. In addition, GM's net income from 2000 to 2004 would be restated and lowered due to "erroneous" reporting of past transactions.

Wagoner reassured readers when his 2005 letter was finally released in midyear that the company was "moving aggressively to strengthen [its] internal accounting resources." He apologized for these errors on behalf of GM's management team and wrote that management was working diligently to fix them. However, he never described what needed to be fixed or explained if this would require a material adjustment to the company's financial results.

In other words, Wagoner educated readers about the company's problems but did not consistently provide the context needed to build confidence in his reporting.

CLUE 2: OFFER MEANINGFUL CONTEXT

The word *context* is defined by Merriam-Webster as "the parts of a discourse that surround a word or passage and can throw light on its meaning."[5] It comes from Latin and refers to the weaving together of words to achieve coherence. While the importance of offering context to educate investors and build trust seems obvious, the word *context* has been used infrequently in shareholder letters.

Over the entire 10 years of the study by Rittenhouse Rankings, less than half of the companies in the survey have used the word *context*. General Electric was one of these companies. In his 2001 inaugural shareholder letter, GE CEO Jeff Immelt provided passionate context to answer a question he imagined was uppermost on investors' minds: "Can such a thing as a $126 billion growth company exist?" He wrote:

> It does exist, because GE always plays offense. *We don't run this Company as a "$126 billion blob."* We run it as an $8.4 billion Medical Systems business . . . a $1 billion Ultrasound business within it . . . and as seven separate operations within Ultrasound, ranging in size between $50 million and $250 million. *These operations are run by people who are obsessed with growth and achieve*

it by creating new markets and technology. Backing them are our systems, our initiatives and a strong balance sheet that allows them to take risks for growth, knowing that the occasional miss or failure is not only unpunished, but is also "no big deal" in the context of a $126 billion company. [author's emphasis]

Immelt paints a powerful image of the strategic value of scale when he writes that an "occasional miss or failure is . . . 'no big deal' in the context of a $126 billion company."

The word *context* appeared most frequently in the 2002 and 2003 shareholder letters written just after the Sarbanes-Oxley legislation was enacted. The new law imposed significant financial and criminal penalties on executives for releasing inaccurate financial statements. Executives now had good reason to provide context to protect executive and corporate reputations.

CEO Michael Dell's 2003 shareholder letter was a bravura performance. As Figure 7.1 shows, it scored among the top decile in the 2004 survey, the highest ranking in the decade.

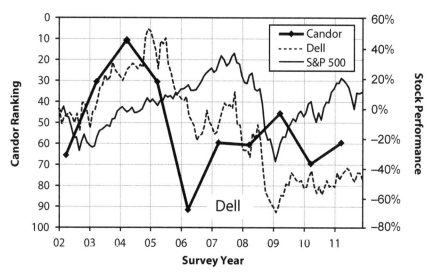

Figure 7.1   **Dell Culture and Candor Rankings and Performance 2002–2011**

Case Study: Dell's Bravura Context

Michael Dell's 2003 shareholder letter began by praising the company's customers, who enthusiastically embraced Dell's products. Because of their support, the company had reported its most financially successful year since its founding. These customers included: "global corporations" making critical data center purchases, "governments, schools and small businesses" wanting to more efficiently serve their constituents, and also individual consumers who wanted to gain the benefits of digital communications.

CEO Dell framed the company's financial results in the context of competitors' results:

> Dell product shipments grew 26 percent, *nearly three times the average of other companies.* Our revenue increased 17 percent, to $41.4 billion; *total sales by the rest of the industry declined.* Operating expenses accounted for just 9.7 percent of revenue, the lowest full-year rate in our history, and were 9.6 percent for the last three quarters. Earnings per share were up 26 percent, to $1.01; *competitors lost money in their computer-systems businesses.* [author's emphasis]

Michael Dell reminded readers that in April 2002, the company had announced a goal "to double sales to more than $60 billion in about five years." While skeptics doubted this goal could be reached, he reported, "two years later we are ahead of pace toward the target." Dell described each of the company's "four strategic initiatives: driving **global growth**, attaining **product leadership**, continuously improving the **customer experience** and enhancing Dell's **winning culture**." He provided context to show the relevance of each initiative.

Global growth was accelerating thanks to Dell's unique direct business model, which allowed it to bypass retailers and sell personal computers directly to consumers. Dell stressed that this was not an exclusively American, European, or Asian concept. The company succeeded because individual customers got more value for their money.

To provide context for *product leadership*, Dell described specific product advantages:

> Dell's PowerEdge servers are being selected more and more for critical applications within the data centers of businesses and other organizations. Based on Microsoft Corp. and Linux operating systems, and using standards-based applications such as those from Oracle Corp. and SAP A.G., our systems are dramatically lowering the cost of computing while providing customers with tremendous power, flexibility and reliability.

He explained how the company used its own products to operate the company website:

> Our Web site, www.dell.com, is one of the world's highest-volume, most-dynamic Internet commerce sites. With more than 1.4 billion page requests per quarter and growing, it runs robustly and cost effectively on PowerEdge servers and PowerVault and Dell | EMC storage products.

To support claims of Dell's "great *customer experience*," CEO Dell reported that the company had "earned more than 100 awards for product and service quality and reliability the last year alone." He described specific customer service metrics, such as: (1) accuracy of order fulfillment, (2) timeliness of deliveries, (3) product quality, and (4) correcting customer problems the first time and treating them "with courtesy and respect."

But when it came to describing the company's *winning culture*, Dell's commentary hit a speed bump. This passage was riddled with clichés, jargon, platitudes, and unsupported statements:

> We have a *constructive passion for winning* in everything we do. *Continuous improvement* is a basic element of our culture, and manifests itself in how we *build a work force with diverse backgrounds and skills* worldwide, maintain the highest standards of integrity, develop leaders, and *encourage personal accountabil-*

ity by all of our people. . . . Our ultimate objective is to be a great company in all ways. We maintain very high expectations for operational excellence. [author's emphasis]

This appearance of FOG was disconcerting. It did not match the candor at the beginning of Dell's letter. But in the context of the company's overall candor score that year, the points for FOG totaled only 23 percent, within the range of best practice (0 to 25 percent of FOG in a letter communication). In fact, Dell's letter ranked 10th in overall candor in our 2004 survey.

Then in July 2004, Michael Dell named President and Chief Operating Officer Kevin Rollins as the company's new CEO and announced that he would serve as the company's chairman. CEO Rollins declared in his 2004 letter that the company was making progress on its "plan to achieve annual revenue of $60 billion by the end of fiscal 2007."

But in the next year's Rittenhouse Rankings survey, the company's candor ranking dropped from 10th to 30th. We wondered if Rollins had the skills to guide the company on its journey. Would he need more time to grow into the CEO spot? In the 2006 survey, Rollins's candor ranking dropped like a hot potato to 91st. Now we were considerably alarmed. Consider too that during this period, the stock price tumbled 58 percent from its all-time high of $58.12 on March 22, 2000.

In fact, Figure 7.2 shows that even as Dell's rankings were falling, HP's candor rankings were climbing under the leadership of Mark Hurd. HP was ranked 33rd in the 2006 survey, up from 81st in the 2004 survey, while Dell had fallen to 91st, down from 10th in 2004. In other words in just three years, the two rivals had virtually swapped rankings.

On January 31, 2007, Dell Inc. announced that Michael Dell would return as CEO. Rollins was out. Dell published his 2007 shareholder letter just two months after his return. For the first time since we began following Dell, the company's shareholder letter cited problems. CEO Dell was taking the first step to restore investor trust.

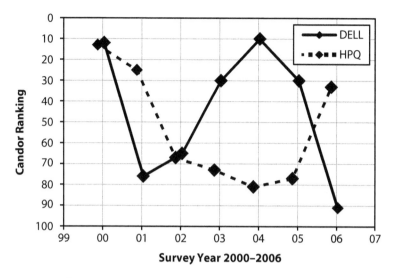

Figure 7.2   Dell (DELL) versus Hewlett-Packard (HPQ) Candor Rankings

CLUE 3: REPORTS COMPANY PROBLEMS

Investors often tell Rittenhouse Rankings they are surprised to learn that CEOs report on company problems in shareholder letters and other communications. In fact, we code commentary about company problems as "What Went Wrong." Our research shows that, on average, about 50 percent of the CEOs in our decade-long survey have reported on this topic. This strong showing suggests that at least half of these executives believe that confession is good not only for the soul, but also for the bottom line. In his first letter after returning, CEO Dell acknowledged the company's disappointing customer service:

> [W]e recently have not met the standards we set for ourselves and our investors. Our business operates in a very competitive environment, and *for the first time in many years, we began to lose share, while our growth slowed and our profitability declined.* Consumers told us that the *customer experience we were providing them, once the benchmark for the industry, had started to slip.* [author's emphasis]

Dell also reported another problem. The audit committee of Dell's board of directors had initiated an independent investigation into the company's financial reporting and found accounting errors and irregularities. As a result, the company had to restate its financial reports for fiscal 2003, 2004, 2005, 2006, and the first quarter of 2007. CEO Dell was disappointed, but he put on his game face. He wrote that the investigation and remedial actions would make Dell a "far stronger company and provide a solid foundation on which to move the business forward and focus our energy on serving our customers."

Then in August 2007, an SEC investigation revealed that throughout 2003 and 2006, the company's accounting results had been inflated to meet investors' quarterly earnings expectations.[6] To his credit, CEO Dell continued to report on company problems in his 2007 and 2008 letters. However, this practice stopped in 2009 and 2010. As a result, he failed to report the 43 percent drop in diluted earnings per share between fiscal years 2008 and 2010 that appeared on the company's financial statements.

Leaders who set an example of candid communication, like Ford's Alan Mulally, build cultures of accountability. These executives gain clearer sight when they balance reports of company successes with failures. They are more decisive and execute more quickly. They are alert to emerging business risks. A CEO who airs company problems exposes his vulnerability, a quality that inspires creativity and also builds trust.

Warren Buffett, for example, not only reports on company problems in his letters, but also takes personal responsibility for these missteps. The phrase "I was wrong" or "dead wrong" has appeared seven times in his letters between 2000 and 2011. This "mea culpa" excerpt from Buffett's 2008 letter is typical:

> Without urging from Charlie or anyone else, I bought a large amount of ConocoPhillips stock when oil and gas prices were near their peak. I in no way anticipated the dramatic fall in energy prices that occurred in the last half of the year. *I still believe the odds are good that oil sells far higher in the future than the current*

$40–$50 price. But so far I have been dead wrong. Even if prices should rise, moreover, the terrible timing of my purchase has cost Berkshire several billion dollars. [author's emphasis]

Buffett is not alone in consistently reporting on "What Went Wrong." Cleveland-based Sherwin-Williams CEO Christopher Connor also ranks high in reporting on company problems.

The Value of Consistent and Balanced Reporting

Case Study: Sherwin-Williams

Called "America's Paint Company," Sherwin-Williams was founded in 1866 by Henry Sherwin and Edward Williams. The Sherwin logo, an image of the Earth being covered with paint, was adopted in 1905, long before "global growth" became a strategic mantra. Over the years, Sherwin-Williams has built a reputation for technical innovation and for consistency in balanced reporting.

The first pages of CEO Christopher Connor's shareholder letters from 2001 to 2010 consistently feature reports on financial results and cash flow discipline. The following excerpts from the company's 2007 shareholder letter illustrate five examples of detailed reporting of financial metrics found in other Sherwin Williams letters:

1. Company results as "strong," "solid," "record," or "challenging":

   We are pleased to report on another record year for The Sherwin-Williams Company. For the first time in our company's long and illustrious 141-year history, we surpassed the $8 billion sales mark. This record sales performance was matched with record achievements in earnings per share, net income and net operating cash. [author's emphasis]

2. The year's consolidated net sales:

   Consolidated net sales for the year grew 2.5% to $8.0 billion. Net income increased 6.9% to $615.6 million, and diluted net income per common share reached $4.70 per share, an increase of 12.2%. [author's emphasis]

3. Cash flow discipline and the amount of company cash flow:

Cash from operations came in at $874.5 million, an increase of nearly $60 million over 2006, and better than 10 percent of sales for the second consecutive year. This strong cash flow performance was *achieved through a combination of improved profitability and continued stringent working capital management.* [author's emphasis]

4. Uses of net operating cash flow:

We prudently reinvested this cash.... During the year we completed seven acquisitions to strengthen our store presence and expand our family of technologically superior coatings products.... Additionally, during the year we invested $165.9 million in capital expenditures to increase our manufacturing capacity, expand our store network and enhance the productivity of our existing facilities. [author's emphasis]

5. Returning cash to shareholders:

We also continued *our long-standing practice of returning a portion of the cash we generate to our shareholders through treasury stock purchases* and dividends. In management's opinion, *Wall Street's reaction to the slowing domestic housing market resulted in our stock being significantly undervalued.* The company took advantage of this opportunity and purchased a record 13.2 million shares of our common stock in the open market. [author's emphasis]

Sherwin-Williams's decision in 2007 to repurchase a record 13.2 million shares of common stock may not have appeared to be significant, but Connor's reporting that the company took advantage of the stock's low market price in 2007 was unique. Consider that between 2001 and 2010, on average, 34 percent of all the Rittenhouse Rankings survey companies reported on share repurchases. However, only 4 percent of these companies reported on buying back *undervalued* shares [author's emphasis].

Sherwin Williams—"What Went Wrong" in 2008 and 2009

CEO Connor's 2008 shareholder letter began uncharacteristically by describing Sherwin-Williams's depressed financial results:

> *Consolidated net sales finished the year at $7.98 billion, down $25 million from the prior year.* Net income declined 22.5% to $476.9 million and diluted net income per common share declined to $4.00 per share from $4.70 per share in 2007. [author's emphasis]

The letters written in 2009 produced the largest number of citations of what went wrong in our decade-long survey. These included reports of disappointing sales and earnings, and other corporate troubles.

Connor's 2009 letter was among this group. As Figure 7.3 shows, his letters in 2008 and 2009 included the largest number of reports on company problems.

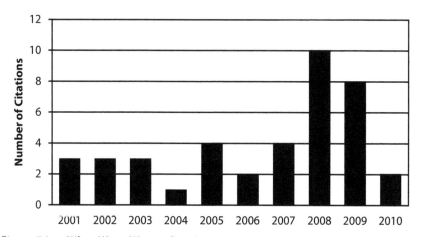

Figure 7.3 **What Went Wrong Citations in Sherwin-Williams 2001–2010 Shareholder Letters**

His 2009 communication began by describing a very challenging year:

> U.S. architectural paint industry *volume plunged* more than 11 percent in the year and total coatings industry shipments, including protective and marine coatings and finishes used in manufacturing, *fell even more. Domestic new construction activity continued to spiral downward* while *commercial vacancy rates and residential foreclosures continued to rise.* Conditions in most markets outside the U.S. *were only marginally better.* [author's emphasis]

But Connor offered context to frame the impact of these challenges:

> As a result of these *difficult market conditions, our results declined for the second consecutive year.* Consolidated net sales finished the year at $7.09 billion, down $885 million, or 11.1 percent, from the prior year. Net income declined 8.6 percent to $435.8 million and diluted net income per common share declined 5.5 percent to $3.78 per share from $4.00 per share in 2008. [author's emphasis]

The italicized words in the previous extract illustrate Connor's ability to deliver straight-up, no-apologies facts. There was no sugar-coating these results.

Connor's 2010 letter was mixed. While consolidated company sales were up to $7.78 billion, he reported that prices for raw materials had risen dramatically and shortages had forced the company to ration supplies. He credited the quick responses from employees with mitigating the costly impact. As a result, the company posted a 6.1 percent gain in consolidated net income and an 11.4 percent increase in diluted net income per common share.

Disclosures like these build investor confidence because they are candid and show that a CEO can think dualistically—seeing both problems and opportunities.

CLUE 4: EMBRACES DUALITIES
Case Study: Coca-Cola Managing Complexity

A leader's capacity to manage complexity is aided by his or her ability to balance two opposing ideas. We code examples of this kind of thinking as "duality." Rittenhouse Rankings first observed this dual mindset in Coca-Cola CEO Roberto Goizueta's 1995 shareholder letter when he described the ability to see "opportunity others cannot see." He had observed throughout the world that when Coke employees entered a room, they didn't just see where Coca-Cola was; they saw where it was *not*.

Goizueta believed this ability to hold the tension between opposing ideas could be developed: "'Seeing where Coca-Cola is not' has to be more than just a knack that some people have and some people don't. It must be a required, self-sharpening skill."

Juxtaposing metaphors in one sentence can also reveal dualistic thinking. Consider the paradoxical truth in this statement from former Toyota President Watanabe's 2008 letter: "The strongest grass is revealed after swift wind." In this sentence, Watanabe describes how unseen strengths can be revealed in difficult situations.

CEOs who use both a prism and a magnifying glass to see the world can lead with a steadier hand. Was this true of Ford and GM? Both companies had weathered the global crisis in 2008 and 2009 and were now writing their 2010 shareholder letters.

In his 2010 letter, GM CEO Duane Akerman reported:

> It was a good year for GM, but we have a lot of work ahead of us. *Although great opportunity abounds around the globe, risks do as well.* In a still-recovering global economy, uncertainty surrounding the crisis in Japan, a volatile oil price environment, higher commodity prices and an increasingly competitive automotive marketplace, we will build on our 2010 progress by concentrating on three critical areas. [author's emphasis]

In his 2010 letter, Ford's Alan Mulally echoed this view of reporting operating improvements in the context of world events:

> *Along with improvements in our operating results,* we continue to make significant progress on *issues that impact the world around us, such as fuel economy and CO2 emissions.* [author's emphasis]

In both examples, the CEOs combine reports on company operations with reporting on social, environmental, and economic world issues. The ability to articulate a worldview reveals a CEO's ability to expand his vision.

CLUE 5: ARTICULATES A WORLDVIEW

Rittenhouse Rankings research shows that CEOs of non-U.S. companies, such as Toyota, Siemens, and Novartis, or non-U.S-born CEOs, such as Citigroup's former CEO Vikram Pandit, have offered noteworthy commentary on balancing the needs of business and society.

In his 2005 shareholder letter, Toyota's Chairman Hiroshi Okuda devoted this entire paragraph to describing his views on business and society:

> As I have said in the past, I am convinced that the automobile industry will grow vigorously in the 21st century. The advent of full-fledged global motorization is bound to continue expanding the automotive market. At the same time, *the new social priorities of the emerging era* will call for radically new approaches to vehicles. . . . Automakers have to address *the issue of coexistence with society,* particularly in relation to environmental preservation and safety. *And, the outcomes of those efforts will determine companies' competitive success.* [author's emphasis]

Because of this dual focus, Toyota was the first company to manufacture hybrid models, releasing the Toyota Prius to Japanese buyers in 1997 and to U.S. buyers in 2000. Ford and GM did not launch hybrid vehicles until 2004.

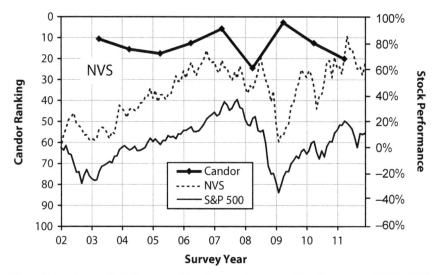

Figure 7.4   Novartis Culture and Candor Rankings and Performance 2003–2011

Case Study: Novartis's Worldview

Swiss-born Daniel Vasella trained as a doctor, but discovered that he liked business more than medicine. He joined Sandoz pharmaceuticals in 1988 and in 1994 became its CEO. When Sandoz merged with Ciba-Geigy to create Novartis in 1996, Vasella was named CEO.

Between 2006 and 2012, *Fortune* magazine ranked Novartis among the top three most respected pharmaceutical companies. The company's stock appreciated 67 percent from 2002 to 2012, outperforming Pfizer, Johnson & Johnson, Merck, and the S&P 500. From 2003, when it was added to the Rittenhouse Rankings survey, until 2011, Novartis consistently ranked in the top quartile of our CEO candor rankings (see Figure 7.4).

Vasella described three demographic forces in his 2007 shareholder letter that were impacting the global pharmaceutical industry:

1. *Dramatic growth in aging populations in developed nations:*
   This shift would require new treatments for elderly patients with chronic conditions such as degenerative diseases of the

joints, the cardiovascular system and the central nervous
system, as well as a heightened risk of cancer.

2. *Unhealthy, sedentary lifestyles and increasing environmental
    pollution:* This trend affected populations in both developed
    and developing nations, as they would be further exposed
    to diseases such as obesity, chronic cardiovascular disorders,
    diabetes, cancer and pulmonary disease. These could
    potentially reach "pandemic levels."

3. *Middle-class growth in developing nations:* The increasing
    incomes enjoyed by populations in China, India, Russia,
    Brazil, and other rapidly growing nations were increasing
    demand for services to prolong and improve the quality
    of life.

To meet these increased demands for global healthcare, Vasella
believed that scientific and medical innovations were essential. But he
feared that public and private support would be insufficient to support
innovative medical research. In addition, the time it took to develop
new medicines—as long as 12 to 15 years—was too long to interest
investors.

In his 2009 shareholder letter, Vasella offered a view of "globalization" that contrasted the short-term planning horizon in the West with
the longer-term Eastern view of progress:

> A company that acknowledges that Asia will shape our society
> and economy in the future has the potential to base its actions
> on the ramifications of this shift. Projects in China are typically
> approached systematically, strategically and with a long-term
> horizon—in contrast to the West, where politics, economics and
> financial analysis are often short-term and characterized by a
> hasty response to risks and opportunities.

He repeated his prediction that short-term thinking in Western
countries would result in poorly planned responses to risks. Vasella
hoped that policy makers and financial leaders in the West would
return to values "such as trust in the future and belief in progress."

Case Study: Citigroup: Emerging Market Power

Former Citigroup CEO Vikram Pandit had similar views on globalization.

Born and educated in India until 1973, Pandit came to study engineering at Columbia University at the age of 16. In his 2010 shareholder letter, he described the "rise of the emerging-market consumer" and how this was driving global growth:

> [I]n China and India alone, middle class households are expected to grow by more than 300 million over the next decade. Last year, 70 million people living in emerging markets entered the middle class. According to one estimate, by 2020, three-quarters of incremental consumer spending will come from emerging markets.

Pandit predicted that if this estimate proved to be correct, Asia could overtake North America to become the world's largest consumer bloc by 2020. He then described another factor in emerging market growth—"the vast increase in trade and capital flows":

> The share of global trade from emerging markets rose from 21% in 1995 to 35% in 2009, and that share is rising slightly faster than their share of the global economy. While intra-emerging market flows represent less than 15% of global trade today, these flows are increasing rapidly—rising from 6% of world trade to 13% between 1995 and 2009. By contrast, the advanced economies' share of global trade is now 65%, down from 79% in 1995.

He imagined the impact of a "new generation of globally minded and tech-savvy people" that was preparing to enter the financial system and realized that these new banking customers had more in common with their urban counterparts in other nations than they did with the nonurban people in their own. Pandit considered the social networking challenge to come from this demographic shift:

> More than 750 million people around the world now use social networking sites, which are radically changing the way consum-

ers communicate—with each other and with businesses. What used to be simple messages are now interactive and ongoing dialogues. Industries and businesses that succeed in the new environment are harnessing social network technology to offer highly personalized service and virtual, online communities.

He regarded the effort to meet the networking and technology needs of these "globally minded and tech-savvy" young consumers as being as much of a challenge to the banking industry as was complying with post-2008 Dodd-Frank banking regulations. Pandit predicted that technology would reshape the banking industry by driving down processing costs close to zero and expanding data storage and analytic capabilities.

Pandit welcomed the cost reduction and efficiency opportunities, but he also considered the importance of trying to meet new security challenges. He expected that Citi's future would be defined by people who valued a new standard of "Responsible Finance." This required Citigroup to act "in ways that are in our clients' interests and that are systemically responsible."

Understanding Systemic Risk

Pandit's use of the term "systemically responsible" was unusual. Over the past decade of shareholder letters in the Rittenhouse Rankings survey, only 14 companies have used the word *systemic* to describe a holistic view of the business environment. Four were financial firms and five were healthcare companies. The others were Boeing, IBM, Nike, CSX, and Alcoa.

In 2002, for instance, the CEO of Wells Fargo at the time, Richard Kovacevich, wrote that the collapse of Enron and other companies was due to "individual greed" and not to "*systemic business corruption*" [author's emphasis].

In his 2010 letter, Novartis Chairman Vasella noted:

Political debate all too often ignores the fact that medical problems have heavy costs for healthcare systems, but also have various socioeconomic cost implications. Far more political attention should be paid to indirect cost savings realized through preventing or treating disease with innovative therapies and procedures. Because the indirect cost of illness is not covered by government budgets, however, it rarely receives *systemic cost-benefit analysis* or is the subject of debate. Who calculates the economic benefits of a quicker recovery and faster reintegration into work? [author's emphasis]

The virtual absence of the word *systemic* from CEOs' vocabulary indicates a widespread corporate myopia that threatens the safety of our increasingly interconnected and mutually dependent planet. The inability or refusal of CEOs and directors to imagine systemic risk led to the massive housing bubble meltdown in 2008 and the resulting feeble recovery.

Looking at recent efforts to restore confidence in the world's economic institutions has not inspired confidence. New thinking and new vocabulary are needed, a view famously expressed by Albert Einstein, who wrote: "The significant problems we face cannot be solved at the same level of thinking we were at when we created them."

We need twenty-first-century executives who tackle problems using their left-brain capabilities (rational, analytic, and quantitative reasoning) as well as their right-brain capabilities (emotional, intuitive, symbolic, and inductive thinking). We need leaders who are strategic and visionary, who are curious about both the unknown and the unexpected.

Consider that during the 2011 Occupy Wall Street actions, only one CEO publicly offered to meet with the protest organizers. It was Vikram Pandit.

On October 16, 2012, Pandit was asked to step down by Citibank's board of directors. Media reports cited highly visible missteps that may have weakened the board's confidence in his leadership. But questions remain about his abrupt departure from the company. In his 2010 letter, Pandit wrote repeatedly about the need for Citibank to return to the business of banking. Perhaps his vision of the bank's future had clashed with those of others in the company. "Vision" is the fifth system in the Rittenhouse Rankings Sustainable Business Model.

CHAPTER 8

Vision

Vision, noun

1a. Something seen in a dream, trance, or ecstasy.

  b. Thought, concept, or object formed by the imagination.

  c. A manifestation to the senses of something immaterial.

2a. The act or power of imagination:

  b. (1) mode of seeing or conceiving; (2) unusual discernment or foresight.

  c. Direct mystical awareness of the supernatural, usually in visible form.

[Origin Middle English, from Anglo-French, from Latin *vision-*, *visio*, from *vidēre*, to see. First known use: 14th century.][1]

More than 700 years ago, the word *vision* was introduced into the English language. It meant having prophetic, even mystical abilities to see into the future. Visions such as those described in the Bible were received in dreams, in trances, or even in "ecstasy."[2]

By the twentieth century, however, the definition had shifted from a focus on mystical awareness to a more pragmatic interpretation. Today, vision refers to "the ability to conceive what might be attempted or achieved." In the twenty-first century, forming such a vision requires the "power of imagination" and "unusual discernment or foresight." Recall that the capabilities to articulate corporate visions are part of the right-brain system in the Rittenhouse Sustainable Business Model. This system embraces Vision and Leadership. These capabilities include emotional intelligence, creativity, and inductive reasoning, which are typically described as "feminine" qualities.

Smart investors know that visions are essential to corporate success. A corporate vision of a desired future state points a company in a particular direction. Well-crafted visions can motivate and inspire large numbers of people to work together to realize this future state. Great vision statements balance emotional awareness with strategic discipline.

Unfortunately, corporate vision statements are not often great. Many are stated as platitudes and rightly ridiculed. This was evident in *Fortune* reporter Tom Stewart's 1996 tongue-in-cheek description of a time-saving process to create vision statements at corporate retreats:

> You know the drill. Carry your coffee from breakfast to the meeting room, find a seat at a table, play with the pile of markers and Post-its, admire the vacant sheets of brown paper on the walls. Tee time is 1 p.m. To make sure you get there, try this Handy-Dandy Vision Crafter, an exclusive for FORTUNE readers. Select one to three items from each group below, add your logo, marinate overnight in Scotch and red wine, and serve with a straight face.
>
> *OUR VISION is to be a:*
> a. premier / leading / preeminent / world-class / growing company that provides
> b. innovative / cost-effective / focused / diversified / high-quality
> c. products / services / products and services
>
> *to*

d. serve the global marketplace / create shareholder value / fulfill our covenants with our stakeholders / delight our customers

in the rapidly changing

e. information-solutions / business-solutions / consumer-solutions / financial-solutions industries.[3]

His story makes us laugh because we see the truth in his parody. Now consider these vision statements from shareholder letters in the 1990s. As you read, imagine that each begins with: "Our vision is to be":

- ". . . the World's Leading Energy Company—creating energy solutions worldwide for a better environment." (Enron, 1995)
- ". . . a financial services company that offers whatever our customers want today." (First Union Bank, 1996)
- ". . . the leading bank of the 21st Century." (NationsBank, 1998)
- ". . . the world's most recognized and admired financial services brand." (Merrill Lynch, 1999)

Who believes such statements? More important, who cares? Rather than demonstrating "unusual discernment or foresight," these platitudes invite cynicism. The fact that each company just mentioned either declared bankruptcy or was merged into another company is not coincidental.

Management guru Peter Drucker often observed that "the best way to predict the future is to create it." Consider that words are the building blocks of the future. To create the future, leaders must use meaningful words, not clichés or platitudes. Meaningless vision statements like those above put these companies at a strategic disadvantage.

CASE STUDY: IBM—NOT GIVING UP ON "BIG BLUE"

In 1993, shortly after being named IBM's CEO, Lou Gerstner made headlines when he declared, "The last thing IBM needs right now is a vision."[4] He knew the company had to deal with immediate problems: it was running out of cash. When he arrived, a plan was already in place to break up it up. IBM was considered too big and bureaucratic to manage. But Gerstner wasn't ready to give up on "Big Blue." To prove the company's worth, he first had to cut costs and grow profits.

In his second shareholder letter, in 1995, Gerstner reported on IBM's progress. That year revenues had grown 12 percent, the most in 10 years. Excluding special charges, the company's earnings had doubled to $6.3 billion. Sales were up in all four business segments. At year-end, IBM's cash totaled $7.7 billion—and this was after spending $5.7 billion to repurchase stock and another $2.9 billion to buy Lotus, a Massachusetts-based software company that was a leader in personal computing.

Since his arrival, Gerstner reported, IBM's total market value had increased by almost $27 billion. These improving financials allowed the company to acquire other businesses, hire 15,000 new employees, and invest in "high-growth semi-conductor manufacturing and services."

But Gerstner wasn't finished. When he was asked, "What will IBM do next?" Gerstner reminded people how he had earlier mocked the company's need for a corporate vision. He recalled how the media had "whooped and hollered" as they imagined IBM "wandering visionless, through the wilderness."[5] Ironically, he now admitted that IBM needed a vision more than ever.

His vision imagined IBM as the leader in *network-centric* computing. In his 1995 letter, he described advances in digital technologies that allowed "video, high-resolution images, voice and music" to flow seamlessly over a faster Internet. Gerstner imagined new technology that would allow *real people* thousands of miles apart to collaborate in *real time*. He noted that already "people and organizations were moving from surfing to working, from browsing to buying." This would change commerce, education, and the distribution of entertainment and government services.

In this networked world, IBM would be the go-to place for businesses that wanted to tap its power. This bold vision was based on analysis of industry trends. While investors might expect most CEOs to anchor their corporate visions in projections of future trends, they would be disappointed. Rittenhouse Rankings research between 2002 and 2011 found that only a handful of shareholder letters were published by companies that described vision statements supported by trend analysis data.

CLUES TO SPOT VISION IN SUSTAINABLE BUSINESSES

What are the clues that readers can search for to spot compelling, motivating, and credible corporate visions? Rittenhouse Rankings recommends searching for leaders who demonstrate the ability to:

1. Write simple, but not simplistic statements
2. Report on innovative ideas, practices, and results
3. Tell stories that entertain and teach
4. Display emotional intelligence
5. Articulate a convincing corporate purpose and mission

CLUE 1: WRITE SIMPLE, BUT NOT SIMPLISTIC STATEMENTS

The best vision statements are simple and profound. Peter Drucker was a master at this. He gathered simple words together so that others could instantly see the world in new ways. For example, he connected leadership and curiosity in these sentences: "Leaders of the past knew how to tell. Leaders of the future will know how to ask."[6] Employing original vocabulary creates a powerful competitive advantage.

When CEOs ask, "What is ahead?" they start to build a blueprint of the unknown. Over time, this design will change, sometimes dramatically. The creators of this vision must be alert to changes in the environment that require course corrections. Without such a blueprint, however, a company *is* wandering directionless in a corporate desert, just like Lou Gerstner described. In the Rittenhouse Rankings 2002 survey, Intel, Boeing, and IBM all scored high in explaining how events and industry trends were shaping their companies' visions of the future.

Intel and the Premature Death of Technology

In their 2001 letter, Intel Chairman Andy Grove and CEO Craig Barrett described Intel's tough challenges as the technology industry continued to reel from the implosion of dot-com businesses. They wrote that investors "wondered if technology was dead." Their reply was a "resounding no." Grove and Barrett advised taking the long view. "The history of technology revolutions," they reminded readers, "is told in cycles of boom, bust and build-out."

The two leaders reaffirmed their confidence in the growth of digital technologies to power the Internet: "Guided by our vision of the ongoing digital revolution, we continue to introduce new products and invest for the future so that we will be ready to ride the recovery."

Boeing's 20-Year Vision

In Boeing's 2001 letter, CEO Phil Condit and Vice Chairman Harry Stonecipher wrote that they were shocked and angered to see their company's planes being used for acts of terror. After the 9/11 attacks, Boeing's orders for new planes dropped precipitously as air travel went into a tailspin. Nevertheless, Condit and Stonecipher stuck to the company's long-term vision as they confronted the continuing challenge of operating in the boom/bust aircraft industry cycle.

> ... we have been getting ready for this challenge since 1996. That is when, as a new CEO, I set out a 20-year vision for Boeing that would define the company when it reached its 100th anniversary in 2016. That vision led us to build a broader, more balanced portfolio of aerospace businesses. *A portfolio of businesses that could connect and protect the world.* [author's emphasis]

IBM Passes the Torch

In his 2001 shareholder letter, CEO Gerstner described how IBM's customers were now integrating business and information technology strategies rather than keeping them apart in separate divisions. He observed that information technology investments were supported not only by chief information officers ("CIOs"), but also by business managers with profit and loss responsibility.

Gerstner also reported on IBM's progress in rebuilding information systems for multiple applications. As the company shifted its focus from proprietary software to open standards, he boasted, "Absolutely every piece of IBM hardware and software today is a fundamentally different beast (and a more socialized one) than it was ten years ago." At the end of his letter, Gerstner passed the baton to IBM's new CEO, Sam Palmisano, a career IBMer who had started as a salesman at the company in 1973.

In his letter, Palmisano described how the industry downturn was affecting sales in IBM's Technology and Personal Computer Groups. While cost cutting and other measures had helped to boost profits, Palmisano still expected a slow recovery in 2002. Despite this dim outlook, however, IBM was fully focused on creating its future. The company would continue to (1) "help customers to thrive in this [slow growth] environment"; (2) "gain share against our competitors"; (3) "drive turnarounds in our underperforming businesses"; and (4) "keep advancing productivity gains."

Palmisano predicted that during periods of cataclysmic industry change, companies like IBM would not only gain market share, but also set the technical agenda of the future. Don't believe that IBM's 2001 market share gains are due just to the bankruptcies of pure-play dot-com companies, he warned readers. In fact, the company's share growth was improving as "the reality of e-business" was finally taking hold.

To support "a new computing infrastructure for e-business," IBM was building technologies for systems that could "regulate, protect, configure and even heal themselves." Why was this needed? Palmisano imagined a future in which the coming flood of "transactions, operations and complexity" would outstrip the supply of technologists in the world who could support this growth.

Creating spontaneous, self-regulating systems energized IBM's scientists and engineers. It was the "kind of challenge," Palmisano wrote, "that gets the juices flowing across IBM's technical communities." In 2001, IBM became the "first enterprise to earn more than 3,000 new U.S. patent awards." In fact, the company's actual total— 3,411—"exceeded the combined total of 12 of the largest I/T companies in the United States."

Consider that the strength and resilience of American business and the U.S. economy have always been spurred on by great inventors such as Thomas Edison, Henry Ford, Alexander Graham Bell, Samuel Morse, and the Wright Brothers. Given this inventive heritage, it is not unreasonable to expect most companies to report on their patent and innovation progress. In fact, over the past decade, only 34 percent of companies in our survey reported on this topic. IBM and Swiss pharmaceutical giant Novartis have reported on their patents more than other companies in the Rittenhouse Rankings Surveys.

Palmisano continued to extol IBM's inventiveness. Not only were his letters noteworthy for reports on patent progress, but the letters themselves were innovative.

CLUE 2: INNOVATIONS

Case Study: Wells Fargo—Innovation in the Broadest Sense of the Word
It may surprise readers to learn that a "stodgy" bank has consistently scored high in the Rittenhouse Rankings Culture and Candor Surveys for reporting on commentary about unique and innovative corporate practices, ideas, and results not found in other CEO letters. We code these passages as "Innovations."

How has Wells Fargo managed to do this? It has built a culture where the commonplace is seldom treated as common or ordinary.

Each of the innovations below, taken from the 2003 shareholder letter by then-CEO Richard Kovacevich, illustrates how Wells Fargo turned the ordinary into extraordinary. In the first example, Kovacevich dusted off traditional banking performance metrics and compared these to baseball stats. In the second, instead of using platitudes to describe customer services, he described actual services provided by the bank to meet special needs. And in the third, Kovacevich explained why investors should consider the happiness of employees.

Innovation 1: Compares Banking Performance Metrics with Baseball Statistics

> Even a game that's been around as long as baseball is changing the way it measures success. As Michael Lewis points out in his best-seller, Moneyball, statistics such as batting average and stolen bases traditionally were considered most important. Today, it's on-base percentage, runs scored, and slugging percentage. So, too, we must change how we measure success in our industry. Traditionally, asset size and return on assets were most important. Today, it's revenue growth and products per customer.

Innovation 2: Forgoes Platitudes and Describes Actual Customer Services

> Wells Fargo is proud to lead an industrywide pilot to help victims of identity theft quickly regain control of their financial information and restore their credit ratings. In partnership with the Financial Services Roundtable, we're providing coordination and resources for the Identity Theft Assistance Center, expected to open in 2004. It will provide victims with a single point of contact to report identity theft and one process to record victim information. This means victims will have to tell their story only once—to their primary financial institution.

Kovacevich even mentioned how Wells Fargo had added spoken content to the company's website to help visually impaired customers bank online. One such customer, he wrote, told her service representative that online banking now took only 15 minutes, instead of hours.

Innovation 3: Links Employee Happiness to Customer Loyalty and Profits

Many companies describe how important employees are to corporate success, but few do this as consistently in each letter as does Wells Fargo. In his 2003 letter, Kovacevich linked specific measures of employee satisfaction and happiness to company profits:

The quality of our customer service begins with our team members. They're the single biggest influence on our customers. If our team members are happy and satisfied, our customers will be more loyal to us and give us more opportunities to earn all their business. We regularly measure the engagement of our team members—to find out, for example, if they have the opportunity to do what they do best every day, if they've received recognition and praise for doing good work in the last seven days, if they have someone at work who encourages their development, if they have opportunities at work to learn and grow.

This commentary is important because it is easy for investors to test the truth of these claims. Go to your local Wells Fargo branch and look for happy employees. Figure 8.1 tracks the candor rankings of important financial services companies from 2002 to 2008. As shown, Wells Fargo consistently outscored Wachovia, Merrill Lynch,

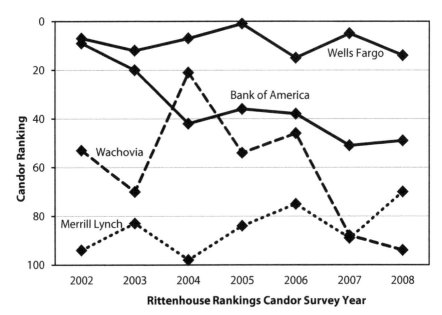

Figure 8.1   **Financial Services Companies**
Rittenhouse Rankings Culture and Candor Rankings 2002–2008

and Bank of America. It ranked in the top quartile of the survey in each of those years.

IBM Case Study: Leading the Industry in All the Ways a Business Should Lead

Consider that IBM's letters have scored among the top-performing companies reporting on innovation between 2001 and 2010. These excerpts from Palmisano's 2002 letter illustrate how IBM's culture is reflected in its "innovations."

Innovation 1: Taking the Market by Storm

Palmisano reported again on IBM's patent performance in his 2002 letter. That year IBM earned "3,288 U.S. patents, nearly double the number of the next closest company." Still, he was quick to remind investors that technical innovation alone would not ensure IBM's competitive edge. The company also had to show customers how to use the technology it was inventing:

> [A]lthough IBM pioneered the mainframe model of computing, it would not have taken the market by storm if we had only brought customers a new machine. We had to bring them a new idea about business, and we had to show them how to apply mainframe systems to transform back-office functions like accounting, payroll and inventory management.

Realizing that clients wanted help to build "infrastructures that connected them with other businesses and people" led Palmisano to a powerful insight: "If customers are going to look to you as the leader in computing, you have to be able to drive forward the entire computing agenda, not just a piece of it."

Innovation 2: Creating Intuitive Systems to Counter Threats from Hackers to Hurricanes

Palmisano described specific applications that supported "on demand businesses." These allowed clients to manage inventory profitably and respond more quickly to meet customers' needs. Palmisano described how IBM Global Services provided business process and industry expertise for clients to help them build enterprises that:

> are almost intuitive in their responsiveness to changes in demand, supply, pricing, labor, capital markets and customer needs. This requires a great deal of integration—of business processes and operations, and of applications and the underlying IT systems. It means making them resilient in the face of changes and threats, from hackers to hurricanes.

The words in this excerpt—"almost intuitive in their responsiveness," "a great deal of integration," "making them resilient," and "threats from hackers to hurricanes"—are seldom found in other shareholder letters. These create vivid pictures of business opportunities that penetrate readers' minds. They reveal Palmisano's vocabulary advantage.

Innovation 3: Managing Aspirations as Business Priorities

Palmisano described his vision for IBM to lead the industry—"in all the ways that a business should lead." Not only would IBM aspire to achieve technical and sales leadership, but it would be "a great employer" and "a responsible citizen." Meeting these goals would be given the same attention as meeting business priorities like "managing R&D, manufacturing and sales."

Palmisano believed that failing to be a great employer, investment, and community member could be "as damaging [to IBM's business] as failure to stay abreast of markets or technology."

Innovation 4: Stepping into the Shoes of Employees

In his 2002 letter, Palmisano offered a new employee innovation. He began by describing changing employee expectations:

> We know that employees today value flexibility and mobility, yet they want to feel part of a team, a community of colleagues. They value skill enhancement, but they want lifelong learning, not just classroom training. Most of all, while they are attracted to IBM's breadth and global presence, they don't want to get lost in a

big company. They want to make a difference, have impact. *All of this represents opportunities for us once again to* innovate *as an employer.* [author's emphasis]

Not only was the opportunity to "innovate as an employer" a shareholder letter innovation, but so too was Palmisano's use of the word *innovate*. Consider that this verb has been used only 145 times in the 10-year survey, while the noun *innovation* has been used 1,428 times.

Why should investors care? It stands to reason that CEOs who populate their shareholder letters with action verbs are more likely to engage and motivate their stakeholders. This will increase execution and performance and give a CEO a narrative advantage.

CLUE 3: STORIES TO GAIN NARRATIVE ADVANTAGE

"Narrative advantage" refers to a CEO's ability to report information as a story. CEO stories entertain and engage readers. They can also impart important lessons. Telling stories requires a writer to imagine the beginning, middle, and end of critical events or results. Stories can reveal the consequences of actions, provide insightful context, and often contain memorable imagery. Stories can reveal a company's execution strength, and even its morality.

In his 2003 letter, Palmisano offered a story about the decision to reexamine IBM's values, which had been in place since 1911. He believed this effort was long overdue and was vital to the company's success. He reminded readers:

> When IBMers have been crystal clear and united about our strategies and purpose, it's amazing what we've been able to create and accomplish. When we've been uncertain, conflicted or hesitant, we've squandered opportunities and even made blunders that would have sunk smaller companies.

To gain more certainty throughout the enterprise, Palmisano wanted all IBM employees to be involved in reassessing the company's "reason for being, what sets [it] apart and what should drive our actions as individual IBM-ers." "Something as vital and personal as values," he wrote, "could [not] be dictated from the top."

But how could more than 300,000 employees around the world simultaneously get engaged in this effort? IBM created a unique online experience called "Values Jam":

> [F]or 72 hours last summer, we invited all 319,000 IBMers around the world to engage in an open "values jam" on our global intranet. IBMers by the tens of thousands weighed in. They were thoughtful and passionate about the company they want to be a part of. They were also brutally honest. Some of what they wrote was painful to read, because they pointed out all the bureaucratic and dysfunctional things that get in the way of serving clients, working as a team or implementing new ideas. But we were resolute in keeping the dialog free-flowing and candid. And I don't think what resulted—broad, enthusiastic, grass-roots consensus—could have been obtained in any other way.
>
> In the end, IBMers determined that our actions will be driven by these values:
> - Dedication to every client's success
> - Innovation that matters, for our company and for the world
> - Trust and personal responsibility in all relationships

Palmisano explained why the process was meaningful to him:

> We are getting back in touch with what IBM has always been about—and always will be about—in a very concrete way. And I feel that I've been handed something every CEO craves: a mandate, for exactly the right kinds of transformation, from an entire workforce.
>
> Where will this lead? It is a work in progress, and many of the implications remain to be discovered. What I can tell you is that we are rolling up our sleeves to bring IBM's values to life in our policies, procedures and daily operations.

This inspiring story offered a vivid picture of what sets IBM apart from other companies: an original vocabulary, a moral vision, and a CEO who highlights personal responsibility to others as a corporate value.

Finding CEOs who tell stories in their shareholder letters with a beginning, a middle, and a moral at the end is rare. Typically we read letters with narratives that are disguised as PowerPoint presentations, in which information is stated, but not connected. Such disjointed narratives reveal strategic weakness.

Case Study: Connecting the Dots at American International Group

Rittenhouse Rankings first noticed the PowerPoint style of reporting in American International Group's (AIG's) letters. More than most companies, AIG offered plenty of data in the early days of the Rittenhouse Rankings surveys, but seldom connected them to provide strategic, meaningful context. For instance, this excerpt from then-CEO Hank Greenberg's 2000 shareholder letter described the company's progress in growing its insurance business in Vietnam:

> As reported last year, early in 2000 American International Assurance Company, Ltd. [AIA] received a life insurance license from the government of Vietnam to operate a wholly owned life company in that country, the first insurance license granted by Vietnam to a U.S.-based company. Our new Hanoi and Ho Chi Minh City offices opened in October. We now have an agency force of approximately 1,800 and the new company is achieving faster growth than its original business plan.

Greenberg's story offered a lot of information, but also raised questions: Why did he believe that Vietnam was an attractive place to do business? How was AIG's overall strategy advanced by becoming the first U.S.-based company to get an operating license in Vietnam? Where were the sales numbers that supported his claim of "faster growth than [the] original business plan"? In other words, Greenberg won points for providing data, but he lost points for failing to connect this data. More evidence of this PowerPoint narrative style was evident in AIG's 2008 shareholder letter, written in the midst of the global economic collapse.

To appreciate this commentary, some background is needed. Recall that by 2004, approximately $157 billion of *collateralized debt obligations* or "CDOs" had been sold to investors around the world. CDOs represented an owner's claim on the revenues that came from a portfolio of mortgages that were divided into tranches ranked from highest to lowest in risk.

Incredibly, these baskets of mostly sketchy mortgages had been given the highest ratings by Wall Street credit agencies. This may have comforted unsophisticated investors, but savvy holders knew these securities were shaky. They were happy to buy the *credit default swaps* or "CDSs" offered by AIG to protect them in the event that the CDO tranches began to lose value as the underlying mortgages defaulted.

AIG's CDSs securities acted like an insurance policy. In the event that a CDO tranche began to lose value, AIG would pay the holder for their losses. Because AIG called these CDS insurance policies "swaps" instead of "insurance policies," it appeared that the company was not required to set aside reserves. In other words, they may have been sold like traditional insurance, but they were not treated as such.

So when the daisy chain of CDOs defaulted, holders came to AIG asking them to post more and more collateral. But AIG had none to give. On September 16, 2008, AIG received an $85 billion taxpayer loan from the Federal Reserve, using special authority granted to the agency under the Federal Reserve Act.

Edward Liddy, who was named AIG's CEO on September 18, 2008, at the height of this crisis, described the situation in his 2008 shareholder letter. He wanted readers to understand the reasons for granting AIG a taxpayer bailout, which he called an "investment from the U.S. government."

> Because of its size and substantial interconnection with financial markets and institutions around the world, the government recognized that a failure of AIG would have had severe ramifications. In addition to being one of the world's largest insurers, *AIG was providing more than $400 billion of credit protection to banks and other clients around the world through its credit default swap*

business. AIG also is a major participant in foreign exchange and interest rate markets.

To stabilize AIG and prevent reverberations throughout the economy, the *government extended to AIG a two-year emergency loan of $85 billion on September 16, 2008*. [author's emphasis]

Liddy explained that in return for this loan, taxpayers would receive quarterly interest payments, "a commitment fee of 2 percent on the loan principal," and "a fee on the undrawn portion of 8.5 percent." Furthermore, the government now owned 79.9 percent of the company through a preferred stock investment. When this loan solved AIG's immediate liquidity crisis, Liddy next turned his attention to figuring out how to repay taxpayers and shore up the company's financial foundation:

> With the loan in place, the management team developed a plan to enable AIG to sell many of its leading businesses around the world to pay back the government loan with interest. However, with this divestiture and restructuring plan in place, AIG still had to address its two principal liquidity issues: the multi-sector credit default swap portfolio and the securities lending program.

While investors and taxpayers may not have liked the dots that Liddy was connecting, he was admirably linking them to explain what had been done and why.

Liddy then told the story of what it was like for him to join AIG on September 18, 2008, when "less than 12 months after reporting record results, [the company was] on the brink of collapse." After accepting U.S. Treasury Secretary Hank Paulson's request to lead AIG, Liddy described what he found at the company:

> [It was] an organization full of proud, talented and dedicated people who were stunned and bewildered to see their life's work—and in many cases their life's savings—a shambles. The swift decline of AIG seemed all the more incongruous because most of our businesses were healthy and operating normally— as they are today. But the implosion of the U.S. housing market

exposed AIG's risk concentration in mortgage-backed securities. That concentration, combined with tumbling asset values and dysfunctional credit markets, led to a sudden and severe cash crisis.

Although Liddy served only 11 months as CEO, he accomplished a great deal. On August 10, 2009, Robert Benmosche, the just-retired CEO of insurance giant MetLife, was named AIG's CEO. AIG's candor rankings have not strengthened, although the company's market price has increased 38 percent during this period.

Benmosche's 2010 shareholder letter scored 122 points for strategy, but only 10 points for vision. We noted his unique commentary on the importance of "checks and balances."

> AIG entered 2011 poised to emerge as a company independent of government support. We have worked hard to enhance our businesses and functions so that the U.S. government—and the investment community—will have confidence in our ability to operate without government financial assistance . . . the significant progress we have made with oversight and controls will enable us to grow with the right checks and balances.

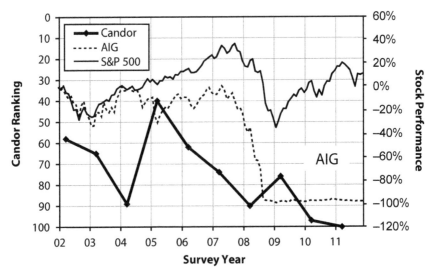

Figure 8.2   **AIG Culture and Candor Rankings and Performance 2002–2011**

As Figure 8.2 shows, AIG's candor ranking began to fall in the 2006 survey (2005 letter). It hit a low in the 2008 survey and improved in 2009. Over the study period, AIG's stock has declined 98 percent.

CLUE 4: EMOTIONAL INTELLIGENCE: PERSONAL AND AUTHENTIC

In their seminal 1990 article, "Emotional Intelligence (EI)," researchers Peter Salovey and John D. Mayer described four factors or abilities that indicate EI:

1. "Perceiving emotion" based on body language, facial expressions, and other clues
2. "Reasoning with emotion" when this helps us to focus our attention on what seems to be most important
3. "Understanding the context of emotions" in others and ourselves
4. "Managing or regulating emotions" to respond appropriately to the emotions of others[7]

The clue to spotting emotional intelligence in shareholder letters is to find commentary that "creates emotion," such as Liddy's description of what he found when he arrived at AIG. Hard-wired investors tend to dismiss emotional intelligence. However, Rittenhouse Rankings has learned to respect this indicator of CEO vision. Consider that Nike, a top scorer in emotional intelligence, has seen its stock market value increase more than 262 percent over the decade of our candor surveys.

In fact, CEOs who are business founders typically score higher on expressing emotion in their letters than CEOs who are professional managers. Nike founder and former CEO Phil Knight's shareholder letters, for example, stand out not just because they are emotional and authentic; his writing is quirky, original, and even reflective. Among the letters written after the 9/11 attacks, Knight's 2002 commentary stood out as the most reflective:

We entered FY '02 with a 1% decline in U.S. futures orders. We had our work cut out for us. Then came September 11, and with it a bow wave of uncertainty. Restaurants, stadiums, theme parks, malls, all thinner of crowd, showed the wan face of anxiety. We were at a threshold, one of those defining moments that pop up out of nowhere in every life, both individual and corporate. You can cross that threshold with courage or turn away in fear. Either way, you change forever.

Only 17 percent of the companies in our annual surveys have used the word *fear* in their shareholder letters, and Nike has used it three times. In contrast, 31 percent have used the words *courage* or *courageous*. Reebok has used them more times than any other in describing the recipients of its annual Human Rights Awards in 2001, 2003, and 2004.

In his 2007 shareholder letter, Knight emotionally reaffirmed his commitment to stewarding investor capital. He recalled how he felt when the company went public in December 1980. Consider that over our 10-year survey, Phil Knight is the only CEO to have ever used the word *scared*:

[W]e had 7,500 shareholders, and in a word it *scared* me. I can remember getting that first list, 7,500 people long, that had invested in this company. I put that list on a credenza in back of my desk, and it was the last thing I looked at every morning before I sat down at my desk, thinking, These people have invested their savings in you. . . . Today we have 300,000 shareholders, and I've really never lost that feeling. We really have an obligation to do well not only for ourselves but for them.

Knight could always get emotional when reporting on sports. This story from his 2009 shareholder letter about the Beijing Olympics tells how Nike developed new products for specific athletes and also described the company's long standing relationship with China.

For three years we worked with athletes all over the world to design new products for nearly every competitive event. We created new technologies like Flywire and LunarFoam that continue to drive product innovation. We turned the Hyperdunk basketball shoe into one of the highest profile and most dramatic shoes in Olympic history. For two weeks in August we watched our products and athletes from all over the world compete and win on the biggest stage in sports. It was a great moment for Nike and for sports.

If there were any lingering doubts that China should be considered an emerging market, the Olympics responded with a thunderous, "No!" China is not an emerging market. It is an emerged market that combines power and potential critical to the future of any global company.

We sold our first shoes in China in 1984 when we placed 200 pairs in a 50-square-foot shop called The Friendship Store in Beijing. They sold out in 11 days. Today, nearly a year after the closing ceremony in the Bird's Nest, the appetite for Nike products and athletes continues to grow. The brand is known and, more importantly, understood among many of the 500 million Chinese consumers under 25 years old. That's a billion feet that we're going after just as fast as we can.

Knight's letters stand out because they are informative, emotional, and personal.

A Vision of Personal Technology

When Google went public in 2004, its founders, Larry Page and Sergey Brin, used Warren Buffett's shareholder letters and *Owner's Manual* as a model to write their Founder's Letter and "'An Owner's Manual' for Google's shareholders." Back then, they vowed to take turns writing a shareholder letter each year. The unique voice of each founder is evident in each year's letter. For example, Page's style is cerebral, while Brin's writing is more personal and emotional.

Here is how Brin opened his 2010 letter:

My father did not have the freedom to pursue the career of his choice in the Soviet Union. Nevertheless, he produced copious research on dynamical systems, a branch of mathematics, in his spare time.

When I was four years old, there was an international conference on the subject in Warsaw—a rare event in any scientific field behind the Iron Curtain. Even though he was not officially allowed to attend and it was challenging to get permission to travel, my father was able to make the trip with the help of supporters in Poland. What he learned there went well beyond mathematics, and dramatically changed the course of our lives.

Contrary to what my father had been taught, the mathematicians from the other side of the Iron Curtain were not monsters. They were fellow scientists who shared the same passions. The key difference was that they were free: free to pursue the career of their choice, free to voice their opinions, free to travel, and above all they were free from fear of their own government. That small but powerful piece of information drove my family to flee the Soviet Union two years later and start a new life in the United States.

Today the vast majority of the world's population has access to mobile phones, and over two billion people are connected to the Internet. As a result, the trickle of information that made its way into closed societies such as the USSR when I was a child has now become a torrent—and millions of people living under totalitarian regimes are able to glimpse freedom every day of their lives, albeit virtually.

Cynics may dismiss this story as public relations pabulum. Over the past decade, however, Rittenhouse Rankings has seldom found writing that is as personal, purposeful, and visionary as this. In his letter, Brin explained how technological innovation can give power to the powerless:

Technology has also democratized communication and creation of information. Capabilities that were once available only to the largest corporations are now available to businesses, political movements, governments, and individuals alike. There is no longer a need to manage servers, updates, and patches; instead, users simply refresh their browser. In addition to Gmail, our most-used communications app, our broader suite of apps is now used by over three million businesses and 10 million students.

Brin offered examples to show how small start-ups were gaining global visibility:

A panama hat maker in Bolivia is now selling in 84 markets and has grown to 50 employees across Latin America using AdWords.

The owner of a baby products store in Nigeria had such a response to her AdWords campaign that she literally ran out of stock.

Displaced by Hurricane Katrina, the founder of a fitness boot-camp was able to completely rebuild, and then grow, his customer base with AdWords when he returned to New Orleans and started over.

Brin also reported on a city in Florida that had moved its website to Google Apps. This allowed people "more time to focus on open government initiatives." Now city council meetings can be live-streamed on YouTube—another Google product.

All these examples supported Google's corporate purpose to provide "access to information." In the following passage, Brin placed this purpose in a powerful context:

As I write this letter, a wave of change is passing through the Middle East and North Africa. I cannot predict what countries it will touch, or what the state of the world will be by the time you read this in two months. But I can be certain of one thing: access to information will play a key role.

CLUE 5: CORPORATE PURPOSE AND MISSION

Brin connected his stories to Google's purpose and mission. Consider that a mission statement answers the question, "Why do we exist and what do we contribute?" The answer is based in the present time. Vision statements are different. They describe a company's future aspirations.

For example, Costco's mission, as described in founder and former CEO Jim Sinegal's 2010 letter, is to "continually bring quality goods and services to our members at the lowest possible prices, while being responsible corporate citizens, taking care of our members and our employees, and respecting our vendors." Sinegal believed that by "building a company that will be here fifty, sixty, and more years from now," he and the company were honoring their responsibilities to shareholders, members, employees, and suppliers.

Costco's long-term mission to offer quality goods and services at the lowest prices may not seem groundbreaking, but it is. Rittenhouse Rankings research shows that Costco is the only company in our decade-long survey that defines *value* in its shareholder letters as combining "the highest quality goods and services at the lowest possible prices."

In his 2009 letter, Walmart CEO Michael Duke reported on his company's simple and compelling mission to "save people money so they can live better."

In Target's 2001 letter, CEO Bob Ulrich used words like "upscale discount store," "new design partnerships," and "attractive prices" to describe Target's essential mission:

> Discipline also plays a role in our ability to satisfy our guests' expectations for merchandise excitement and value, and for in-stock reliability. It helps us avoid complacency and preserves our competitive advantage. Reflecting our fundamental mission as an upscale discount store, we remain vigilant in offering attractive prices, receptive to fostering new design partnerships and focused on managing inventories to meet our guests' demand and to optimize sales and markdowns.

Case Study: IBM Building a "Smarter Planet"

IBM's Sam Palmisano devoted an entire section on "The Purpose of a Business" in his 2002 letter. He described how IBM's focus on business and global societal needs attracted people who want to work at "a big, complex company" so they could help solve big issues.

Palmisano described his vision of returning IBM to a position of leadership. The strategy was simple: IBM's remarkable scientists, managers, and analysts—"some of the best minds on the planet"—would dedicate themselves "to help local, national, and international communities solve problems and stimulate economic growth." In his 2003 letter, an optimistic Palmisano expanded on this vision:

> In today's world, where everyone is so interconnected and inter-dependent, it is simply essential that we work for each other's success. If we're going to solve the biggest, thorniest and most widespread problems in *business and society*, we have to inno-vate in ways that truly matter.

In his 2008 shareholder letter, Palmisano explained how IBM was expanding this vision to deploy information technologies that could build a "Smarter Planet." This would be accomplished by infusing "intelligence into the way the world actually works: the systems and processes that enable physical goods to be developed, manufactured, bought and sold; services to be delivered; everything from people and money to oil, water and electrons to move; and billions of people to work and live."

The disastrous collapse of the global financial system in 2008 was evidence of the growing instability in the current "systems by which the world works." Creating a networked world was just part of the job. Now IBM wanted to deliver intelligent data and technology over these connections that would more efficiently deploy capital and improve the quality of life for millions of people. He described some of these Smarter Planet innovations:

> SMARTER TRAFFIC: Stockholm's intelligent traffic system, cre-ated by IBM, has resulted in 20 percent less gridlock, a 12-percent drop in emissions and a reported 40,000 additional daily users of public transport. IBM is building smart traffic systems in cities

from London to Brisbane to Singapore—with many more being planned. . . .

SMARTER HEALTHCARE: The cost of therapy is being lowered by as much as 90 percent. For example, IBM technology is being used to monitor the proper delivery of injections and vaccines to more than 2 million patients in 38 states.

SMARTER FOOD SYSTEMS: IBM built a system for Norway's largest food supplier that uses RFID technology to trace meat and poultry from the farm, through the supply chain, all the way to supermarket shelves. . . .

SMARTER WATER: We can even use computer modeling to simulate, monitor—and potentially manage—the behavior of river basins around the world, as Water for Tomorrow, a collaboration between IBM and The Nature Conservancy, is now doing in Brazil, China and the U.S.

Palmisano's 2003 vision of solving worldwide problems by innovating "in ways that really matter" was being realized. Achieving this vision, he had written, required IBM's employees to make decisions reflecting the corporate values. Importantly, he expected them to take *"personal responsibility* for all of our relationships—with clients, colleagues, partners, investors and the public at large. This is IBM's mission as an enterprise, and a goal toward which we hope to work with many others, in our industry and beyond" [author's emphasis].

When you read a shareholder letter, how can you tell if a CEO is taking personal responsibility for building relationships with all those having a stake in the company's success? Rittenhouse Rankings looks for reports that describe the breadth and depth of "Stakeholder Relationships." This is the sixth system in the Rittenhouse Rankings Sustainable Business Model.

CHAPTER 9

Stakeholder Relationships

Person, noun

1. A living human.
2. An individual of specified character: a person of importance.
3. The composite of characteristics that make up an individual personality; the self.
4. The living body of a human.

[Middle English, from Old French *persone*, from Latin *persōna*, mask, role, person, probably from Etruscan *phersu*, mask.]

Personal, adjective

1. Of or relating to the private aspects of a person's life.
2. Of or relating to a person's body, its care, or its appearance.
3. Belonging to or intended for a particular person and no one else.
4. Undertaken by an individual himself.
5. Referring to, concerning, or involving a person's individual personality.[1]

Why did CEO Sam Palmisano advise IBM's thousands of leaders to assume *personal* responsibility for their relationships with important company stakeholders? Perhaps he did so because business *is* personal. We give as much as we can trust to give. The more we trust, the more we give.

In business, as in life, first impressions are important. Read the opening paragraphs of a shareholder letter to see if the CEO is focused on the quality of stakeholder relationships. For example, consider these three airline company letters written after the 9/11 attacks. Each introductory paragraph reveals clues about the quality of personal relating at each company:

Richard Anderson, CEO of Northwest Airlines in 2001, started his letter with this emotional story:

> Everyone at Northwest Airlines breathed easier when Flight 22, a Boeing 747 from Tokyo's Narita Airport, landed in Honolulu at 2:13 p.m. It was Tuesday, September 11, 2001. The arrival signified that all our aircraft were safely on the ground.
>
> More than six hours earlier we had learned of the terrorist attacks on the United States. We had immediately directed all flights to land at the nearest suitable airport, even before the order came from the Federal Aviation Administration to ground all U.S. aircraft. After Flight 22 landed, we gathered our key leaders to assess the situation and plan immediate tactics.

This drama draws us in. Readers share Anderson's relief when all the company's aircraft are on the ground. However, the passage also raises questions: Who decided to wait until six hours after the terrorist attacks to assemble the company's key leaders? Who directed the landing of all the company's planes? Who was in charge?

In contrast, the opening of Southwest Chairman Herb Kelleher and CEO Colleen Barrett's shareholder letter left no doubt about who took responsibility. It began with a quote by Todd Beamer, the passenger on United Flight 93 who organized passengers to seize control of the plane from the terrorists on board.

"Are you guys ready? Okay. Let's roll."—Todd Beamer

These heroic words, flung into the macabre face of impending tragedy, were a luminous reflection of the iron character, unquenchable spirit, and inspiring altruism of a noble team leader and player. Todd Beamer's words and actions, in the scarifying context of the horrific events of September 11, helped to galvanize America into a state of "terrible, swift resolve.

This writing puts us inside that doomed flight. Verbs build suspense: "let's *roll*" and "helped to *galvanize* America." Words like *scarifying* and phrases such as "flung into the macabre face of impending tragedy" were raw and original. Southwest dramatized an extreme example of personal responsibility.

In contrast to these narratives, the shareholder letter by the then-CEO of Continental Airlines, Gordon Bethune, was tame. Unlike the other CEOs, Bethune put the company's stakeholders at the start of his letter. He reassured readers that this tragedy would not shake the company's commitments to them:

> During this past year of unimaginable challenges, Continental relied even more heavily on the fundamentals that have made us successful. Although no one could have anticipated the events of last year, our culture of Working Together developed over the last seven years, including relationships with employees, customers, vendors and distribution partners, proved to be our most valuable resource for weathering the storm precipitated by the terrorist attacks of Sept. 11.

First, he wrote that just hours after the attacks, the management team had used every possible communication vehicle to update employees on progress in restoring the system.

Second, Bethune imagined the anxiety of employees who realized that a reduction in flights due to the attacks would mean job losses. He wrote:

> Our corporate culture under the Go Forward Plan has always dictated that we communicate openly, honestly and frequently

with our co-workers, and Sept. 11 was no exception ... When we knew that a 20 percent capacity reduction would result in the elimination of 12,000 positions, we did not hide from the hard facts by saying that we were studying staffing issues; instead, we proactively and quickly let our co-workers know that furloughs were coming, and we implemented them as quickly as possible.

Bethune also wrote that the company would honor severance provisions for all contract and noncontract employees. He and the leadership team were designing programs that would "avoid as many involuntary furloughs as possible" and "treat our coworkers with the dignity and respect they deserve." Already, more than 4,000 employees had come forward to take voluntary furloughs.

Bethune thanked Congress and the president for passing the Air Transportation Safety and System Stabilization Act that provided emergency funds to cover the costs of the immediate shutdown of all airlines and offered loan guarantees. He was the only airline CEO to do so in his letter.

At the end of his communication, Bethune asked readers to support the Continental team:

Continental survived a uniquely turbulent set of events beyond its control, and is well positioned to enjoy the benefits of an economic recovery. Every member of our employee group responded with an effort that exemplifies our Work Hard. Fly Right. slogan. Our team's outstanding performance will allow us to Go Forward in 2002, smaller than before, but the same company, with the same commitment and vision. Bigger isn't better, better is better. *Stick with us, as we stick with our plan. As the future unfolds, you'll be glad you did.* [author's emphasis]

How can you tell if a CEO is assuming personal responsibility for strengthening stakeholder relationships? Look for these clues in his or her communications. Find leaders who: (1) build ownership cultures; (2) engage stakeholders; (3) balance stakeholder needs; and (4) anticipate what customers want.

CLUE 1: BUILD OWNERSHIP CULTURES

Personally, I had decided to "stick" with Continental long before the 9/11 attacks. As a frequent Continental flyer, I knew that Bethune's words were authentic, not PR spin. Of course, this had not always been true.

Throughout the 1990s, I had avoided Continental. Under previous leadership, the company had been in bankruptcy twice between 1983 and 1993. In 1994, Bethune, an executive and former Boeing mechanic, was named the company's CEO. He made an immediate difference in the company and its culture. He took decisive action to eliminate unprofitable routes, improve service, and win back lucrative business travelers. The year he joined, Continental lost $613 million. In 1995, Continental reported a profit of $224 million.[2]

Reading Bethune's shareholder letter in 1997 impressed me enough to book a Continental flight with my then-toddler daughter. Before boarding the plane on the day of our departure, I checked her stroller on the Jetway. We took off and landed on time. The in-flight service was efficient and pleasant. But when we disembarked and stepped onto the Jetway, I realized the stroller was not in sight, nor was anyone around to help me find it. Suddenly the pilot stepped off the plane and asked what was wrong. I explained the situation, and he promptly retrieved the stroller from the tarmac below. This was impressive. Here was a pilot who landed planes and took personal responsibility for finding strollers. His action showed that Continental had an ownership culture. That day I became a Continental frequent flyer.

In his 1998 letter, Bethune described the company's strategy to "Work Hard, Fly Right." He vowed that the 48,000 men and women at Continental would strive "every day to get you safely to your destination on-time, with your bags, to serve you good food at meal times and, with our new airplanes, to show you movies when you are bored on many long-haul flights."

Three years later, not long after the September 11 attacks, I flew on Continental to attend a business meeting. On the plane, I asked a flight attendant how Bethune was holding up. She replied, "I just sent him an e-mail telling him how things were going." I was surprised. She was writing directly to the CEO? "Did he respond?" I asked. "Sure," she said. "Usually he gets back to us within 24 hours." That was even more startling news! When I asked why she had written, she replied, "I wanted him to know he had my support."

Over the years, I have tried this same experiment on other airlines and asked flight attendants how their CEOs were doing. Often they will say, "Who?" or may scowl and shake their heads. The airline business is tough. It is a service business with commodity-like margins. CEOs are always looking for ways to cut costs, and the two biggest expenses are fuel and labor. As a result, pilots and crew are asked to reduce their pay and benefits. For these employees, the words and actions of CEOs don't matter much.

Case Study: Berkshire Hathaway Honors Promises

Warren Buffett described the attributes of an ownership culture in his 2000 shareholder letter. That year, Berkshire paid about $8 billion to acquire eight companies. These ranged from Seattle-based Ben Bridge Jeweler; Fort Worth–based Justin Industries, a maker of cowboy boots and brick and masonry products; the Benjamin Moore paint company; and MidAmerican Energy Holdings Company, an electric and gas utility serving customers in the Midwest and the United Kingdom.

Although operating in very different industries, these companies shared one characteristic: they built ownership cultures. Buffett described these qualities in his 2000 letter, starting with the example set by the business owners:

> We like to do business with someone who loves his company, not just the money that a sale will bring him (though we certainly understand why he likes that as well). When this emotional attachment exists, it signals that important qualities will likely be found within the business: honest accounting, pride of product, respect for customers, and a loyal group of associates having

a strong sense of direction. The reverse is apt to be true, also. When an owner auctions off his business, exhibiting a total lack of interest in what follows, you will frequently find that it has been dressed up for sale, particularly when the seller is a "financial owner." And if owners behave with little regard for their business and its people, their conduct will often contaminate attitudes and practices throughout the company.

These desired hallmarks—"honest accounting, pride of product, respect for customers, and a loyal group of associates having a strong sense of direction"—also describe the Berkshire culture. Buffett expects the sellers of businesses to honor the promises they make to employees and customers. In turn, the sellers expect Buffett to keep his promise to support and preserve the cultures of these businesses that have been built over a lifetime. In his 2000 letter, Buffett assured sellers that "Berkshire's ownership structure" would allow him to make bankable promises: "When we tell John Justin that his business will remain headquartered in Fort Worth, or assure the Bridge family that its operation will not be merged with another jeweler, these sellers can take those promises to the bank."

This promise is based on Principle 11 in Berkshire Hathaway's *Owner's Manual*:

> Regardless of price, we have no interest at all in selling any good businesses that Berkshire owns. We are also very reluctant to sell sub-par businesses as long as we expect them to generate at least some cash and as long as we feel good about their managers and labor relations. . . . [G]in rummy managerial behavior (discard your least promising business at each turn) is not our style.

This is not just a high-minded rule. As Buffett reminded the more than 35,000 investors at the company's 2012 annual meeting in Omaha, Nebraska, much of the company's success comes from its ability to attract sellers of high-quality businesses who know from experience that he keeps his promises.

Keeping Continental's Ownership Culture Alive

Bethune was not a business founder like Berkshire's entrepreneur-owners, but he acted like one. He made promises he tried to keep. This commitment was reflected in the service attitudes of the crews I met when I flew Continental.

In December 2004, Bethune's vice-chair, Larry Kellner, was named Continental's CEO. The difference between the two leaders was evident in Kellner's shareholder letters. From 2001 to 2003, Bethune's candor rankings had averaged fourth highest in our survey. Kellner's average shareholder letter ranking between 2004 and 2006 was 14th, a very respectable score, but nonetheless revealing increasing amounts of FOG.

Now when I boarded Continental flights and asked flight attendants how Kellner was doing, I would often hear, "He's not like Gordon Bethune." In fact, after 2006 Kellner stopped writing a shareholder letter altogether. In 2010, Continental announced that it would merge with United Airlines, a company that had not written a shareholder letter since it went into bankruptcy in 2002.

In 2011, only two major U.S. airline companies published shareholder letters: Southwest and JetBlue. Not only do both companies continue to nurture stakeholder-responsive cultures, but since 2009 these companies have reported positive financial results. Employees at these companies take personal responsibility for their actions. They treat passengers respectfully. They act like owners.

CLUE 2: ENGAGE STAKEHOLDERS

Case Study: Home Depot

While most companies focus on serving customers, some companies go the extra mile. Their leaders imagine the experience they want customers to have when they connect with the company. They meet obvious and special needs. This defines the quality of stakeholder engagement at Home Depot, which has been a huge force in the company's early and later success.

Founders Bernard "Bernie" Marcus and Arthur Blank began Home Depot in Atlanta in 1980. The company grew by buying up local home improvement stores and tucking them under the Home Depot logo. It offered top-notch service. By 1996, the company reported $20 billion in sales. As the company grew, the founders were committed to building a culture that engaged employees and customers. In fact, Home Depot's 1996 annual report included three shareholder letters: one signed by Chairman and CEO Marcus, a second from President and Chief Operating Officer Blank, and a third letter signed by "The Home Depot Store Associates."

Marcus's letter included a question asked by skeptical investors: "How does a $20 billion company that is already the world's largest retailer in its category continue a pattern of unprecedented growth?" He replied by reporting on Home Depot's 1996 success metrics, which fortified the company's sound financial base:

- Sales growth of 26 percent or $19.5 billion, compared to $15.5 billion in 1995
- Market share increase of 14 percent, up from 12 percent
- Comparable store-for-store sales increase of 7 percent over the 3 percent the previous year
- Passing the 500-store milestone to reach a total of 512 stores in operation by year-end
- Adding 18 new markets in the United States and one new market in Canada

In addition to these "tangible measures of success," Marcus wrote about "intangible [success] measures." These were evident in customer comments praising the company for "'low prices,' 'best assortment,' and 'great service.'" He described four growth strategies: (1) penetrating existing domestic markets; (2) extending the Home Depot brand to include remodeling and design consulting services; (3) acquiring new businesses to attract professional business customers; and (4) expanding into global markets starting with Chile.

Arthur Blank's letter described improvements to company operations. These included efforts to (1) increase efficiencies from new information systems; (2) improve the supply chain by speeding up deliveries; (3) create more satisfied customers by offering great value; and (4) lowering the cost of goods and maximizing sales opportunities. The success of these efforts was evident in "weekly sales per store [that] increased 2% to an average of $803,000, and sales per square foot [that] grew 2% to $398." These measures of "sales productivity" allowed Home Depot associates to "provide higher levels of service to our customers."

Blank reminded investors that "With every change we make, we keep in mind that the customer relationship, not just the transaction, drives our business. This relationship is the key to creating a bond of trust with each of our customers and it is one of the most important catalysts of our growth." The Home Depot Associates letter reflected these same attitudes:

> Customer service is *the* bottom line at The Home Depot [emphasis theirs]. Pricing and merchandising will get customers through the front door once, but superior customer service builds the loyalty and trust necessary to keep them coming back. It creates added value for our customers. It drives same-store sales growth. It sets us apart from our competitors. It prompts word-of-mouth advertising. . . . We may appear uniform in our orange aprons, but we value individuality, creativity and fresh thinking. We teach each other.

The Home Depot Store Associates explained how they had "more influence on a customer's shopping experience than any other group." Taking personal responsibility for offering customers expert advice resulted in increased sales and repeat visits. The employee letter concluded with these words:

> Bernie and Arthur have always told us, "Take care of the customer, and the stock price will take care of itself." We know that if we continue to build strong relationships with our customers,

then we will reap the rewards as stockholders. We are proud that our role has played a part in The Home Depot's success, and we are committed to perpetuating the "orange-blooded spirit" into the future.

Other consulting and academic studies have shown that engaged employees are vital to business success. Why is this true? Engaged employees are more focused and aligned with the company strategy. They contribute more and are likely to assume personal responsibility for results. This self-reinforcing process—known as the virtuous cycle—starts with leaders who genuinely care about employees. These engaged employees create loyal customers, who buy more of the company's products and services. Committed customers increase company sales, which in turn leads to higher profits that can be passed on to investors as a return on their investment.

Home Depot's Emerging Problems

Like other customer-facing businesses, it was easy to conduct due diligence to test the strength of Home Depot's annual report promises. At a 1997 industry conference, I shared the podium with a Home Depot executive who had joined the company in its early days. His enthusiasm for the company, both in his prepared remarks and in private conversation afterward, reflected the promises made in Home Depot's shareholder letters. On visits to Home Depot stores, I found the "associates" I met to be personable and informed.

By 1998, however, the letters signed by Blank as president and CEO and Chairman Marcus began to change. Marcus wrote about the "healthy economic and housing environment," an indicator that macro factors might now be influencing the company's growth. He wrote about the need "to squeeze more productivity out of our assets to enhance returns." Marcus admitted that getting results in 1998 was no "piece of cake. . . . [T]he bigger and better we get, the higher the hurdles become." Despite these warnings, Home Depot's stock increased 134 percent between 1998 and 2000.

Then, on December 5, 2000, Blank announced he would resign from the company. Robert Nardelli, a former GE executive, was tapped to become Home Depot's CEO, the third in the company's history. With GE's reputation for tight, efficient operations and high investor returns, it seemed probable that the board wanted Nardelli to instill greater financial and organizational discipline at Home Deport.

After the Nardelli announcement, Home Depot's stock soared 27 percent. The Rittenhouse Rankings analysis of Nardelli's 2000 shareholder letter, however, raised questions about whether the GE veteran's management style was aligned with Home Depot's culture. Unlike other company letters, Nardelli's opening paragraph was marred by redundancies, such as an honor *and* a privilege, and meaningless adjectives, such as *powerful* culture. Instead of engaging stakeholders, the style was disengaging:

> It is *an honor and a privilege* to write this letter for the first time as President and CEO of The Home Depot. I come to this Company *with respect for its past,* a *deep* appreciation of its *powerful* culture and *tremendous* enthusiasm for the *great* opportunities that are in front of us. I am eager to expand upon our history of *unparalleled* growth, *enviable* trust and brand recognition built on *outstanding* customer service, broad merchandise assortments and the lowest prices in the industry. [author's emphasis]

Nardelli wrote that when he considered the job, he "looked at this business as would any investor." This raised a simple question: if he had had such a deep appreciation of the Home Depot's multistakeholder culture, why didn't he also look at the business from the customers' and employees' perspectives?

Nardelli added, "By every standard I could find, I joined a runaway winner. Now that I am here and *have met every Home Depot store manager,* I am more convinced of that than ever" [author's emphasis]. Here was another red flag. Instead of meeting with the orange-blooded associates of the company who had published their own shareholder letter four years earlier, Nardelli chose to meet with the company's managers.

The pie charts in Figure 9.1 compare the content allocations in Blank's 1999 letter and Nardelli's 2000 letter.

The size of Blank's larger pie shows that his letter contained 50 percent more content than did Nardelli's letter. In addition, the content was more balanced. Nardelli's Capital Stewardship score accounted for only 1 percent of total content, down from 11 percent, and Vision dropped to 5 from 16 percent. Most significantly, his letter registered a large increase in FOG.

While Blank's 1999 shareholder letter ranked 14th in our survey, Nardelli's 2000 letter ranked 41st. Of course, Nardelli needed time to

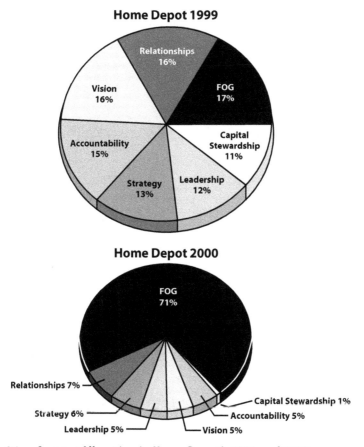

Figure 9.1   **Content Allocation in Home Depot's 1999 and 2000 Shareholder Letters**

settle into his job. As new CEOs get their feet on the ground, candor rankings often increase.

As Figure 9.2 shows, however, Nardelli's 2002 letter scored even more FOG points than his earlier letters. This letter ranked 81st in the Rittenhouse Rankings survey compared to archrival Lowe's 12th-place ranking. Not only did Lowe's 2002 letter boast higher content scores than Home Depot's, it was also better balanced and had significantly less FOG—only 10 percent compared to Home Depot's 43 percent. In other words, Lowe's had gained a communication advantage over Home Depot.

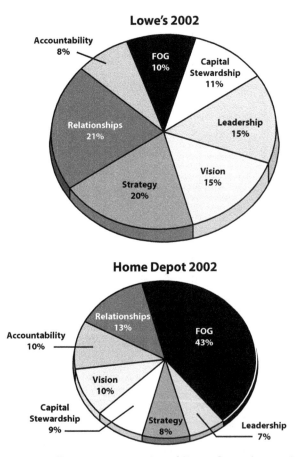

Figure 9.2 **Content Allocation in Lowe's and Home Depot's 2002 Letters**

The drop in Home Depot's stock price tracked its falling candor rankings. Under Marcus and Blank's stewardship, between 1996 and 2000, Home Depot's stock had increased 330 percent compared to the 114 percent increase in the S&P 500 and a gain of 167 percent in Lowe's price.

Now consider that between 2000 and 2004, Home Depot's stock dropped 10 percent versus a decline of 16 percent in the S&P and a gain of 181 percent in Lowe's stock.

In 2003, a colleague of mine shopped at a Home Depot store and watched a distressed customer walk out shouting: "Where is the nearest Lowe's store?" In 2004, I visited a Home Depot store outside of Manhattan looking for bathroom fixtures. When I could find only three of the eight I needed, I asked an associate if she could find more in the stockroom. She laughed and replied, "I can't. This is Home Depot."

Despite anecdotal stories like these, Nardelli was praised on Wall Street for almost doubling sales and operating income between 2001 and 2006. He centralized reporting and relentlessly cut costs. He replaced the company's knowledgeable full-time associates with part-time inexperienced employees. Still, by the end of 2005, Home Depot's stock had declined 19 percent since the announcement that Nardelli would be CEO.

Nardelli also alienated investors. Home Depot's 2006 annual meeting marked a low point in the history of U.S. corporate governance. As the only board member in attendance at the meeting, he informed owners that it would last only 30 minutes and each shareholder question would be limited to one minute. After this allotted time, the speaker's microphone would be cut off. Investors in attendance faced a giant clock placed in the front of the room to mark the passing seconds. Reporters and investors at the meeting were flabbergasted by the board's absence and Nardelli's arrogance.[3]

Eight months later, on January 2, 2007, Nardelli was fired by the Home Depot board for refusing to adjust his compensation agreement.[4]

CLUE 3: BALANCE STAKEHOLDER NEEDS

By then, Home Depot was suffering. During the Nardelli era, the stock had underperformed and the company's famous customer-centric culture had been seriously weakened. In the wake of this highly public firing, the board named Francis Blake, Home Depot's vice chairman, as the new CEO. Blake's mission was clear: to be attentive to and balance the needs of stakeholders, and to restore the company's culture. This would not happen overnight. In fact, the content in his 2006 shareholder letter, as shown in Figure 9.3, was similar to Nardelli's final one.

Each year after, however, Blake's candor rankings improved. His 2009 shareholder letter included exemplary commentary about the

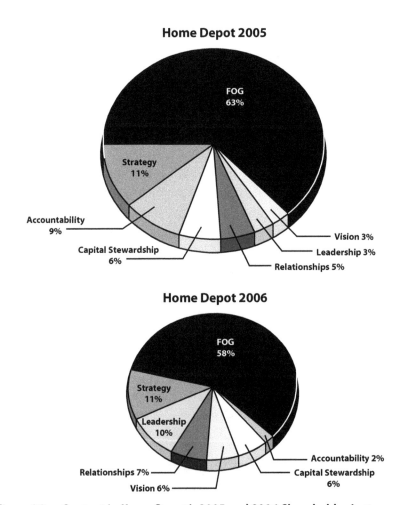

Figure 9.3   **Content in Home Depot's 2005 and 2006 Shareholder Letters**

importance of balancing stakeholder interests, an idea largely absent in the Nardelli era:

> At The Home Depot, our goal is to provide the best customer service and product authority in home improvement retail. *Taking care of our associates is an important part of taking care of our customers.* . . . Our strategy remains simple and straightforward: We are passionate about customer service. We are—and must continue to be—the number one authority on products in the home improvement market. And we will drive shareholder return through disciplined capital allocation. [author's emphasis]

Blake bolstered these comments about taking care of associates by reporting on the amount of "success sharing checks" or bonuses that were paid to hourly associates. This totaled more than $146 million, a company record. He described how customers had saved over $600 million thanks to the company's "'New Lower Price' campaign." He also noted that price was not all that mattered to customers:

> More than ever, our customers expect *great value*. They also expect new products that will simplify their home improvement projects, like our new line of paint, Behr Premium Plus Ultra˚, which is paint and primer in one can. Through our focus on everyday low pricing and innovation, we are committed to meeting those expectations. [author's emphasis]

Blake reported that Home Depot had retired debt and repurchased about $200 million of outstanding shares. In addition, the board of directors voted to raise the dividend by 5 percent, the first such increase since 2006.

At the end of his 2009 letter, Blake invited readers to spend time in Home Depot's stores and notice continuing improvements. His growing confidence was even more evident in the 2010 letter, published in March 2011. In this letter, FOG represented only 25 percent of the total content. That year's letter earned the highest ranking in the candor survey since Arthur Blank's 1999 shareholder letter.

As Blake's candor scores strengthened, so did the stock price. By mid-2011, Home Depot's stock began to outperform Lowe's.

Today on visits to a clean and well-stocked Home Depot store in Manhattan, I meet helpful and knowledgeable associates. This improvement is reflected in the annual rankings of the University of Michigan's Customer Satisfaction Index. As shown in Figure 9.4, the gap between Home Depot's and Lowe's customer satisfaction scores has narrowed between 2005 and 2011.

Balancing and Engaging Stakeholders

Top-scoring companies Siemens and Costco frequently report on the importance of engaging and balancing the needs of stakeholders.

In his 2010 shareholder letter, Siemens CEO Peter Löscher reported that as "an infrastructure provider, a major employer and an economic force in the regions where we do business," he believed the

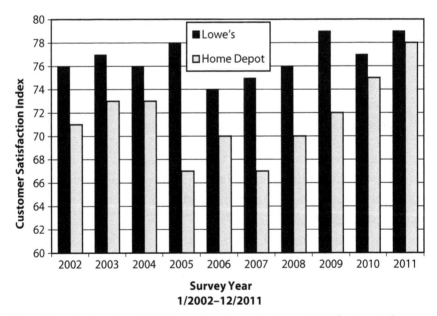

Figure 9.4   **University of Michigan American Customer Satisfaction Index: Lowe's and Home Depot 2001–2011**

company had an obligation "to earn the respect of all our stakeholders—our shareholders, our employees and our customers." As a result, the company was actively engaged "in dialogue with governments, organizations and people all around the world." Löscher noted in his 2010 letter how the success of this approach was evident:

> The true value of a company's accomplishments becomes apparent only when these achievements are recognized. At our company, this recognition takes various forms: first, the confidence that you, our shareholders, demonstrate when you make long-term investments in our company; second, the pride of our employees, who are not only committed to their company but also recommend it as an attractive employer; and finally, the acceptance and loyalty of our customers, whose orders sustain our business.

Case Study: Costco and "How's Jim Doing"?

Costco's 2010 shareholder letter began with statements about stakeholder service and quality goals. The Costco founders apparently cared a great deal about balancing stakeholder needs. The company was among the top five to score in this topic in both 2009 and 2010. They wrote:

> We enter the second decade of the 21st century poised to expand our operations, increase our sales, reduce our costs, and continue to lead our industry while rewarding you, our shareholders. We will accomplish these goals by doing what we have always done—concentrate on our mission to continually bring quality goods and services to our members at the lowest possible prices, while being responsible corporate citizens, taking care of our members and our employees, and respecting our vendors. We are in business for the long haul, and we are committed to continually building a company that will be here fifty, sixty and more years from now. We owe that to our *shareholders,* our *members,* our *employees,* and our *suppliers.* [author's emphasis]

The three Costco executives who signed the letter invited investors to attend the company's annual meeting, naming the date and the place—the only company in our survey to do so. On behalf of the management team and "all of our 150,000 employees around the world," Brotman, Sinegal, and Jelinek thanked investors for their support. The company's personal touch was evident in the letter's closing:

> We wish you, your associates and your families joy and peace over the holiday season. May we all greet the new year with optimism for the future.
>
> Warm Regards,
> Jeff Brotman, Chairman of the Board
> Jim Sinegal, Chief Executive Officer
> Craig Jelinek, President & COO

These are personal statements. Did Costco's presumed stakeholder friendliness hold up in real life?

Years before the company opened its first Manhattan warehouse in November 2009, I was a card-carrying Costco member. On visits to locations throughout the United States, I often would ask a manager or clerk, "How is Jim doing?" "Jim" was Jim Sinegal, the CEO and a Costco founder. Almost every time, either I was told that Jim had recently visited or I would hear about the number of visits that he and other executives had made throughout that year. Not once did I hear, "Jim who?" These employees even seemed to welcome these visits.

The company's shareholder letters rank high because they imagine what customers want: a fun place to shop where they can find quality merchandise at the lowest possible prices. In the 2008 shareholder letter, Sinegal described the customer experience that Costco tries to create:

> Every day is "High Theatre" in a Costco warehouse, with every aisle and every employee "showtime ready" to delight our members and, hopefully, exceed their expectations. This attention to detail is one of the many things that we believe sets us apart from our competition.

> Shoppers enjoy being able to save on the basics and take advantage of high-end luxury items; and we provide plenty of both with great prices and excellent quality. We pride ourselves on our trend-setting merchandise mix, where shoppers can find everything from bath tissue to multi-carat diamond rings.
>
> People come to Costco for the treasure hunt—the search for that special item among our new and ever-changing merchandise and services presentations.

The letter described how the company was combating supplier price inflation. Before anticipated price increases were announced, Costco would buy more inventory than usual and then pass the savings along to customers. In addition, readers learned more about Costco's employee practices:

> Our labor practices are routinely held up as a model for other companies, and our employee wage and benefit packages lead the retail industry. Just recently, a long-time Costco employee said, "it's nice to work for a company that is not only successful and growing . . . but is also liked and trusted by both its employees and its customers."

Sinegal, Brotman, and Jelinek noted that investors wanted a company with a healthy balance sheet, strong cash flow, and lean operations. They were proud of employees who had reduced operating expenses as a percentage of sales. The company had invested \$3 billion to build new warehouses and remodel old ones, spent \$900 million to repurchase common stock, and paid out \$265 million in dividends to shareholders.

The high ranking of this letter in the 2009 candor survey and in other years reflected the positive growing gap between Costco's share price and the S&P 500 (see Figure 9.5).

2008: A Year of CEO Successions

In 2008, the same year that Costco was writing about stakeholder experiences and management continuity, two other world-class retailers

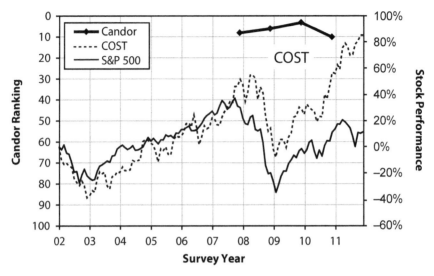

Figure 9.5   Costco Culture and Candor Rankings and Performance 2008–2011

were transitioning to new CEOs. On November 21, 2008, Walmart announced that CEO Lee Scott would step down and Michael Duke, vice chairman of Walmart International, would serve as the company's new CEO. At Target, CEO Bob Ulrich, who had served 21 years as CEO, passed his baton on to Gregg Steinhafel, a 29-year Target veteran.

Both Duke and Steinhafel started their new jobs at a time when consumer confidence and the stock market were hitting historic lows. As the Federal Reserve worked around the clock to save the U.S. banking system from collapse, unemployment in the United States was reaching historic levels. To assume leadership during this perfect economic storm required courage and resilience.

Walmart: Save Money and Live Better

Walmart published two shareholder letters in its 2009 annual report, one by Michael Duke and the other by Walmart Chairman Rob Walton.

Duke's letter began by praising former CEO Lee Scott and the Walmart management team. In the second paragraph, Duke described what he imagined customers were seeking when they shopped at

Walmart: "Our U.S. stores are delivering faster checkouts, a friendlier shopping experience and cleaner presentations. Simply, they are just operating better. . . . People who have never shopped with us previously are now loyal customers."

In the third paragraph, Duke described the company's financial results. Earnings per share from continuing operations were up 6 percent, and total net sales were up 7.2 percent. He connected this strong performance to helping "customers save money so they could live better."

In the sixth paragraph, Duke praised the company's 2.1 million associates around the world who "made the difference for Wal-Mart shareholders." Toward the end of the letter, Duke mentioned how the company had created 33,000 jobs in the United States and thousands more in other countries. He wrote:

> These good jobs offer competitive wages and benefits and the opportunity to advance. *We plan to create tens of thousands of jobs again this year.* And, we'll continue to be a force for inclusiveness everywhere we operate. We need our associates more than ever. [author's emphasis]

A critical reader might have paused after reading the excerpt above. It was not surprising to find commentary that praised Walmart's employees, particularly given the legal challenges facing the company at that time from female employees alleging they were denied promotions and other employees who asserted they were not paid competitive wages. But there were no supporting details in the letter to counter these claims. Instead, Duke described his visits to Walmart stores and a customer's home:

> As vice chairman responsible for Walmart International, I saw firsthand how much our business model resonates around the world. I make it a habit not only to walk our stores, but also to visit our customers in their homes. I remember one woman's tiny house in Costa Rica. She told me that everything she needs is at our Pali store.

Here was a stakeholder innovation: a CEO who visited a customer in her "tiny house." But this story raised questions: Could a woman living in a tiny house in Costa Rica afford all she needed to buy from Walmart? What strategic intelligence did Duke gain from this visit? Was this visit the best use of his valuable time or a PR stunt?

To his credit, however, Duke anticipated investor anxiety about the leadership transition and reassured investors it would be smooth:

> Although there will continue to be many changes at Wal-Mart, there is one thing that will never change—our culture. Wal-Mart associates operate with honesty and integrity. We respect people as individuals and strive for excellence. And, most important, we obsess about our customers and ways to serve them better than ever before.

Despite the strengths in this letter, it also scored FOG points. As a result, Walmart's candor ranking dropped from 33rd to 68th.

What was different about Walmart's 2008 letter? Three things stood out. First, then-CEO Lee Scott began by praising "The hard work and exceptional efforts of our two million associates, managers, and leaders around the world." Guided by the company's mission of "saving people money so they can live better," associates around the world helped to make Walmart the unbeatable price leader. He wrote: "Our customers appreciated it and our shareholders understood it."

Second, Scott reported on Walmart's efforts to improve associate benefits in the United States. In 2008, the number of associates with "some form of health insurance," had increased to 92.7 percent up from 90.4 percent in 2007. Walmart also helped customers save money through its $4 prescription program and in-store health clinic services.

Third, Scott connected Walmart's responsibilities as "the world's largest private employer" with the progress made to hire and promote women in China. He underscored the company's commitment to "achieve a more diverse workforce in all [U.S.] demographic groups." Finally, Scott reaffirmed the core value of working hard "to move up the economic ladder." He wanted Walmart's "price leadership position" to support these efforts.

In his 2011 letter, Duke similarly demonstrated his ability to step into the shoes of his customers and articulate their needs:

> Our customers remain pressured, particularly in mature markets, about job security and personal finances. In emerging markets, the economic recovery is stronger and fueling a growing middle class. All of this points to the incredible opportunity we have with the Next Generation Walmart and our mission of saving people money so they can live better.

But while Duke rightly addressed the economic pressures facing Walmart's customers, he missed the opportunity to describe the experience of what it was like to work and shop at Walmart. Both the 2010 and 2011 shareholder letters earned more negative than positive candor points in the Rittenhouse Rankings surveys.

Target's Promise: Expect More and Pay Less

In 2010, Target was the eleventh largest retailer in the world. It's price-based slogan is: "Expect More and Pay Less."

In his 2006 shareholder letter, former CEO Bob Ulrich described the shopping experience he wanted Target's customers to have in the company's stores. He wrote that customers, whom he called "guests," would discover three things: (1) merchandise that was "distinctive, exclusive and unexpected in its design"; (2) a brand promise reflected "in each store's design and aesthetics"; and (3) the experience of "Target-friendly service and fast checkout, and . . . the fresh look of our new shopping cart. . . ."

This attention to detail was unique. No other CEO wrote about a minor thing such as the new look of the company's shopping carts or the aesthetics of its store designs. By balancing fashion and value, Target strove to create "an intuitive shopping environment that emphasizes convenience and conveys a sense of fun and discovery." Ulrich wanted guests to make repeated visits and find "the excitement they expect and the Target experience they love."

He wrote about employees and explained that the company wanted to "attract and retain a diverse team of highly motivated and talented individuals." To do this, Target would create "a desirable and rewarding workplace [that] reinforces our brand, strengthens our organization and helps Target sustain its advantage in an extremely competitive environment." These were important statements, but no details were provided to explain how the company created "a desirable and rewarding workplace."

In this same 2006 letter, Ulrich described what investors could expect from Target:

> Over the past 10 years, Target has generated a total annualized return to shareholders of nearly 22 percent, well above the S&P 500 and nearly all of our large retail competitors. . . . As we look to the future, we remain confident in our direction and believe that Target is well positioned to build on our past success and generate profitable market share growth for many years to come.

Around the time this letter was published in early 2007, Bill Ackman, founder and CEO of hedge fund Pershing Square Capital Management, shared Ulrich's belief in the company's past success but questioned Target's promising future. By mid-July of that year, Ackman announced that his fund had accumulated 81.8 million Target shares, giving him a 9.6 percent ownership in the company.[5] He used this investment stake to engage the company's board of directors in conversations about his proposals to create more value in the company. These required the company to sell off its credit card receivables and leverage the value of company-owned land under its stores. He wanted Target to put this land into a real estate investment trust (REIT) security and spin it off to investors. To fulfill these goals, on March 17, 2009, Ackman proposed a slate of five new directors and invited shareholders to vote for them rather than management's nominees.

Named Target's CEO in May 2008, Gregg Steinhafel had to face down the Ackman challenge. On May 28, 2009, after the shareholder votes from the annual meeting had been tallied, Target announced that the Pershing slate of directors had all been defeated. Still, the effort required to fight this challenge (along with a weakening economy) took a toll on the company, which Rittenhouse Rankings observed in the

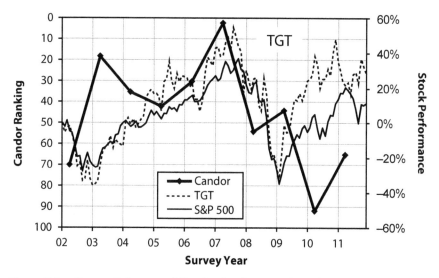

Figure 9.6   **Target Culture and Candor Rankings and Performance 2002–2011**

2010 Culture and Candor Survey. Steinhafel's 2009 shareholder letter fell to 92nd place from 44th (see Figure 9.6).

Steinhafel's 2010 letter, however, climbed back up to 58th place in the 2011 Rittenhouse Rankings survey. In the first paragraph of this letter, Steinhafel described new elements of the Target brand promise, which included "a more personalized shopping experience."

Steinhafel explained that by listening to its guests, Target was determined to make the company's brand experience "more personal, relevant and rewarding than ever." He described the company's efforts to remodel its stores, add new merchandise, and expand into fresh food. He promoted a 5 percent discount for customers who used Target debit and credit cards at its stores and on Target.com.

Recognizing the "new frugality" of Target's guests, Steinhafel reminded readers that Target would back up the company's "Low Price Promise" by matching competitors' advertised lower prices on similar items. He reported on other efforts to create "industry-leading mobile applications and web strategies—including the . . . launch of [a] new Target.com site [that] summer—offering a Target experience that fits guests' lives and shopping styles, whether in store, at home or on the go."

These new digital customer offerings were impressive. A careful reader, however, might wonder if these initiatives were designed to combat a threat greater than the one posed by Pershing Square's shareholder activism—the retailing challenge posed by Amazon.com.

Case Study: Amazon.com

In 1995, Jeff Bezos started an online bookseller in a Seattle garage. His vision compelled him to see a large volume of book sales, and therefore, so one story goes, he called the company Amazon, after the most voluminous river in the world—and also because he wanted a name that began with "A."[6]

By 2011, Amazon posted sales of $48 billion and had become the customer go-to site for product reviews and the lowest prices. This resulted in a practice called "showrooming," in which customers would visit physical stores to try out new products, but would then buy them on Amazon.com.

Bezos, who employs sophisticated programs to track product pricing, is able to drive loyal traffic to his site by giving customers the savings that come from Amazon's digital business model. This model creates loyal customers in a way that traditional retailing cannot support. While physical store retailers Target and Walmart aspire to be price leaders and Costco is acknowledged to be a pricing authority, Amazon offers more.

Giving customers both product and service quality and pricing intelligence, creates long standing relationships. Amazon's famous customer product reviews hold other retailers accountable for their prices and product quality. Accountability and customer empowerment are at the heart of Amazon's success. "Accountability" is the seventh system in the Rittenhouse Rankings model.

CHAPTER 10

Accountability

Account/accountability, noun

1. A narrative or record of events; a reason given for a particular action.

2. A formal banking, brokerage, or business relationship established to provide for financial transactions; a precise list or enumeration of financial transactions; money deposited for checking, savings, or brokerage use; a customer having a business or credit relationship with a firm.

3. To provide an explanation or justification for.

4. To hold answerable for.

[Middle English, Old French *acont, aconter* (to reckon); from Latin *ad + cunter* (to count).][1]

Ellen Kullman was named CEO of DuPont on January 1, 2009. She had joined the company in 1988 after a stint at GE and advanced by taking unpopular assignments and turning them into profitable businesses. As CEO, Kullman has earned DuPont's highest rankings in the Rittenhouse Rankings Culture and Candor Surveys.

In her inaugural letter in 2009, Kullman used words not typically found in shareholder letters. She wrote, "We will hold ourselves accountable." Then she listed the goals the company expected to meet by 2012:

- Over the period 2009 to 2012, our target compound annual growth rate (CAGR) for sales is about 10 percent, and for earnings, our target CAGR is about 20 percent.
- We will deliver another $1 billion in fixed cost productivity and $1 billion in working capital productivity over the next three years. Cost productivity is now a way of life at DuPont.
- We will continue research and development investments, which will vary by reporting segment from 2 percent to 9 percent of sales, so our businesses can add value and create new ways to solve customer problems.
- We will allocate research and development funds, capital expenditures, and sales and marketing expenditures to the opportunities that offer us maximum growth.
- We will extract maximum return on our investments by being paid for the value of new products that we bring to the market or for extending the use of existing products into new markets, new applications and new geographies.

Then Kullman described how the company had advanced these goals in 2009:

- We redeployed hundreds of employees into mega-projects focused on productivity in inventory and receivables which allowed us to retain highly talented people during the downturn and create real value for our company.
- We reorganized the company, eliminating cost structurally and building capability by integrating our 23 strategic business units into 13 businesses. We removed layers of management and moved decision-making closer to our customers. The resulting realignment reduces organizational complexity, provides greater transparency, increases productivity, and allows DuPont to be more nimble and more responsive to customer needs.

- Our engine of innovation never slowed down. We continued research and development investment during the recession at the same level as pre-recession. We introduced more than 1,400 new products in 2009—or about 60 percent more than in 2008—and filed 2,086 U.S. patent applications, the most ever in a single year for our company.

In her 2010 letter, Kullman reported that DuPont had met its goals for improving fixed cost and working capital productivity. As a result, in 2011, DuPont would strive to achieve an additional $300 million of improvements in each productivity category. Kullman also added a fourth goal: DuPont would exceed a target of "greater than $1.7 billion" free cash flow.

CEOs like Kullman who set goals and hold themselves accountable for meeting them are master builders of trust. As Figure 10.1 shows, the rise in her candor scores mirrored the increase in DuPont's stock price from the first quarter of 2012.

To find CEOs who blaze accountability trails, Rittenhouse Rankings searches in shareholder letters and other corporate commu-

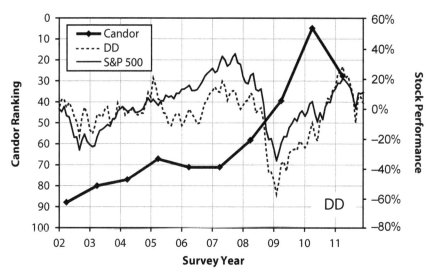

Figure 10.1   **DuPont Culture and Candor Rankings and Performance 2002–2011**

nications for these clues. We look for leaders who: (1) link goals with results; (2) report consistent financial results; (3) focus on the bottom line; and (4) combine low FOG with high principles.

CLUE 1: GOALS LINKED WITH RESULTS

Case Study: Burlington Northern Santa Fe Railroad

Overall, only 38 percent of the CEOs meaningfully linked their results with their goals or promises in the 2001 Rittenhouse Rankings Culture and Candor Survey. That year, CEO Matthew Rose of the Burlington Northern Santa Fe Corporation (BNSF) earned the highest points for providing information on meeting goals. He wrote:

1. Safety goals:

   We believe safety and efficiency go hand-in-hand. *Our goal is to have an injury-free, accident free workplace.*

   Our progress toward this goal since 1995 has been out-standing. Employee injury frequency and severity (lost work days) ratios, as measured per 200,000 hours worked, have dropped 12 percent and 52 percent, respectively, in this five-year period. This reduction in severity reflects approximately 22,000 fewer lost workdays in 2000 compared with 1995, or the equivalent of 110 full-time employees. [author's emphasis]

2. Customer service goals:

   Providing consistent on time service to our customers is the key to revenue growth and realizing our potential. . . . We invested more than $500 million since 1995 to develop, expand and enhance our real time integrated information system as well as to constantly expand our suite of web-based applications. [author's emphasis]

3. Operating efficiency goals:

   Since 1995, BNSF has increased the annual number of gross ton miles (GTMs) it handles at a faster rate than other Class I rail-

roads. Gross ton miles, a standard industry measure, reflect the total tons of freight hauled and the distance the freight was moved. Over the past five years, GTMs increased 17 percent to 875 billion. For the same period, adjusted operating expense per 1,000 GTMs declined 14 percent to $7.20 adjusted for inflation. [author's emphasis]

From 2004 to 2008, BNSF's shareholder letters on average ranked 19th in our candor surveys compared to rival CSX, which on average ranked 65th over the same period. But we were not alone in spotting CEO Rose's insistence on candor and performance. On November 3, 2009, Berkshire Hathaway announced that it would acquire BNSF for $26 billion.

Goals Linked with Results Amnesia: Enron

If Rose represented the alpha of CEO accountability at that time, then Kenneth Lay and Jeff Skilling represented the omega. Remember that in the fall of 2001, Enron faced a massive liquidity crisis. The company's leaders knocked on many doors requesting help. But no one answered.

Enron's spectacular fall from grace would not have surprised critical readers of the company's shareholder letters. From 1996 to 2000, they could have spotted obfuscation clues that foreshadowed this outcome.

In its 1996 annual report, Enron announced it had earned $13.2 billion in sales and $584 million in net income. That year, co-CEOs Lay and Skilling offered a forthright and detailed outlook for each of Enron's business segments:

Our infrastructure business currently has three large power projects valued at $3 billion in construction. Three more power projects, targeted to start in 1997, are valued at over $1 billion. They're part of a backlog of more than $20 billion in high quality projects.

Our wholesale and retail electricity marketing activities are off to a tremendous start. So are our LNG infrastructure projects, which are working to deliver clean natural gas to India, the Middle East and Puerto Rico.

Co-CEOs Ken Lay and Jeff Skilling next reported on what these new businesses would contribute to the company's net income by 2001. They made bold predictions that each of these new businesses, as well as the company's renewable energy business, would produce $1 billion in net present value and contribute 40 percent more to Enron's net income in five years.

But five years is a long time to wait. Unless the company reports on progress in meeting these goals (or failing to meet them) over time, they become meaningless. In Enron's case, neither goal was ever mentioned again in shareholder letters published after 1996.

In fact, Enron's shareholder letter in the 1997 annual report featured a new financial goal: "We also are committed to delivering earnings growth from our core businesses in 1998 and target an approximate 10 percent increase over 1997 earnings. This growth will exclude one-time earnings items." But this goal, too, had a limited shelf life. It was never again mentioned. Enron's 1999 and 2000 shareholder letters introduced new perishable goals. As well, investors who searched Enron's shareholder letters looking for consistent financial results—Rittenhouse Rankings' second accountability clue—would have been equally disappointed.

CLUE 2: CONSISTENT FINANCIAL RESULTS REPORTING

To evaluate the consistency of financial results reporting, take a red pen or pencil and circle or otherwise mark all the financial results numbers in a shareholder letter or other executive communication. These may include the following:

- Revenues
- Operating income
- Net income
- Earnings per share
- Diluted earnings per share

Revenues and sales are called top-line items. If these numbers increase over time, you know that the business is growing, not shrinking. The earnings number—sales minus expenses—will tell you if a company is making or losing money. Reported earnings can be positive or negative. Positive earnings are reported in black ink; negative earnings are reported in parentheses or red ink. A positive number tells investors that the company's growth is profitable. This number is like a CEO report card. It is so important that Rittenhouse Rankings penalizes companies with extra point deductions when they fail to report diluted earnings per share.

After circling these numbers in the letter, go and search in the annual report to find the company's audited *income statement*. It should be toward the middle of the report. After this, you will find the company's *balance sheet* report and *cash flow* statement.

Recall from Chapter 4 that the *balance sheet* matches assets and liabilities. It reveals information that allows you to judge the creditworthiness of a company. The *cash flow statement* tells you how the company invested its cash from business operations and whether it had any left over to reinvest in the business or to return to investors. It also reports on activities that increase company cash, such as private or public financings.

Try to match all the numbers circled in the shareholder letter with the numbers in one of these three reports. If the numbers do not match those in the letter, be on the alert.

The following excerpts from Enron's shareholder letters show why this test is so important. Inconsistencies found in Enron's financial results reporting could have warned critical readers of internal problems.

1996: Enron Omits Earnings Results

In the 1996 letter, Enron failed to report on the company's earnings. Instead, management set a future target "to achieve compound annual growth in earnings per share of at least 15 percent from 1996 through the year 2000." It told investors to "expect minimum double digit earnings per share growth every year" during this period.

1997: Enron Reports Net Income per Diluted Share

Enron missed meeting the new double-digit growth rate target, but never mentioned this fact in the 1997 shareholder letter. In fact, earnings per share had dropped like a hot potato to $0.32, down from $2.14 in 1996. Once again Enron introduced another new financial metric: "net income per diluted share."

> Our net income of $0.32 per diluted share included $1.82 per share of non-recurring charges primarily attributable to the renegotiation of a North Sea gas contract. These financial results adversely affected our stock price performance, as 1997 total return to shareholders of (1.5) percent was our first annual negative return since 1991—a year where the S&P 500 also showed a negative return. [author's emphasis]

Enron's opening sentence was illogical. How could the company report net income of $0.32 that included $1.82 per share of nonrecurring charges due to the renegotiation of a contract? Other questions were raised. How did this loss qualify as an extraordinary loss? Renegotiating contracts is supposed to be a normal, not an extraordinary, act of business. Furthermore, losing $1.82 per share from one contract reflects either a whopping failure of judgment or bad luck. Without any clear explanation, investors could only scratch their heads and wonder if such losses could occur in the future.

1998: Enron Reports a 36 Percent Increase in Operating Income

In its 1998 letter, Enron introduced yet another new earnings metric— "earnings from operations":

> In 1998, the business platform we have built to achieve that status delivered record earnings and excellent shareholder returns,

outpacing our industry group and the broader stock market. *Earnings of $698 million from operations represent a 36 percent increase compared to 1997,* and our return to shareholders of almost 40 percent beat the 2.9 percent return of our peer group and the S&P 500 return of 28 percent. [author's emphasis]

Applying the Rittenhouse Rankings matching test, we found that the operating income number reported in the letter—$698 million—did not match the number in Enron's 1998 financial statement. The auditors had blessed a higher number: $703 million. This discrepancy sent us searching the footnotes that accompanied the financial statements. In a section titled "After-Tax Results Before Items Impacting Comparability," we discovered that the difference was due to $5 million of "non-recurring events" in 1998. Again we wondered why Enron chose to report a lower number in the shareholder letter than the higher audited number in the financial statements. In the face of all these questions, there was one fact that could not be disputed—finding Enron's earnings was like looking for the pea in a shell game.

GAAP Versus Non-GAAP

In Chapter 4 we described how, despite its basis in mathematics, accounting is an art as well a science. While it is easy to count earnings that have been turned into cash, it is more difficult to decide how to report earnings from customer receivables or long-term service contracts that have not yet been turned into cash.

Remember that companies and their auditors are required to follow the Generally Accepted Accounting Principles (GAAP) set by the Financial Accounting Standards Board (FASB). Terms such as "GAAP earnings" or "reported earnings" mean that the numbers reported by a company conform to these FASB rules. On the other hand, terms such as "pro forma" or "continuing" earnings do not follow these rules. These numbers indicate that human judgment is required to interpret the GAAP rules. These interpretations give companies latitude in deciding what to count and when to report gains and losses. They allow companies to use discretion in reporting earnings.

Be on the lookout for companies that report large and recurring differences between GAAP and non-GAAP earnings. Is the company being excessively creative with its interpretations of accounting rules? Consider that most companies want to present their earnings in the best possible light. This may lead to more aggressive than conservative interpretations of the rules.

Case Study: Reporting the True Picture of Business Value

Critics argue that these aggressive interpretations distort the true picture of business value. In 2001, for instance, networking giant Cisco Systems wrote off $2.5 billion in inventory that was judged to be obsolete, even though some experts argued that inventory misjudgments are a routine cost of business.[2] These experts believed that liquidating inventory by taking annual charges against income would more accurately reflect the ongoing value of Cisco's business. Accounting for restucturing charges creates similar challenges. In his 1998 letter, Buffett noted that managers rationalize potentially imprudent interpretations because: (1) everybody else is engaged in "accounting shenanigans" and (2) to do otherwise might depress the company's stock price, its currency for doing deals:

> The distortion du jour is the "restructuring charge," an accounting entry that can, of course, be legitimate but that too often is a device for manipulating earnings. In this bit of legerdemain, a large chunk of costs that should properly be attributed to a number of years is dumped into a single quarter, typically one already fated to disappoint investors. In some cases, the purpose of the charge is to clean up earnings misrepresentations of the past, and in others it is to prepare the ground for future misrepresentations. In either case, the size and timing of these charges is dictated by the cynical proposition that Wall Street will not mind if earnings fall short by $5 per share in a given quarter, just as long

as this deficiency ensures that quarterly earnings in the future will consistently exceed expectations by five cents per share.

How significant was this activity? Buffett cited a study that compared the amount of special restructuring charges reported by Fortune 500 companies in 1998 to total corporate earnings in 1997. Incredibly, the researchers calculated that the amount of special charges represented almost one-fifth of the total 1997 Fortune 500 company net earnings.

Case Study: Earnings at Enron

We have seen how Enron changed its definition of earnings each year between 1996 and 1998. This practice continued in 1999 and 2000.

1999: Net Income Before Non-Recurring Items

Enron introduced another new earnings term in its 1999 shareholder letter: "net income before non-recurring items":

> We reported another round of impressive financial and operating results. In 1999 revenue increased 28 percent to $40 billion, and *net income before non-recurring items increased 37 percent to reach $957 million.* [author's emphasis]

Looking at Enron's audited 1999 income statement, however, Rittenhouse Rankings could not find the $957 million reported above. Instead, $893 million was listed as net income before non-recurring items, Returning to the financial footnotes, we learned that "non-recurring" charges in 1999 netted out to negative $64 million. In other words, Enron reported earnings in its letter that ignored these non-recurring charges.

2000: Net Income Reached a Record $1.3 Billion

As expected by now, Enron introduced another new earnings term in its 2000 shareholder letter. It was simply: "net income." That year, as we learned in Chapter 1, Enron's net income "reached a record $1.3 billion."

You may recall that the net income figure in the audited income statement—$979—did not match this number. In fact, the difference between the net income in the letter and in the audited income statement had ballooned from $64 million to $326 million.

Further evidence of management's creative accounting appeared in this excerpt: "Enron is increasing earnings per share and continuing our strong returns to shareholders. *Recurring earnings per share* have increased steadily since 1997 and were up 25 percent in 2000."

Why does Enron pick the year 1997? Remember, that was the year that Enron posted earnings of $0.32 due to a contract renegotiation problem. Management was practicing one of the techniques Buffett had described: pick a year when earnings are poor so that future earnings will look better.

Five years of inconsistent and unclear earnings reports ought to have given a prudent investor reasons to question management's accounting integrity. In fact, at the time that Enron's 2000 shareholder letter was published, the stock was trading at $80. Having failed Rittenhouse Rankings accountability tests over five years, it seemed obvious that the question was not *if* Enron would fail, but *when*. By November 2001, the stock had fallen to $0.60. Company investors who had listened to pundits and advisors who ignored these obfuscating clues paid a stiff price for their misplaced trust.

CLUE 3: FOCUS ON THE BOTTOM LINE: THE CEO REPORT CARD

If cash is the lifeblood of a business, then earnings are its oxygen. Given their importance, investors might expect to find earnings reports in every shareholder letter. Rittenhouse Rankings research shows that they would be disappointed.

In the 2001 Rittenhouse Rankings Culture and Candor Survey, 42 percent of the company letters omitted a report on company earnings, while 30 percent failed to do so in the 2011 survey. Investors might justifiably wonder if such an omission is deliberate or an oversight.

Rittenhouse Rankings candor research shows that companies scoring high in financial earnings reporting often score high in overall candor.

Case Study: Dominion Energy

In its 2007 shareholder letter, Virginia-based Dominion Energy reported GAAP earnings of $3.88, which included a large one-time after-tax gain:

> Earnings per share under Generally Accepted Accounting Principles (GAAP) in 2007 rose 98 percent over 2006 earnings thanks in large part to a one-time, after-tax gain of $2.1 billion generated by the sale of substantially all of our E&P properties. As a result, we reported GAAP earnings of $3.88 per share in 2007, compared with GAAP earnings of $1.96 per share in 2006, recast for the 2-for-1 stock split.

In the next paragraph, CEO Tom Farrell reported "operating earnings" of $2.56 a share, which excluded the $2.1 billion of E&P (Exploration and Production) sale proceeds and explained the advantages of reporting operating earnings:

> Dominion recorded operating earnings of $2.56 per share in 2007, up from 2006 operating earnings of $2.53 per share, excluding the benefit from the E&P sales under GAAP, among other items.*
>
> Management uses operating earnings as the primary performance measurement because we believe it provides a more meaningful representation of the company's fundamental earnings power. However, last year's corporate refocusing, E&P sales and significant share repurchases make a year-to-year comparison of operating earnings not particularly meaningful.

Dominion's careful reporting leaves no doubt about the difference between GAAP and non-GAAP earnings. The shareholder letters by

---

* Based on non-GAAP financial measures.

General Mills CEO Ken Powell also stand out for clear and consistent financial reporting.

Case Study: General Mills

Minneapolis-based General Mills traces its origins back to 1857. This iconic company, which invented Bisquik in the 1950s and other convenience foods, is now the sixth largest food company in the world, according to the company's website. General Mills, whose stock trades as GIS, has scored at the top of the Rittenhouse Rankings Culture and Candor Surveys for both "Goals Linked with Results" and "Financial Results" reporting, the only company to do so in our decade-long survey.

The company's top candor scores were earned by CEO Ken Powell. Joining General Mills in 1979, Powell worked in various positions. In 1990, he helped launch a joint venture with Nestlé called Cereal Partners Worldwide (CPW), and then took on various assignments before returning to headquarters in 2004. In 2008, Powell was named CEO.

One impression left by Powell's inaugural 2008 letter was surprising: it lacked sizzle. There was no resounding "Grrreat!"—the iconic cry of Kellogg's Frosted Flakes' mascot Tony the Tiger. Instead, Powell used neutral adjectives and verbs, such as *strong, broad-based, pleased*, and *good*. He wrote:

> Fiscal 2008 was a *strong* year for General Mills. We generated *broad-based* sales and earnings growth, and *strengthened our position* in markets around the globe.
>
> We're *pleased* to give you this report on our progress in 2008, and our plans for continuing growth in fiscal 2009 and beyond. Our results in 2008 reflect particularly *good* sales performance.
>
> Net sales for the year ended May 25, 2008, increased 10 percent to $13.7 billion. This was *strong* growth on top of a 6 percent sales increase the previous year. And each of our major operating divisions contributed to this year's sales gain.... [author's emphasis]

Table 10.1   **General Mills 2008 Net Sales Percentage Change by Business Segment**

Broad-Based Sales Growth	
Operating Division/Segment	**2008 Net Sales % Change**
Big G Cereals	+ 5
Meals	+ 5
Pillsbury USA	+ 5
Small Planet Foods	+ 6
Baking Products	+ 9
Yoplait	+ 10
Bakeries and Foodservice	+ 11
Snacks	+ 12
International	+ 21
Total General Mills	+ 10

However, Powell scored Innovation points when he added a table showing "Net Changes in Sales Growth for Each Operating Division or Segment" (see Table 10.1). Not only is General Mills one of the few companies in the Rittenhouse Rankings survey to provide such information, but it has done so consistently since 2008. This allows investors to track company sales trends by business segment over time.

In subsequent letters, Powell added more charts and tables in the body of the letter. These included a table on "Long-Term Growth Model Financial Results" and another on "Leading Market Positions." The information in these tables, not typically found in other letters, was woven into Powell's narrative.

The following excerpts from Powell's 2008 shareholder letter show how he linked goals with results.

Goal 1: Meet High Single-Digit Growth in Diluted Earnings per Share

The excerpt below shows how thoroughly General Mills describes its financial results. Unlike most other companies, GIS reported "diluted earnings per share" results both before and after non-recurring gains:

Diluted earnings per share grew 17 percent to reach $3.71. This figure includes non-cash gains totaling 19 cents per share from mark-to-market valuation of certain commodity positions and a favorable court decision related to a tax matter. *Excluding these non-cash items* from fiscal 2008 results, diluted earnings per share would total $3.52, up 11 percent from $3.18 per share last year. These sales and profit results exceeded our original financial targets for fiscal 2008. *They also measure up very well against the goals we established three years ago for General Mills' long-term growth.* [author's emphasis]

Goal 2: Give Shareholders Above-Market Returns Over Time

In the commentary below, Powell described how the company would meet its goal to give shareholders above-market returns:

We believe that this sales and profit growth, coupled with a dividend yield of between 2 and 3 percent of our stock price, *should result in returns to our shareholders that meet or exceed the broader market's return over time.* [author's emphasis]

During the prior three-year period through fiscal 2008 to 2010, General Mills shareholders had earned a total return (stock price appreciation plus reinvested dividends) averaging 10.1 percent. This compared to just a 6.7 percent return for the S&P 500 and a food industry average return of 4.4 percent.

Goal 3: Increase Average Annual Total Return on Capital

Few companies report on their average returns on capital (ROC), and even fewer set total return goals. General Mills did both. The company set a goal to increase returns on capital by 50 basis points each year. To succeed, GIS had to grow earnings each year and spend capital wisely. Note also that Powell was careful to remind readers that in meeting this goal, the company would "exclude non-cash commodity and tax gains."

Our long-term performance goals also include a commitment to increase the return we generate on capital invested in the business. Specifically, our goal is to increase return on average total capital (ROC) by 50 basis points per year. We've kept pace with that goal in recent years. For 2008, reported results exceeded that goal, and excluding the benefits of our non-cash commodity and tax gains, *we met our 50-basis point improvement target.* [author's emphasis]

Goal 4: Return Cash to Shareholders as Dividends and Share Repurchases

Powell explained how the company had met its goal to return cash to shareholders through dividends and reduced outstanding company shares by an average of 2 percent annually. He even reported in his letter on the changes in year-end average shares outstanding:

> Beyond this capital investment, we return a significant portion of the cash our businesses generate to shareholders. Dividends in fiscal 2008 totaled $1.57 per share, up 9 percent for the year. Our ongoing share repurchase program has a goal of reducing the number of shares outstanding by an average of 2 percent per year. In fiscal 2008 we exceeded that target: Average shares outstanding were 347 million, down nearly 4 percent from 360 million shares the previous year.

As Figure 10.2 shows, the stock of General Mills has consistently outperformed the S&P 500 since 2008, when Powell was named CEO. The company's candor rankings have shown similarly high performance.

Powell's clear and detailed explanations throughout this and other letters revealed a fourth clue in measuring accountability in shareholder letters—finding CEOs who deliver straight talk and low FOG. Consider that over the ten-year Rittenhouse Rankings survey period, General Mills has placed 17th out of 100 companies.

Of course, a solid, time-tested company like GIS might be expected to turn in candid and consistent performance. So it may surprise some investors to learn that a much younger company, Amazon .com, placed 12th in the overall Rittenhouse Rankings survey.

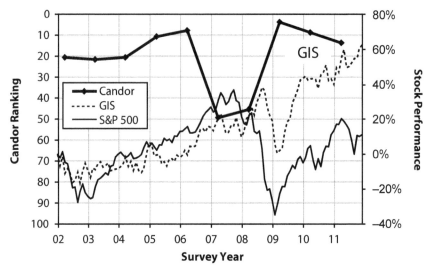

Figure 10.2   **General Mills Culture and Candor Rankings and Performance 2002–2011**

CLUE 4: LOW FOG AND HIGH PRINCIPLES

Case Study: Amazon.com

The letters that CEO Jeff Bezos writes for Amazon.com are original, even quirky. Consider that he began his 2000 shareholder letter with, "Ouch."—his reaction to the dot.com meltdown. Then he asked: why had Amazon.com's stock dropped 80 percent?

To reassure investors that this share price loss was temporary, Bezos wrote that "by almost any measure, Amazon.com the company is in a stronger position now than at any time in its past." To support his claim, Bezos listed key customer sales and financial metrics:

- We served 20 million customers in 2000, up from 14 million in 1999.
- Sales grew to $2.76 billion in 2000 from $1.64 billion in 1999.
- Pro forma operating loss shrank to 6% of sales in Q4 2000, from 26% of sales in Q4 1999.
- Average spend per customer in 2000 was $134, up 19%.

- Gross profit grew to $656 million in 2000, from $291 million in 1999, up 125%.
- Almost 36% of Q4 2000 U.S. customers purchased from one of our "non-BMV" stores such as electronics, tools, and kitchen.
- International sales grew to $381 million in 2000, from $168 million in 1999.
- We ended 2000 with cash and marketable securities of $1.1 billion, up from $706 million at the end of 1999, thanks to our early 2000 euroconvert financing.

Importantly, Bezos boasted that the company had earned a score of 84 on the American Customer Satisfaction Index, the "highest score ever recorded for a service company in any industry."

Here was a shareholder letter first—blending customer and financial results in one list. This innovation underscored a key Amazon.com principle: financial success starts with customers who save time and money on visits to Amazon's virtual store and become repeat buyers.

Bezos posed another question in his letter for hard-core skeptics: "[I]f the company is better positioned today than it was a year ago, why is the stock price so much lower than it was a year ago?" In reply, he invited readers to remember that Amazon was in business for the long haul. He quoted Warren Buffett's mentor, Ben Graham, who wrote: "'In the short term, the stock market is a voting machine; in the long term, it's a weighing machine.'"

Bezos added: "[T]here was a lot of voting going on in the boom year of '99—and much less weighing. We're a company that wants to be weighed, and over time, we will be—over the long term, all companies are. In the meantime, we have our heads down working to build a heavier and heavier company." He expected Amazon.com to be a company where gross profit defined success, not the ratio of advertising spending to sales, a practice that launched many short-lived initial public offerings of dot.com stocks.

To become a heavier company, Bezos wrote that Amazon.com had made "bold bets," investing in companies and technologies that lost a lot of investor money. Bezos admitted that he had underestimated the time needed to "enter these categories" and "to achieve the scale necessary to succeed." Shutting down these businesses was painful, he wrote, but the alternative—keeping them afloat—"would have been an even bigger mistake."

Bezos learned from these failures. To succeed, he knew that Amazon .com had to grow sales to cover its high fixed costs, including technology investments, marketing, and the cost of fulfilling orders. Once Amazon .com had covered these fixed costs, it could compete aggressively against physical store retailers that had to pay costs such as property taxes, store maintenance, in-store inventory management, and other brick-and-mortar store expenses. Meanwhile, Amazon.com would pass on these "virtual store" savings to customers and further discount products. This would lead to more sales, expanded services, and strengthened customer loyalty.

Amazon.com Shareholder Letters: Evolution of an Online Giant

In July 1995, Amazon.com started shipping books ordered online from a two-car garage outside of Seattle. The books were packed on a table made from a door. In 1997 the company went public, and Bezos wrote his first shareholder letter. He described his vision for the company, using phrases not found in other letters: "execute well," "precious time," "personalization," and "the very process of discovery." His words made the future visible and possible:

> [T]his is Day 1 for the Internet and, if we execute well, for Amazon.com. Today, online commerce saves customers money and precious time. Tomorrow, through personalization, online commerce will accelerate the very process of discovery. Amazon. com uses the Internet to create real value for its customers and, by doing so, hopes to create an enduring franchise, even in established and large markets.

Bezos described the competitive landscape in online purchasing and Amazon.com's "window of opportunity." He named the company's game plan, "It's All About the Long Term."

> We believe that a fundamental measure of our success will be the shareholder value we create over the *long term*. This value will be a direct result of our ability to extend and solidify our current market leadership position. The stronger our market leadership, the more powerful our economic model. Market leadership can translate directly to higher revenue, higher profitability, greater capital velocity, and correspondingly stronger returns on invested capital. [emphasis theirs]

Bezos cautioned investors that this long-term focus would require Amazon.com to make decisions and weigh trade-offs differently from other companies. For example: "When forced to choose between optimizing the appearance of our GAAP accounting and maximizing the present value of future cash flows, we'll take the cash flows."

Bezos's 2001 letter announced that Amazon.com had finally reached the critical breakeven point—the company's sales were now covering its fixed costs. He explained how this led to cost improvements and higher sales:

> We lowered prices again in January when we offered a new class of shipping that is free (year-round) on orders over $99. Focus on cost improvement makes it possible for us to afford lower prices, which drives growth. Growth spreads fixed costs across more sales, reducing cost per unit, which makes possible more price reductions. Customers like this, and it's good for shareholders. Please expect us to repeat this loop.

This announcement signaled a new era in Amazon.com's shareholder letters. Beginning in 2002, each Amazon.com letter would henceforth focus on a "Big Idea" that was vital to the company's success.

Big Ideas: Amazon.com's Shareholder Letters from 2002 to 2011

The "Big Idea" in the 2002 letter explained why Amazon.com was not a "normal" store. Bezos listed seven radical practices that accounted for the company's unique retailing strategy:

1. Because it is not constrained by shelf space, Amazon.com was able to turn its inventory 19 times in one year.
2. We personalize the store for each and every customer.
3. We trade real estate for technology (which gets cheaper and more capable every year).
4. We display customer reviews critical of our products.
5. You can make a purchase with a few seconds and one click.
6. We put used products next to new ones so you can choose.
7. We share our prime real estate—our product detail pages— with third parties, and, if they can offer better value, we let them.

The Big Idea in the 2003 shareholder letter was Bezos's critique of the short-term, portfolio-churning practices of Wall Street investors:

> Long-term thinking is both a requirement and an outcome of true ownership. Owners are different from tenants. I know of a couple who rented out their house, and the family who moved in nailed their Christmas tree to the hardwood floors instead of using a tree stand. Expedient, I suppose, and admittedly these were particularly bad tenants, but no owner would be so short-sighted. Similarly, many investors are effectively short-term tenants, turning their portfolios so quickly they are really just renting the stocks that they temporarily "own."

In his 2004 letter, Bezos explained the limitations of focusing on earnings and earnings growth. Writing it like a business case that would have made Ben Graham proud, he explained why Amazon.com's free cash flow per share was the company's most important success measure:

> Why not focus first and foremost, as many do, on earnings, earnings per share or earnings growth? The simple answer is that earnings don't directly translate into cash flows, and shares are worth only the present value of their future cash flows, not the present value of their future earnings. Future earnings are a component—but not the only important component—of future

cash flow per share. Working capital and capital expenditures are also important, as is future share dilution.

Bezos challenged Wall Street's love affair with earnings metrics, even though Amazon was growing earnings for the first time in its history. He took shots at analysts and companies that focus on EBITDA—earnings before interest, taxes, depreciation, and amortization—which, he cautioned, leads to "faulty conclusions about the health of a business." It is a practice that Warren Buffett has compared to believing in the tooth fairy.

The big idea in Amazon.com's 2005 letter was the difference between data-driven and intuitive judgments. But the opening of this letter was different. Instead of writing in his usual confident style, his writing seemed tentative. For the first time ever, his letter introduction scored FOG points. He wrote:

> Many of the important decisions we make at Amazon.com can be made with data. There is a right answer or a wrong answer, a better answer or a worse answer, and math tells us which is which. These are our favorite kinds of decisions.

This paragraph raised questions: What were these "important decisions"? Why was Bezos writing about something that seems so obvious—that some decisions have a right and a wrong answer?

In the next paragraph, Bezos gave an example, showing how the company made the decision about opening "a new fulfillment center." But then he never explained the importance of a fulfillment center. He failed to step into the shoes of his readers and imagine what they didn't know. He seemed to have forgotten his audience. As well, strange Orwellian terms appeared like "proactive experimentation" and "The heavy lifting is done by math."

Curious to know what might be going on behind the curtain at Amazon.com, Rittenhouse Rankings examined the company's financial statements and found new trends. While sales continued to grow, income from operations dropped 2 percent in 2005 down from a 63 percent increase in 2004. The numbers were trending down, not up.

In addition, two of the three major company expense categories—
"fulfillment" and "marketing" expenses—were declining as a percentage of total expense. But the third expense category, "technology and
content," was growing. At the end of 2005, technology spending had
grown to 28 percent of total expenses, up from 24 percent in 2004.

It appeared that Amazon.com was ramping up technology spending faster than any other expense. Was Bezos making a bet on some
new technology invention?

Curiously, the beginning of Bezos's 2006 letter asked investors
to be patient:

> *At Amazon's current scale, planting seeds that will grow into mean-*
> *ingful new businesses takes some discipline, a bit of patience, and a*
> *nurturing culture.*
>
> Our established businesses are well-rooted young trees.
> They are growing, enjoy high returns on capital, and operate in
> very large market segments. These characteristics set a high bar
> for any new business we would start. Before we invest our share-
> holders' money in a new business, we must convince ourselves
> that the new opportunity can generate the returns on capital our
> investors expected when they invested in Amazon. And we must
> convince ourselves that the new business can grow to a scale
> where it can be significant in the context of our overall company.
> [author's emphasis]

It seemed as if Amazon was contemplating some new business, but
Bezos never explained what it was. Describing a strategy of "planting
seeds that will grow into meaningful new businesses" sounded mysteri-
ous. But there was one reason for increased confidence. Amazon's FOG
score in this letter had dropped to 35 percent, down from 54 percent
in the 2005 letter. Perhaps the company was making progress in this
technology investment.

In 2007, the mystery was solved. Bezos trumpeted the release of
Kindle. This was the seed he had referred to in the 2006 letter. As in
earlier letters, Bezos's voice was now confident and engaging:

November 19, 2007, was a special day. After three years of work, we introduced Amazon Kindle to our customers.

Many of you may already know something of Kindle—we're fortunate (and grateful) that it has been broadly written and talked about. Briefly, Kindle is a purpose-built reading device with wireless access to more than 110,000 books, blogs, magazines, and newspapers....

Folks who see the display for the first time do a double-take. It's thinner and lighter than a paperback, and can hold 200 books. Take a look at the Kindle detail page on Amazon.com to see what customers think—Kindle has already been reviewed more than 2,000 times.

How important was Kindle? Bezos devoted his entire letter to the new product. Only toward the end of his letter did Bezos mention financial results:

[We are] fervent about driving free cash flow per share and returns on capital. We know we can do that by putting customers first. I guarantee you there is more innovation ahead of us than behind us, and we do not expect the road to be an easy one. We're hopeful, and I'd even say optimistic, that Kindle, true to its name, will "start a fire" and improve the world of reading.

Amazon.com's 2008 shareholder letter omitted reports about the company's free cash flow and returns on capital, but it did report on the release of Kindle 2.

Amazon.com's 2009 letter began with a reaffirmation of the Amazon.com strategy: "The financial results for 2009 reflect the cumulative effect of 15 years of customer experience improvements: increasing selection, speeding delivery, reducing cost structure so we can afford to offer customers ever-lower prices, and many others." Just as he did in the 2000 letter, Bezos listed highlights:

- Net sales increased 28% year-over-year to $24.51 billion in 2009. This is 15 times higher than net sales 10 years ago when they were $1.64 billion in 1999.

- Free cash flow increased 114% year-over-year to $2.92 billion in 2009.

But unlike the 2000 letter, which listed six financial results and four customer results, the 2009 letter included nine customer/product results and just two financial results. Again, Bezos anticipated investor questions and offered this commentary about the company's financial results:

> Senior leaders that are new to Amazon are often surprised by how little time we spend discussing actual financial results or debating projected financial outputs. . . . Our annual goal setting process begins in the fall, and concludes early in the new year after we've completed our peak holiday quarter. Our goal setting sessions are lengthy, spirited, and detail-oriented. We have a high bar for the experience our customers deserve and a sense of urgency to improve that experience.
>
> We've been using this same annual process for many years. For 2010, we have 452 detailed goals with owners, deliverables, and targeted completion dates. . . .
>
> A review of our current goals reveals some interesting statistics:
>
> - 360 of the 452 goals will have a direct impact on customer experience.
> - The word *revenue* is used eight times and *free cash flow* is used only four times.
> - In the 452 goals, the terms *net income*, *gross profit* or *margin*, and *operating profit* are not used once.
>
> Taken as a whole, the set of goals is indicative of our fundamental approach. Start with customers, and work backwards. Listen to customers, but don't just listen to customers—also invent on their behalf. We can't assure you that we'll meet all of this year's goals. We haven't in past years. However, we can assure you that we'll continue to obsess over customers. We have strong conviction that that approach—in the long term—is every bit as good for owners as it is for customers. [emphasis theirs]

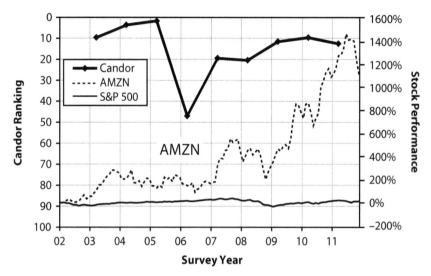

Figure 10.3   **Amazon.com Culture and Candor Rankings and Performance 2002–2011**

As Figure 10.3 shows, Amazon.com's annual scores have ranked at the top of the Rittenhouse Rankings Culture and Candor Survey over the past decade. The company's stock has increased almost 700 percent. In fact, the only time the stock has underperformed the S&P 500 was in 2006, the only time when Amazon failed to place in the top quartile of our candor rankings.

The Grandfather Test

In 2012, an analyst writing for *Seeking Alpha* described Amazon.com as one of the least transparent companies in the market.[3] Talking with Amazon.com's suppliers and analyzing other data, he believed that Kindle sales had fallen off dramatically, and also that this had improved the company's gross margin in the first quarter of 2012. How could this happen? He reasoned that the company was not making a profit on Kindle sales. As a result, the drop in Kindle sales improved the company's margin. In his report, this financial analyst was figuring out competitive information that companies do not typically provide.

In fact, Amazon.com's letters have never ranked high in financial results reporting. Like Buffett, Bezos is keeping his eye fixed on economic results, not accounting. He stays true to the principles on which the company was founded. And as he has done every year since 1998, Bezos ended his 2010 letter with these words:

> As always, I attach a copy of our original 1997 letter. Our approach remains the same, and it's still Day 1.

In that 1997 letter, Bezos wrote:

> [W]e are working to build something important that matters to our customers, something that we can all tell our grandchildren about. Such things aren't meant to be easy. We are incredibly fortunate to have this group of dedicated employees whose sacrifices and passion build Amazon.com.

Bezos has built a company that many believe is the dominant online retailer in the world. He continues to evolve and so does the company. Bezos manages to look both forward and backward. He lays out a model for business in the twenty-first century that is truly unique: how to build a company "we can all tell our grandchildren about." He is one of only six CEOs to use the word *grandchildren* in the decade-long Culture and Candor Survey.

CHAPTER 11

Candor and Accountability Crisis

Crisis, noun

1a. A crucial or decisive point or situation; a turning point.

 b. An unstable condition, as in political, social, or economic affairs, involving an impending abrupt or decisive change.

2.   A sudden change in the course of a disease or fever, toward either improvement or deterioration.

3.   An emotionally stressful event or traumatic change in a person's life.

4.   A point in a story or drama when a conflict reaches its highest tension and must be resolved.

[Middle English, from Latin, *judgment*, from Greek *krisis*, from *krīnein, to* separate, judge; see *krei-* in Indo-European roots.][1]

Crises can be personal or public. News about public crises is delivered 24/7 through iPads, Google Alerts, and CNN screen crawls. What did you read about recently: the euro currency crisis, Middle East turmoil, the war on terror, climate change, or continuing global financial chaos? The United States has a smorgasbord of crises: political polarization; a widening gap between the rich and the poor; the student loan burden, healthcare, and social security crises; and also an enormous national debt. There is one crisis, however, that will not show up on your screen crawl. This is the "corporate candor crisis." It refers to executive communications that are increasingly unclear, evade the truth, and can further destabilize economic conditions.

As illustrated in Figure 11.1, Rittenhouse Rankings research shows that over the past decade, there has been a dramatic increase in executive FOG. In 2002, FOG points in the Rittenhouse Rankings survey totaled 9,600. By 2010, these points had more than tripled to over 32,000.

Consider these FOG trends:

1. In 2002, 43 percent of the companies in the Rittenhouse Rankings survey scored in the best practice range, posting

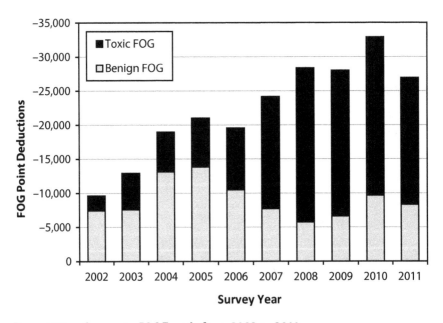

Figure 11.1   **Corporate FOG Trends from 2002 to 2011**

FOG scores of between zero (0) and 33 percent; by 2011, only 21 percent of the companies scored in this range.

2. Similarly, FOG scores among the companies in the bottom quartile of the Rittenhouse Rankings survey have deteriorated dramatically. In 2002, only 8 percent of the companies reported negative FOG scores, accumulating point deductions that exceeded all positive points. By 2010, however, this candor-deficient group included 23 percent of the companies in the survey.

Such trends indicate that executive candor has been declining. This fact is handicapping leaders in finding and executing effective solutions to our multiple crises. Why? We have seen in earlier chapters that excessive FOG can blind leaders to both wealth-destroying risks and new, profitable opportunities.

BENIGN AND TOXIC FOG

Over the years, Rittenhouse Rankings has developed special codes for benign and toxic FOG. Benign FOG includes obfuscating statements coded as: (1) spin; (2) clichés; (3) jargon; and (4) platitudes. These word choices shroud problems and avoid facts. Like junk food, these phrases may offer instant satisfaction, but they lack the necessary sustenance to grow a healthy business.

> Find *opportunities to standardize connectivity.* An ATM card works anywhere because the banking industry had the insight to realize that *a proprietary productivity gain could be leveraged into a far more valuable revenue and profit-generator, if rivals would cooperate to support a common system.*

> We use technology to enable new products and services, *providing guidance and total solutions for employers and consumers.*

> We engage in research and development *to foster constant innovation, unexcelled service and positive consumer behavior change.*

> From a customer segment perspective, *the commercial market remained very solid and well balanced globally.* We are *continuing to expand our product offerings, services, and distribution capabilities to this strategic market.* [author's emphasis]

In contrast, toxic FOG codes include: (1) confusing and incomplete information about vital business concepts and results; (2) contradictions; (3) excessive hyperbole; and (4) Orwellian nonsense. Consider these nonsensical excerpts from 2006 shareholder letters (the year the housing bubble peaked). All were coded as "Orwellian FOG." They are humorous, but they also provide sobering evidence of a disregard for common sense, clarity, basic grammar—and accountability:

> We maintain relationships with more than 25 research institutions with whom we continuously search for a more profound understanding of the skin we live in.

> While some brands are expanding into new sales points, others are rethinking and revaluating their growth plans . . . this process will speak to our heritage as brand builders and strengthen our impact at retail.

> In all these efforts, listening to customers remains our touchstone. We want our customers to walk our hallways every day via their direct feedback.

Rittenhouse Rankings research shows that benign FOG has declined over time, while toxic FOG has grown. In the 2002 Rittenhouse Rankings Candor Survey, toxic statements represented only 23 percent of total FOG points. By 2008, they represented 80 percent of the total candor points.

TOXIC FOG AND THE FALL OF LEHMAN BROTHERS

The following paragraphs from Lehman Brothers' 2007 shareholder letter included numerous statements that signaled danger ahead.

CEO Richard Fuld began his letter by trumpeting a fifth record-setting year of revenues at the firm. At the same time, he admitted that Lehman's important fixed-income business faced challenges. Because of the housing market collapse, revenues were down 29 percent from 2006, the first significant decline in nine years. In response, the company had closed its subprime businesses and was restructuring its global mortgage origination business. But these facts raised new concerns: Would Lehman continue to post losses from the subprime businesses? More important, which of the company's businesses had overperformed to make up for these fixed-income losses and allow the company to post a fifth year of record total revenues?

In the excerpt below, Fuld shows that he rightly focused on the company's need to manage risk and liquidity, but failed to report on actions or results that supported this effort:

> *We* effectively managed our risk, balance sheet, and expenses. Ultimately, our performance in 2007 was about our "One Firm" sense of shared responsibility and careful management of our liquidity, capital commitments, and balance sheet positions. *We* benefited from our senior level focus on risk management and, *more importantly, from a culture of risk management at every level of the Firm*. It also helped that *our senior leadership team has, on average, worked together for more than two decades and has successfully navigated difficult markets before. This experience proved to be especially valuable this year.*
> [author's emphasis]

This commentary raised questions: What did it mean to have "a culture of risk management at every level of the Firm"? What were the actual risk management policies and practices that supported such a culture? What metrics did Lehman use to measure risk management? While it was interesting to learn that Lehman's senior executives had "worked together for more than two decades," what had they learned about navigating difficult markets, and how were these lessons applied to Lehman's current challenges?

To build investor confidence in the company's ability to meet these challenges, Fuld cited Lehman's industry-leading rankings:

- "Ranked #1 by a leading industry consultant in U.S. fixed income market share, penetration, sales, research, trading, and overall quality."
- "Maintained our leading position in fixed income benchmarks, ranking #1 in fixed income indices by *Institutional Investor* every year since that survey began in 1997."
- "Achieved a #1 ranking for the eighth consecutive year in the *Institutional Investor* All-America Fixed Income Research poll."

All were impressive facts, but they did not address Lehman's current problems. As Warren Buffett often reminds investors, historical performance is not a reliable indicator of future performance. If it were, he notes, "the Forbes 400 would consist primarily of librarians."[2]

Investors in 2008 weren't buying Fuld's arguments. By the middle of 2008, Lehman's stock had lost 73 percent of its value. This crisis of confidence continued even as the company began to raise cash by selling some of its profitable businesses. By September 2008, plans to rescue Lehman were being debated at the New York Federal Reserve. But none were successful. On September 14, Lehman filed for bankruptcy protection. The following day, Barclays announced it would buy the "clean" parts of the company for $1.75 billion.[3]

In hindsight, one sentence from the Lehman 2007 letter stands out. It was: "Notably, our Fixed Income sales credit volumes, a good measure of how we delivered for our clients, rose 40% in 2007." Fuld's use of "sales credits" as a metric to measure customer satisfaction was an odd choice. "Sales credits" is how traders describe their sales commissions. In essence, Fuld was saying that Lehman's fixed-income sales force made a lot of trades that year. This fact, however, had nothing to do with whether or not Lehman's clients had a good year.

In the end, Lehman could not distinguish between the firm's goals and those of its clients. The "me first" culture I had observed at Lehman in the early 1990s appeared to have blinded the leadership to why the company was in business: to serve its customers and other stakeholders.

CANDOR SCORES AND MARKET PERFORMANCE

Since 2005, Rittenhouse Rankings has found that companies with low FOG scores are associated with superior market performance, while companies with high FOG scores are associated with poor market performance. Figure 11.2 illustrates this relationship.

As shown in Figure 11.2, the market returns of companies ranked in the bottom quartile of the Rittenhouse Rankings survey have under-

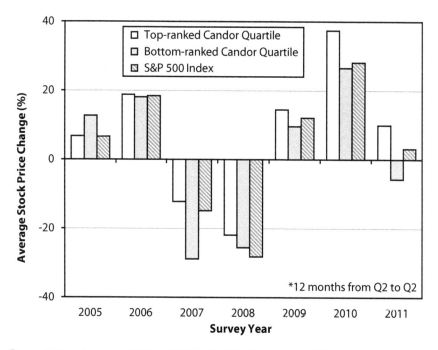

Figure 11.2   Average 12-Month* Market Performance of Companies in Top- and Bottom-Ranked Candor Quartiles versus S&P 500 Index

performed, on average, the top-ranked quartile of companies in six of the seven years from 2005 to 2011. In addition, the quartile of companies that were top-ranked in candor has on average outperformed the S&P 500 in each of the seven years.

Figure 11.3 below shows the two-year market returns of each group. In this case, the bottom-ranked quartile of companies outperformed both the S&P 500 and the top-ranked companies in 2005 and in 2008, but underperformed the top-ranked companies and the S&P 500 in the other four years. Over the entire period, the top-ranked companies returned an average of 59.8 percent compared to only 15.3 percent for the bottom-ranked companies and 36.4 percent for the S&P 500.

Finding such a strong association between candor and market performance is surprising, given the numerous coding judgments made by Rittenhouse Rankings and the factors that determine market per-

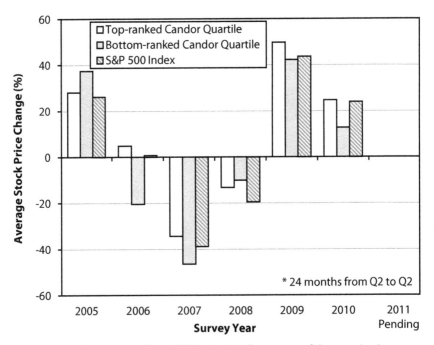

Figure 11.3   **Average 24-Month* Market Performance of Companies in Top- and Bottom-Ranked Candor Quartiles versus the S&P 500 Index**

formance. While this relationship between executive candor and market performance is not causal, it does support this conclusion: strong leadership revealed in candid communications will build employee trust, which furthers the effective execution of strategy and, in turn, leads to superior results and superior market performance. The bottom line: executives' words matter.

WORDS MATTER

In 1949, George Orwell published *1984*, his nightmare novel about the triumph of worldwide totalitarianism.[4] Orwell imagined a world in which books were burned in public bonfires and citizens marched in mass demonstrations chanting slogans like "Ignorance is Strength" and "Freedom is Slavery." The thought police encouraged children to spy on their parents and report statements or acts that challenged the authority of "Big Brother." Expressions of individual freedom were punished by torture or death.

In his 1946 essay "Politics and the English Language,"[5] Orwell connected the destruction of language with political and economic realities.

> Most people who bother with the matter at all would admit that the English language is in a bad way, but it is generally assumed that we cannot by conscious action do anything about it. Our civilization is decadent and our language—so the argument runs—must inevitably share in the general collapse. It follows that any struggle against the abuse of language is a sentimental archaism, like preferring candles to electric light or hansom cabs to aeroplanes. Underneath this lies the half-conscious belief that language is a natural growth and not an instrument which we shape for our own purposes.
>
> Now, it is clear that the decline of a language must ultimately have political and economic causes: it is not due simply to the bad influence of this or that individual writer.

Orwell pointed out that "an effect can become a cause" that can reinforce the original cause. This dynamic is like an alcoholic who drinks because he believes he is a failure, and then this leads to more failure. The same could be said of the English language, wrote Orwell, "It becomes ugly and inaccurate because our thoughts are foolish, but the slovenliness of our language makes it easier for us to have foolish thoughts." He contrasted the purpose of "literary language," intended to "express thought," with that of "political language." The purpose of the latter was to "subvert thought" and "prevent others from thinking." He offered these clues to identify "political language:"

1. Using ugly, stale imagery and imprecise reporting that produces "a mix of vagueness and sheer incompetence"
2. Choosing a passive voice and rejecting active verbs
3. Relying on dying metaphors that "save people the trouble of inventing phrases themselves"
4. Padding sentences "with extra syllables," jargon, and pretentious made-up words such as *deregionalize* and *non-fragmentory*.

In other words, Orwell described many of the clues used by Rittenhouse Rankings to identify and measure CEO FOG.

Why should his writing on political language matter to business leaders? Because his warnings are based on a simple principle: "If thought corrupts language, [then] language can also corrupt thought." In other words, the words we use will determine our thoughts, which lead to future actions. FOG will lead to more FOG.

This caution extends to business leaders, who must be alert to business risks and opportunities. Their failure to do so imperils executive decision making and can waste investor capital. Executives who obfuscate disregard the importance of context, a serious problem analyzed by the late Neil Postman, a professor of media ecology and chairman of the Department of Culture and Communication at New York University.

CONTEXT MATTERS

In *Amusing Ourselves to Death*, published in 1986, Postman described how people rejoiced to find that Orwell's prophecy of worldwide totalitarianism had not been realized.[6] He, however, did not join in this celebration. Postman believed that cultural and technological forces continued to threaten intelligent public discourse and individual freedoms. Instead of Orwell's dark vision, he explained why Aldous Huxley's vision in *Brave New World* was proving to be the more accurate post-1984 prophecy:

> What Orwell feared were those who would ban books. What Huxley feared was that there would be no reason to ban a book, for there would be no one who wanted to read one. Orwell feared those who would deprive us of information. Huxley feared those who would give us so much that we would be reduced to passivity and egoism. Orwell feared that the truth would be concealed from us. Huxley feared the truth would be drowned in a sea of irrelevance. Orwell feared we would become a captive culture. Huxley feared we would become a trivial culture. . . .

Postman believed that cultures are built and shaped by the quality of conversations, which in turn are shaped by the technologies used to transmit them. He argued that the invention of the telegraph and the photograph was instrumental in creating conditions that would endanger public discourse. They set in motion a process called decontextualization. Simply stated, he was concerned that context was disappearing from public discourse.

The *Free Online Dictionary* defines context as "the parts of a piece of writing, speech, etc., that precede and follow a word or passage and contribute to its full meaning" and also "the conditions and circumstances that are relevant to an event, fact, etc." The word *context* is derived from the Latin *contextus*, which means "weaving" or "putting together." In essence, Postman was sounding the alarm that by losing context, our communications were unraveling and becoming meaningless.

The Disappearance of Context

Postman analyzed the impact of television technology on the quality of communications and cultural integrity. He compared the way a book presents reasoned arguments designed to inform and express opinions with television's use of headlines and imagery geared to engaging and entertaining audiences. While books required focused, inquiring, and singular attention, television or screen news welcomed passive attention. Postman worried that information was increasingly becoming a commodity to be bought and sold rather than a means to find "truth." He feared that as "news" became a spectator sport, public discourse would grow ever more trivial.

Postman's analysis may help to explain why Rittenhouse Rankings has witnessed an alarming decline in context in executive communications. Consider this excerpt from Wachovia's 2007 shareholder letter coded for context deficiencies as unanswered questions:

> The conditions in the financial markets that gave rise to excessive risk taking and the use of leverage (controlling a large balance of assets with little capital) were brought about by an unprecedented [**How was this unprecedented?**] increase in concentrated global wealth [**What is concentrated global wealth?**] in an environment where returns on financial instruments were relatively low [**Why were returns on financial instruments relatively low?**] and demand for enhanced returns was feverish [**Isn't feverish a word used during market bubbles?**]. In response, the financial industry [Wasn't Wachovia part of this financial industry?] created new products and business models to supercharge returns through financial engineering. [**Didn't Wachovia sell these new products with supercharged returns?**]. It is now clear that the industry's risk management systems [**What were these risk management systems?**] did not measure up to the new environment. [author's emphasis]

The confusing context that follows was found in General Motors's 2010 shareholder letter. In this communication, investors learned that "[f]or the first time in decades, the playing field in the auto business is level." At the time this letter was published, however, alert readers might have rightly questioned this assertion of a "level playing field." Consider that GM had paid back about $23 billion owed to the American people from its 2008 bailout, but still owed them another $25 billion. When this letter was published, U.S. taxpayers owned 32 percent of the company. They would be repaid when the company sold this stock. However, to recover the full amount of the outstanding loan, GM had to sell this stock for about $53 a share.[7] Unfortunately, the stock had never traded close to this figure since the company had exited bankruptcy. During the 52 weeks of trading ending on October 29, 2012, GM's stock had traded only as high as $27.68 and as low as $18.72.

In contrast, Ford Motor Company had mortgaged all its assets to finance its business and never took taxpayer money.[8] Since then, the company has slowly and steadily reduced its leverage as profits have grown. By claiming that the auto industry was once again a level playing field, GM may well have been transparent in its reporting, but it did not meet the test of candor.

CANDOR IN THE AGE OF "TRUTHINESS"

Postman predicted that television (and television-like technologies), with its bias for episodic imagery, sound bites, and entertainment, would fundamentally change the transmission and content of knowledge. It would endanger context. The truth of his prophecy is revealed in the current success of Jon Stewart's *The Daily Show* and *The Colbert Report*. Each program paradoxically creates "news" by revealing the contradictions, failed logic, and impenetrable obfuscation of political and business reporting. The shows' writers produce satirical sketches that fill in the holes created by television and videos' fragmented and incoherent context.

In 2005, Princeton professor of philosophy Harry Frankfurt published his essay, "On Bullshit." It created so much attention that it was reprinted as a small book and became a bestseller. Frankfurt defined

"BS" as contextless commentary that failed to advance understanding, connection, and truth. He claimed that it is just like "hot air." In other words, he described much of the CEO FOG Rittenhouse Rankings finds in executive communications.

Why should this matter? Frankfurt advanced a counterintuitive argument. He asserted that FOG is worse than lying because a liar respects the truth, while a FOG maker does not. When a liar falsely represents something as being true, he is still connected to truth. This is not so, however, for one who creates FOG. This individual is not likely to care about facts or even "whether the things he says describe reality correctly."

Frankfurt, like others, believed this situation was abetted by the 24/7 news cycle, which requires commentators to talk at times about subjects of which they know little. They substitute opinions for facts. Instead of truth, audiences get "truthiness." This new word was coined by Stephen Colbert in 2005. He defined it as: "What you want the facts to be, as opposed to what the facts are. What feels like the right answer, as opposed to what reality will support."[9]

In today's fogged-in climate, facts, truth, and coherent discourse are increasingly scarce. Citizens, including investors, are less able or willing to do the hard work and critical reading and thinking to separate facts from FOG. Indeed, citizens and investors appear to have grown acclimatized to the new reality of "truthiness." This collective resignation is advanced by forces that work against candor. One of these forces was evident in the increase observed in FOG observed between the 2003 and 2004 Rittenhouse Rankings surveys.

CHAPTER 12

Authenticity

Authentic, noun

1a. Worthy of acceptance or belief as conforming to or based on fact.

  b. Conforming to an original so as to reproduce essential features.

  c. Made or done the same way as an original.

2. Not false or imitation: real, actual.

3. True to one's own personality, spirit, or character.

[Middle English *autentik*, from Anglo-French, from late Latin *authenticus*, from Greek *authentikos*, from *authentēs*, perpetrator, master, from *aut-* + *-hentēs* (akin to Greek *anyein*, to accomplish, Sanskrit *sanoti*, he gains). First known use: 14th century.][1]

On July 30, 2002, responding to the failures of Enron and other prominent companies, U.S. President George W. Bush signed the Sarbanes-Oxley legislation into law. Now CEOs and CFOs were required to personally certify the accuracy of their company's financial statements or face criminal penalties for failing to do so. Many people believed that, by imposing severe consequences for inaccurate financial reporting, this act would improve financial disclosures and reduce fraud. Criminal penalties included awarding fines of not more than $1 million and/or imprisonment for up to 10 years. If executives were found to have willfully falsified information, they could face fines of up to $5 million and sentences of up to 20 years.[2]

Contrary to the intentions of its sponsors, however, Sarbanes-Oxley did not promote higher executive candor scores. In fact, the number of FOG points in the 2004 Rittenhouse Rankings survey jumped 47 percent, the greatest year-over-year increase over the 10-year study period. The passage of Sarbanes-Oxley created a backlash of fear that motivated companies to communicate as little as possible.

As Warren Buffett had prophesied in 2002, more regulations did not lead to greater candor. In fact, corporate FOG measured in the Rittenhouse Rankings research has increased almost every year since 2002. As well, the composition of FOG has changed dramatically. Toxic FOG is now more prevalent than benign FOG.

In this climate, CEOs who consistently rank high in the Rittenhouse Rankings survey deserve investor respect. By offering informed, relevant, and factual reporting on their businesses, these leaders reject the forces that work against candor: (1) "short-term-itis"; (2) excessive CEO compensation; and (3) the high cost of low ethics.

SHORT-TERM-ITIS: ACCOUNTING TRUMPS ECONOMIC GOALS

In 2000, institutional investors held stocks on average for three to five years. By 2011, this holding period had shrunk to six months.[3] As a result, executive teams increasingly focus on meeting consistently growing quarterly earnings guidance to reflect the short-term market bias of their institutional owners.

Buffett described the problems associated with providing guidance in his 2000 letter. He explained that few companies have ever been able to grow consistently at increasingly high rates of double-digit growth—unless they engage in accounting games and allocate capital for short-term earnings benefit. He described these practices just as cracks in the great 15-year bull market were beginning to show. As dot-com stock prices plunged, investors rediscovered the importance of cash on company balance sheets over earnings on their income statements.

At a corporate retreat not long ago, executives laughed when I mentioned the popular business cliché "creating long-term share-holder value." Given the realities of today's capital markets, the more accurate phrase should be "creating short-term trading profits." Consider that as companies grow larger, they gain more opportunities to manage their earnings. Pundits have argued that this consolidation momentum creates not only companies that are too big to fail, but also ones that are too big to manage, too big to innovate, and too big to be held accountable.

In the past, investors who held stocks for extended periods could be expected to "police" CEOs and boards and hold them accountable for their promises. But a 2012 article in the *Harvard Business Review* by Justin Fox and Jay Lorsch described how this connection has grown increasingly tenuous. They asked: "What good are shareholders?"[4]

First, the authors defined the historical shift in share ownership. In 1950, households owned more than 90 percent of the shares in U.S. corporations. Today, small retail investors own only 30 to 40 percent. Domestic and foreign institutional investors who are compensated for turning in short-term results on their managed portfolios have replaced these loyal long-term investors.

In a functioning capital system, investors are expected to provide capital, information, and discipline to executives and boards. Today, however, few investors are true owners. Instead, they are like the rent-ers in Jeff Bezos's story who nailed their Christmas tree to the floor. These stock renters lack pride of ownership.

CEOs are facing shorter tenures, another manifestation of short-term-itis. According to a Booz Allen report, 14.2 percent of the world's top 2,500 companies replaced their CEOs in 2011, up from 11.6 percent in 2010. CEOs, like athletes, are increasingly looking for front-loaded compensation, given this volatility in the executive suite.[5]

CEO COMPENSATION

Supersized CEO pay packages, especially for executives who destroy shareholder value, have undermined investor confidence in the legitimacy of boards of directors. Contrast certain eight-figure compensation packages with Warren Buffett's salary. He continues to pay himself only $100,000 a year and neither gets nor gives stock options, a practice he abhors because it inflates earnings and dilutes the value of the company for existing shareholders.

Both Buffett and Vice Chairman Munger are highly critical of exorbitant compensation paid to CEOs (particularly for nonperformance). They believe this not only fails to motivate executives, but can also corrode CEOs' behavior. In 1998, Munger stated at the Berkshire Hathaway annual meeting that the escalation in CEO pay was creating "a widespread perception that the very top corporate salaries in America are obscene. And it is not a good thing for a civilization when the leaders are regarded as not dealing fairly with those for whom they are stewards."[6]

In 2003, the gap in compensation between large-company CEOs and average workers surpassed 300 to 1.[6] Believing that investors' concerns over CEO pay could distract GE from focusing on its fundamentals, CEO Jeff Immelt provided details about his compensation in both his 2002 and 2003 shareholder letters. In 2002, he linked responsible executive compensation to protecting GE's reputation for "honorable dealings," and provided details to show how he was being compensated:

> [A] substantial portion of my compensation is linked to the performance of GE stock. Nearly 70% of my net worth is in GE stock. I hold my stock options to term (10 years), a practice I adopted when I became chairman and which I will continue. At the same time, I have asked our board's Compensation Committee to explore best practices on linking my pay even more closely with investor interests.

He followed up on this promise in his 2003 letter when he described how the board had adjusted his pay guided by principles of transparency, performance, and investor accountability:

> To reinforce this alignment [with investors], I will no longer receive stock options or restricted stock. Instead, I will receive "performance share units." These units vest in five years based on two metrics: I receive half if GE's total shareowner returns meets or exceeds that of the S&P 500, and the other half if our average annual operating cash flow growth over the vesting period exceeds 10%. If these metrics are not achieved, the performance share units are cancelled. Success will require sustained excellent performance in the long-term interests of GE investors.

Importantly, Immelt tied his compensation to cash flow and total shareholder returns, not to earnings per share.

During the first five years of the Rittenhouse Rankings Candor Survey, only 19 percent of the CEOs reported on their compensation. In the second five years, only 10 percent of the CEOs offered these reports.

As the controversy over CEO pay has intensified, investors voted on more proxies on executive pay in 2012 than ever before. However, according to Compensia, an executive compensation consulting firm, only four companies received a majority negative vote on executive compensation as of April 2012. While nonbinding, these votes put directors on notice that investors expect reasonable, not excessive, executive compensation.[8]

But why would investors who hold stocks for only six months care about long-term performance or the costs imposed by low ethics?

THE HIGH COST OF LOW ETHICS

In 2002, Carl J. Schramm, the former head of the Ewing Marion Kauffman Foundation for Entrepreneurship, published an essay on "The High Cost of Low Ethics: How Corruption Imperils Entrepreneurship and Democracy." He linked the decline in business and political ethics to a failed system of fairly and promptly administered justice.[9]

Schramm noted that in 1938, Richard Whitney, then-president of the New York Stock Exchange, was charged with defrauding his brokerage clients of millions of dollars. Within five months, Whitney was tried, convicted, and sent to Sing Sing Correctional Facility, where he served three years and four months of a 5- to 10-year prison term.

By way of contrast, Schramm observed that it had taken two years to investigate and then indict the top two executives of Enron in 2004. Ultimately, the trial was not scheduled until January 2006. In other words, Richard Whitney was charged, tried, and convicted and had completed his prison term in about the same time it had taken to indict Kenneth Lay and Jeff Skilling.

Just as the Sarbanes-Oxley legislation produced less executive candor, Schramm argued that more rules would fail to create more principled business behavior. He believed that replacing self-regulating standards of common law, common sense, and fair play with legal definitions of right and wrong serves to weaken the moral glue that holds our society together. For instance, after Enron declared bankruptcy in December 2001, a colleague asked a corporate lawyer, "How can executives be held accountable for protecting the savings of hardworking people?" The lawyer replied, "What's the problem? I don't see that Enron executives broke any laws."

In 2012, when investors and taxpayers ask who was responsible for the 2008 collapse of the global economy, leaders point only to empty chairs. Cries for justice have not resulted in actions. Not one individual has been implicated or indicted. And when truth is not connected to consequences, expect to find words and promises growing less relevant and reliable.

INVESTING BETWEEN THE LINES: FACEBOOK INITIAL PUBLIC OFFERING

CEO communications can reveal much useful investor information. For instance, a critical analysis of CEO Mark Zuckerberg's letter to prospective shareholders in Facebook's 2012 initial public offering (IPO) could have tempered investors' enthusiasm and inoculated them from the media hype that accompanied this highly publicized stock offering.

For instance, investors would have learned that Facebook had a clearly defined social mission ("to make the world more open and connected"), but a less coherent business model. Instead of citing business plans and goals, Zuckerberg wrote: ". . . we don't build services to make money; we make money to build better services. And we think this is a good way to build something."

But what were these "better services" and what was this "something"? Instead of addressing these questions, Zuckerberg added:

> These days I think more and more people want to use services from companies that believe in something beyond simply maximizing profits. . . By focusing on our mission and building great services, we believe we will create the most value for our shareholders and partners over the long term—and this in turn will enable us to keep attracting the best people and building more great services.

Nowhere in this description does Zuckerberg describe revenues that might come from "focusing on [this] mission" and "building more great services." In fact, throughout the more than 2,000-word letter, only four numbers were reported. To support the company's services that connect people to businesses and the economy, Facebook would help the over [1] *"800 million people* map out more than [2] *100 billion connections"* [author's emphasis].

Zuckerberg was proud that Facebook's developer platform "had already enabled [3] *hundreds of thousands of businesses* to build higher-quality and more social products," although he failed to offer specific examples. He expected that [4] *"the more than four million businesses"* that currently had pages on Facebook would be joined by more and more businesses to create direct, authentic dialogue with their customers [author's emphasis].

These were admirable intentions, but they were mired in platitudes. This made it difficult to see how the company would achieve long-term profits. Yahoo! blogger and former technology equity analyst Henry Blodget shared these concerns and extracted the following facts that prudent investors could have heeded:

- Facebook's growth rate was decelerating rapidly.
- Facebook's user-base was rapidly transitioning to mobile devices, which produce much less revenue.
- Facebook's operating profit margin was already an astounding 50%, which suggested it had nowhere to go but down. . . .
- Facebook was going public at an astoundingly high price for a company with these characteristics—about 60-times the following year's projected earnings, in a market in which other hot tech companies like Apple (AAPL) and Google (GOOG) were trading at less than 15-times. [10]

Providing context for these facts, Blodget began his *Business Insider* blog by reminding readers that only four months earlier, "Facebook was viewed as 'the next Google.' Now, with no major change in the fundamentals, it's viewed as an overhyped disaster. . . . As I listen to all this whining, I have a simple question: Didn't anyone even read Facebook's IPO prospectus?"

TRUTH MATTERS

Three years after publishing "On Bullshit," Professor Harry Frankfurt published a sequel he called "On Truth." He confessed at the outset that he had mistakenly assumed in 2008 that readers would share a belief that "being indifferent to truth [the opposite of BS] is an undesirable or even a reprehensible characteristic." As a result, he had left out an explanation about why truth matters.

To correct this error, Frankfurt rejected a popular view that truth is merely defined by a person's point of view or determined by what he or she imagines to be true. Instead, he offered commentary about objective truth. This included proven scientific and mathematical principles, as well as engineering and architectural knowledge that is needed to prevent skyscrapers from collapsing. In a similar vein, he cited medical facts that allow surgeons to save lives and nutritional facts that tell us how to keep our bodies healthy.

Frankfurt wrote that advancing human progress requires "a conscientious respect for the importance of honesty and clarity in reporting the facts" as well as "a stubborn concern for the accuracy in determining what the facts are."

This belief is the foundation of the Rittenhouse Rankings research on corporate candor. When people tell me they don't believe that they are smart enough to uncover the truth about executive FOG, I conclude they either are lazy or lack the confidence to use their common sense. Lazy readers are reminded that the search to find candor and truth is vitally important to financial well-being. Readers who lack confidence are offered this advice:

1. *Trust your instincts.* No matter what others might say, if you see the emperor is not wearing any clothes, he is naked. If the communication sounds like nonsense, it probably is.
2. *Read between the lines.* Look to see how the CEO balances the company's profit-making ability with its principles. Look for clarity and consistency in how he or she describes the company's financial results.
3. *Kick the tires.* If a communication seems credible, it's important to check out the CEO's claims in the real world. This will make you a more successful investor.
4. *Look for a CEO's authentic and true voice.*

Warren Buffett and others, like Vanguard's Jack Bogle, remind us of important financial truths or principles, such as the fact that taking on excessive leverage increases risk and treating investors as patsies, not partners, creates unsustainable businesses. Like Amazon.com's Bezos, these leaders believe that creating businesses that matter to future generations is a worthy goal.

AUTHENTICITY AND THE LONG TERM

A few CEOs like Jeff Bezos have referred to this "grandfather test," the desire to pass along something of value to future generations. Duke

Energy's current CEO, Jim Rogers, devoted his predecessor company's 2003 annual report to future generations. It featured employees and their grandkids. The report began with this statement: "Decades from now when our children and grandchildren look back at what we did as a company and the decisions we made, will they think we did the right thing? We want the answer to be yes."

Such leaders are committed to creating a meaningful legacy. Consider that when he retired, Paul Anderson, Alcoa's visionary CEO from 1987 to 1999, asked investors to judge his leadership of the company based not on what had been accomplished during his tenure, but on how the company fared after he left.

On October 3, 2012, HP CEO Meg Whitman met with Wall Street analysts and offered straight talk about the company's prospects. She announced that investors "should expect sharply lower revenue and profits." Furthermore, she projected that the company had considerable work to do to right itself and that results might not be realized until 2016. The *New York Times* reported that while analysts were "taken aback" by this frank assessment of the company's problems,[11] they believed that "Whitman had made the right move in putting [the problems] out in the open."

Patrick Moorhead, President of Moor Insights and Strategy attended the meeting. At the end, he offered these observations:

> In an era where C.E.O.'s watch every word they say, it's refreshing to see complete candor. H.P. is a mess. It will take five to 10 years to fully take care of this, just the way it took I.B.M. to remake itself. [But] Wall Street doesn't like anything longer than a one to three-year horizon. It's too much risk for them.

Whitman paid a price for her candor. While she was talking, HP's stock dropped about 8 percent and closed at the end of the day at $14.91 a share, down nearly 13 percent on very high trading volume. The stock had not been that low in a decade. Nevertheless, Whitman ranks among a small group of CEO heroes who lead with authentic talk and a long-term outlook.

AUTHENTIC AND UNIQUE STYLE

Cynics who learn about the Rittenhouse Rankings model to analyze, quantify, and rank-order CEO communication often say, "Ha! When CEOs figure out your formula, they'll just follow it to get a high score." They forget that the most memorable shareholder letters are those that are original and thoughtful, not formulaic. Those communications are authentic. These authors report their mistakes and strive for the delicate balance between disclosing what is needed so that investors can make responsible, informed decisions and omitting what is unessential.

Writing authentically is not typically expected from a CEO, nor does it conform to public relations and PowerPoint styles. Expressing personal truth is not a manufactured style. In their classic *The Elements of Style*, William Strunk and E. B. White wrote about the hard work of communicating style:

> Writing is, for most, laborious and slow. The mind travels faster than the pen; consequently, writing becomes a question of learning to make occasional wing shots, bringing down the bird of thought as it flashes by. A writer is a gunner, sometimes waiting in his blind for something to come in, sometimes roaming the countryside hoping to scare something up. Like other gunners, he must cultivate patience: he may have to work many covers to bring down one partridge.[12]

While the effort of authoring a communication that is authentic and engaging is considerable, the rewards in building investor trust, motivating employees, creating loyal customers, and achieving superior financial performance are even greater.

In 2001, my then-eight-year-old daughter and I visited Warren Buffett in his Omaha office. After greeting us, he promptly took her to the office copy machine and photocopied her hand. He offered the paper image to her, saying, "Keep this. No one else in the world has a handprint like that." Similarly, when you read an executive communication, look for the CEO's unique handprint. If you find that he or she is authentic and clearly tells a complete story backed up with candid financials and relevant information, you have found someone who merits your trust.

Notes

Chapter 1

1. http://www.thefreedictionary.com/disclosure.
2. Enron Corporation. *2000 Annual Report*. Houston, Texas. 2001.
3. U.S. Securities and Exchange Commission. "Roundtable Discussion on Financial Disclosure and Auditor Oversight." March 4, 2002. www.sec.gov/spotlight/roundtables/accountround030402.htm.
4. Buffett, Warren. Interview by author, June 4, 2001. *Do Business with People You Can Tru$t*. New York: AndBEYOND Communications, 2002.
5. Zweig, Jason. "A Tale of Two Washingtons." *Money*, November 2004, p. 92.
6. Expeditors International of Washington, Inc. FY04-Q2, Form 8-K for the period ending June 30, 2004 (filed August 12, 2004), p. 9. http://www.sec.gov/Archives/edgar/data/746515/000110465904024151/a04-9459_18k.htm (accessed October 10, 2012).

Chapter 2

1. *Merriam-Webster Online*. http://www.merriam-webster.com/dictionary/culture (accessed October 9, 2012).
2. *Online Etymology Dictionary*. http://www.etymonline.com/index.php?term =culture (accessed October 9, 2012).
3. Postman, Neil. *Amusing Ourselves to Death; Public Discourse in the Age of Show Business*. New York: Penguin, 2005, p. 6.
4. Kotter, John P., and James L., Heskett. *Corporate Culture and Performance*. New York: Free Press, 1992.
5. Peters, Thomas J., and Robert H. Waterman, Jr. *In Search of Excellence*. New York: Warner Books, 1982, p. 104.

6. "Excerpts from Decision on Time-Warner Merger." *New York Times,* July 15, 1989. http://www.nytimes.com/1989/07/15/business/excerpts-from-decision -on-time-warner-merger.html (accessed October 9, 2012).

7. Olson, Max. "Wisdom, Virtue and Some Common Sense." *FutureBlind,* February 16, 2009. http://www.futureblind.com/2009/02/wisdom-virtue-and -some-common-sense/ (accessed October 9, 2012).

8. Kass, David. "Notes from 2012 Berkshire Hathaway Annual Meeting." University of Maryland, June 4, 2012. http://blogs.rhsmith.umd.edu/ davidkass/uncategorized/notes-from-2012-berkshire-hathaway-annual -meeting/ (accessed October 9, 2012).

9. Kotter and Heskett. *Corporate Culture and Performance.*

10. Birger, Jon. "Glowing Numbers: Investors Know that General Electric Posts Great Earnings. How It Happens Is More of a Mystery—and It Isn't Always Pretty." *CNNMoney,* November 1, 2000. http://money.cnn.com/magazines/ moneymag/moneymag_archive/2000/11/01/290856/index.htm (accessed October 10, 2012).

11. Kotter and Heskett. *Corporate Culture and Performance.*

Chapter 3

1. http://www.thefreedictionary.com/sustain.

2. Buffett, Warren. Interview with Becky Quick. *CNBC Squawk Box,* March 1, 2010.

3. Munger, Charlie. "A Lesson on Elementary, Worldly Wisdom as It Relates to Investment Management & Business." Lecture, USC Business School, 1994.

4. Housel, Morgan. "Charlie Munger's 30 Best Zingers of All Time." *Motley Fool.* http://www.fool.com/investing/general/2012/06/14/charlie-mungers-30-best -zingers-of-all-time.aspx (accessed October 9, 2012).

5. Munger, Charlie. Wesco 2002 Annual Meeting, Pasadena, California. May 8, 2002. http://mungerisms.blogspot.com/2009/08/wesco-2002-annual-meeting. html.

6. Maranjian, Selena. "Buffett and Munger Answer Questions in Omaha at 2000 Annual Meeting." *Motley Fool.* http://www.fool.com/specials/2000/sp000504a .htm (accessed October 9, 2012).

7. Rhodes, Mark. "Choosing the Words of Strategy." Free Management Library, January 31, 2011. http://managementhelp.org/blogs/strategic-planning/ 2011/01/31/choosing-the-words-of-strategy (accessed October 10, 2012).

8. Lincoln, Abraham. Letter to William H. Seward. June 28, 1862. http:// teachingamericanhistory.org/library/index.asp?documentprint=2233 (accessed October 9, 2012).

9. Cable News Network. "Coke CEO Roberto C. Goizueta Dies at 65." *CNN.com.* http://www.cnn.com/US/9710/18/goizueta.obit.9am (accessed October 9, 2012).

Chapter 4

1. http://en.wiktionary.org/wiki/steward.
2. Bresiger, Gregory. "Mr. Limit Order. Gus Sauter Is at the Vanguard of Roping In Trading Costs." *Traders Magazine*, October 2012, p. 25.
3. Bogle, Jack. Interview by David Serchuk. *Forbes*, December 8, 2008.
4. Ibid.
5. Weisstein, Eric. "Nicolaus Copernicus," *World of Scientific Biography*, 2007. http://scienceworld.wolfram.com/biography/Copernicus.html (accessed October 15, 2012).
6. "Heliocentric Theory—the Triumph of the Heliocentric Theory," 2012. http://science.jrank.org/pages/3276/Heliocentric-Theory-triumph-heliocentric -theory.html (accessed October 15, 2012).
7. "Kant's So-Called Copernican Revolution." *Mind*. vo. 46, no. 182, pp. 214–217. http://mind.oxfordjournals.org/content/XLVI/182/214.extract (accessed October 15, 2012).
8. Alexander, John R. "History of Accounting." Association of Chartered Accountants in the U.S., 2002. http://www.acaus.org/history/hs_pac.html (accessed October 15, 2012).

Chapter 5

1. http://www.merriam-webster.com/dictionary/candor.
2. http://www.beedictionary.com/meaning/candor.
3. Sorkin, Andrew Ross. "Reflecting on Buffett, Business and Politics." *New York Times DealBook*, May 7, 2012. http://dealbook.nytimes.com/2012/05/07/ reflecting-on-buffett-business-and-politics.
4. Edelman. *2012 Edelman Trust Barometer*. http://www.scribd.com/doc/ 79026497/2012-Edelman-Trust-Barometer-Executive-Summary (accessed October 15, 2012).
5. Ferrazzi, Keith. "Candor, Criticism, Teamwork." *Harvard Business Review*, January–February 2012. http://hbr.org/2012/01/candor-criticism-teamwork/ ar/pr (accessed October 15, 2012).
6. Vallicella, Bill. "Kant's Paean to Sincerity." *Maverick Philosopher*, April 4, 2009.
7. *The Invention of Lying*. DVD. Directed by Ricky Gervais and Matthew Robinson. Los Angeles: Warner Brothers Pictures, 2009.
8. Ibid.
9. Kant, Immanuel. *Religion Within the Limits of Reason Alone*. New York: HarperCollins, 1960.
10. Chaplin, Stewart. "The Stained-Glass Political Platform." *Century Magazine*, June 1900. http://www.unz.org/Pub/Century-1900jun-00304 (accessed October 15, 2012).

11. Fox, Justin. "Why the Government Wouldn't Let AIG Fail." *Time*, September 16, 2008. http://www.time.com/time/business/article/0,8599,1841699,00.html (accessed October 15, 2012).

12. Vollmer, Lisa. "Create Candor in the Workplace, Says Jack Welch." *Stanford GSB News*, April 2005. http://www.gsb.stanford.edu/news/headlines/vftt _welch.shtml (accessed October 15, 2012).

13. Harris, Lynn. "Truth-Telling: Confronting the Reality of the Lack of Candor Inside Organizations," 2006–2008. http://www.linkageinc.com/thinking/ linkageleader/Documents/Lynn_Harris_Truth-Telling--Confronting_the _Lack_of_Candor_Inside_Organizations_0506.pdf (accessed October 15, 2012).

14. Hoffman, Bryce. *American Icon: Alan Mulally and the Fight to Save Ford Motor Company*. New York: Crown Business, 2012.

Chapter 6

1. http://www.thefreedictionary.com/strategy.

2. Ohnsman, Alan. "Toyota to Maintain 'Aggressive' Hybrid Car Strategy, Press Says." *Bloomberg*, June 26, 2006. http://www.bloomberg.com/apps/news?pid= 21070001&sid=awyyirna3HVU (accessed October 16, 2012).

3. Ibid.

4. Toyota Motor Coporation. *2006 Annual Report*. Tokyo, Japan, 2007.

5. "Toyota Surpasses Ford as World's No. 2 Automaker." *Economic Times*, January 27, 2004. http://articles.economictimes.indiatimes.com/2004-01-27/ news/27413821_1_toyota-sales-toyota-motor-corp-toyota-city (accessed October 16, 2012).

6. Bunkley, Nick. "Ford Mortgages Assets to Pay for Overhaul." *New York Times*, November 27, 2008. http://www.nytimes.com/2006/11/27/business/27cnd -ford.html (accessed October 16, 2012).

7. "Toyota Knocks Off GM as World's Biggest Car Maker." *Daily News*, July 25, 2012. http://articles.nydailynews.com/2012-07-25/news/32853029_1_gm -sales-global-sales-gm-in-global-vehicle (accessed October 16, 2012).

8. Palmer, Parker. Interview by author. *Executive Talent Magazine*, Spring 2001.

9. Neeley, Tsedal, and Paul Leonardi. "Defend Your Research: Effective Managers Say the Same Thing Twice (or More)." *Harvard Business Review*, May 2011. http://hbr.org/2011/05/defend-your-research-effective-managers -say-the-same-thing-twice-or-more/ar/1 (accessed October 16, 2012).

10. Associated Press. "Toyota Recalls Nearly 1 Million Vehicles." *USA Today*, May 31, 2006. http://usatoday30.usatoday.com/money/autos/ 2006-05-31-toyota_x .htm?csp=34 (accessed October 16, 2012).

11. Ohnsman, Alan, and Kae Inoue. "Toyota Recalls U.S.-Built Tundra Pickup, Sequoia SUVs." *Bloomberg*, January 19, 2007. http://www.bloomberg.com/ apps/news?pid=21070001&sid=a2IyUK.tTwG0 (accessed October 16, 2012).

12. Rogers, David, and Mark Allen. "Bush Announces $17.4 Billion Auto Bailout." *Politico*, December 19, 2008. http://www.politico.com/newsstories/1208/16740 .html (accessed October 22, 2012).

13. Migliore, Greg. "General Motors CEO Rick Wagoner Out, Replaced by COO Fritz Henderson." *Autoweek*, March 29, 2009. http://www.autoweek .com/article/20090329/carnews/903309997 (accessed October 22, 2012).

14. Isidore, Chris. "GM Bankruptcy: End of an Era." *CNNMoney.com*, June 2, 2009. http://money.cnn.com/2009/06/01/news/companies/gm_bankruptcy (accessed October 22, 2012).

15. "Mark Hurd—Rise and Fall of a CEO." *Dayton Business Journal*, August 7, 2010. http://www.bizjournals.com/dayton/stories/2010/08/02/daily73.html (accessed October 16, 2012).

16. LaPlante, Alice. "Compaq and HP: Urge to Merge Was Right." *Stanford Business*, vol. 76, no. 1, November 2007, pp. 28–29. http://www.gsb.stanford .edu/news/bmag/sbsm0711/kn-merge.html.

17. Kotter, John. "Change Management vs. Change Leadership—What's the Difference?" *Forbes*, July 12, 2011. http://www.forbes.com/sites/johnkotter/ 2011/07/12/change-management-vs-change-leadership-whats-the-difference.

Chapter 7

1. http://dictionary.reference.com/browse/lead.

2. Geng, Diane. "GM vs. Toyota: By the Numbers." NPR, December 19, 2005. http://www.npr.org/news/specials/gmvstoyota (accessed October 22, 2012).

3. Ibid.

4. Maremont, Mark. "GM Bookkeeping Errors May Indicate Aggressive Accounting Style." *Wall Street Journal*, March 18, 2006. http://online.wsj.com/ article/SB114264547800801989.html (accessed October 22, 2012).

5. http://www.merriam-webster.com/dictionary/context (accessed October 22, 2012).

6. Lipton, Joshua. "Dell's Investigation Comes to a Close." *Forbes.com*, August 17, 2007. http://www.forbes.com/2007/ 08/17/dell-computer-investigation-markets-equity-cx_jl_0817 markets19.html.

Chapter 8

1. http://www.merriam-webster.com/dictionary/vision.

2. Envisioning Jewish Education. "A 'Biography' of the Word Vision." http:// www.mli.org.il/Visions/Library/Pages/Biography+of+Vision.htm (accessed November 12, 2012).

3. Stewart, Thomas. "A Refreshing Change: Vision Statements That Make Sense." *Fortune*, September 30, 1996. http://money.cnn.com/magazines/

fortune/fortune_archive/1996/09/30/217421/index.htm (accessed October 18, 2012).

4. International Business Machines. *1995 Annual Report*. Armonk, New York, 1996.
5. Ibid.
6. Marquardt, Michael J. *Leading with Questions: How Leaders Find the Right Solutions by Knowing What to Ask*. New York: John Wiley & Sons, 2005, p. 23.
7. http://psychology.about.com/od/personalitydevelopment/a/emotionalintell.htm.

Chapter 9

1. http://www.thefreedictionary.com.
2. Continental Airlines, Inc. *1996 Annual Report*. Houston, Texas.
3. Durpey, Rich. "Home Depot Abdicates Responsibility." *Motley Fool*. http://www.fool.com/server/printarticle.aspx?file=/investingvalue/2006/05/30/home-depot-abdicates-responsibility.aspx (accessed October 26, 2012).
4. Kavilanz, Parija B. "Nardelli Out at Home Depot." *CNNMoney.com*. http://money.cnn.com/2007/01/03/news/companies/home_depot/index.htm (accessed November 14, 2012).
5. Lipton, Joshua. "Target Comes In on Target." *Forbes*. http://www.forbes.com/2007/08/21/target-retail-ackman-markets-equity-cx_jl_0821markets17.html (accessed October 26, 2012).
6. "How Companies Got Their Name." *Did You Know?*, August 8, 2005. http://www.myuniversalfacts.com/2005/08/how-companies-got-their-name.html (accessed October 26, 2012).

Chapter 10

1. http://www.thefreedictionary.com.
2. Pender, Kathleen. "Write-Offs Remove Excess Inventory from Books—Not Shelves." *SFGate*, May 8, 2001. http://www.sfgate.com/business/networth/article/Write-offs-remove-excess-inventory-from-books-2923282.php (accessed October 26, 2012).
3. Santos, Paolo. "Kindle Sales Plunge Made Amazon.com's Gross Margin Look Better." *Seeking Alpha*, May 3, 2012. http://seekingalpha.com/article/557151-kindle-sales-plunge-made-amazon-com-s-gross-margin-look-better (accessed October 26, 2012).

Chapter 11

1. http://www.thefreedictionary.com.
2. Berkshire Hathaway, Inc. *1990 Annual Report*. Omaha, Nebraska, 1991.

3. Smith, Randall, Diya Gullapalli, and Jeffrey McCracken. "Lehman, Workers Score Reprieve." *Wall Street Journal*, September 17, 2008. http://online.wsj.com/article/SB122163100282247355.html (accessed November 1, 2012).
4. Orwell, George. *1984*. New York: Signet Classic, 1950, p. 4.
5. Orwell, George. "Politics and the English Language." *Horizon: A Review of Literature and Art*, vo. 13, no. 76, 1946, pp. 252–265.
6. Postman, Neil. *Amusing Ourselves to Death: Public Discourse in the Age of Show Business*. New York: Penguin, 1986, p. vii.
7. Bennett, Jeff, and Sharon Terlep. "U.S. Balks at GM Plan." *Wall Street Journal*, WSJ.com, September 17, 2012. http://online.wsj.com/article/SB100008723963 904439956045780007540355510658.html (accessed November 1, 2012).
8. Hammond, Lou Ann. "How Ford Did It." *CNNMoney*, January 13, 2011. http://money.cnn.com/2011/01/12/autos/Bill-Ford-Alan-Mulally-carmaker.fortune/index.htm (accessed November 1, 2012).
9. "The Colbert Report." *60 Minutes*, April 30, 2006. http://www.cbsnews.com/8301-18560_162-1553506.html (accessed November 1, 2012).

Chapter 12

1. http://www.merriam-webster.com/dictionary/authentic.
2. "Failure of Corporate Officers to Certify Financial Reports." Legal Information Institute, Cornell University Law School. http://www.law.cornell.edu/uscode/text/18/1350 (accessed November 1, 2012).
3. Fox, Justin, and Jay W. Lorsch. "What Good Are Shareholders?" *Harvard Business Review*, July–August 2012. http://hbr.org/2012/07/what-good-are-shareholders/ar/1 (accessed November 1, 2012).
4. Ibid.
5. Favaro, Ken, Per-Ola Karlsson, and Gary Neilson. "12th Annual Global CEO Succession Study." New York: Booz & Company, 2011.
6. Rittenhouse, L.J., *Do Business with People You Can Tru$t*. New York: AndBEYOND Communications, 2002.
7. "Executive Compensation Scoreboard." *BusinessWeek*, April 19, 2004.
8. Waggoner, John, and Matt Krantz. "Shareholders Don't Often Vote Against Huge CEO Pay." *USA Today.com*, April 20, 2012. http://usatoday30.usatoday.com/money/companies/management/story/2012-04-18/shareholders-say-on-ceo-pay/54397394/1 (accessed November 1, 2012).
9. Schramm, Carl J. "The High Price of Low Ethics: How Corruption Imperils Entrepreneurship and Democracy." *Journal of Markets & Morality*, vo. 9, no. 2, Fall 2006. http://www.questia.com/library/1G1-186469567/the-high-price-of-low-ethics-how-corruption-imperils (accessed November 13, 2012).
10. Blodget, Henry. "It's Becoming Clear that No One Actually Read Facebook's IPO Prospectus or Mark Zuckerberg's Letter to Shareholders." *Business Insider*

SAI, August 31, 2012. http://www.businessinsider.com/facebook-stock-letter
-shareholders (accessed November 1, 2012).

11. Hardy, Quentin. "H.P. Shares Fall as Chief Sees Trouble." *New York Times*,
October 3, 2012. http://bits.blogs.nytimes.com/2012/10/03/h-p-stock-drops
-as-meg-whitman-speaks/ (accessed November 1, 2012).

12. http://grammar.about.com/od/writersonwriting/a/ebwonwriting_2.htm.

Index

About the Author

Wall Street veteran **L.J. Rittenhouse** is president of Rittenhouse Rankings Inc., an investor relations and crisis communications advisory business. Named to the list of "Top 100 Thought Leaders in Most Trustworthy Business Behavior," Rittenhouse advises Fortune 500 executives at the highest levels on developing strategies and communications based on *Executive Candor.*

Building on over 20 years of investment banking and strategic consulting experience, Rittenhouse has developed a groundbreaking, proprietary financial linguistic tool that ranks executive communications based on measures of high and low candor. This tool can be applied to quarterly earnings teleconferences, shareholder letters, investor presentations, and all corporate communications. The annual Rittenhouse Rankings Culture and Candor survey has successfully demonstrated that high levels of executive candor are associated with superior market performance

Rittenhouse Rankings has been featured on CNN, CNBC, MSNBC, and recommended by the *Wall Street Journal, Barron's,* the National Investor Relations Institute, the American Association of Independent Investors, the Directors and Boards Associatio, and the Japanese Investor Relations Association. Rittenhouse is the author of *Do Business with People You Can Tru$t* and *Buffett's Bites* and earned her MBA from Columbia University.

www.ingramcontent.com/pod-product-compliance
Lightning Source LLC
Chambersburg PA
CBHW050731080625
27852CB00015B/108